W9-BXH-235

Above and Below

BOOKS IN THE AMERICAN WILDERNESS SERIES

ABOVE AND BELOW
*A Journey Through Our
National Underwater Parks*
by Helga Sandburg and George Crile, Jr.

FAREWELL TO TEXAS
A Vanishing Wilderness
by William O. Douglas

BY HELGA SANDBURG

THE WHEEL OF EARTH
MEASURE MY LOVE
THE OWL'S ROOST
THE WIZARD'S CHILD
SWEET MUSIC
THE UNICORNS

Children's Books

BLUEBERRY
JOEL AND THE WILD GOOSE
GINGERBREAD
BO AND THE OLD DONKEY

BY GEORGE CRILE, JR.

TREASURE DIVING HOLIDAYS (*with Jane Crile*)
CANCER AND COMMON SENSE
MORE THAN BOOTY (*with Jane Crile*)
A NATURALISTIC VIEW OF MAN

Medical Books

HOSPITAL CARE OF THE SURGICAL PATIENT
(*with F. Shively*)
PRACTICAL ASPECTS OF THYROID DISEASE
BIOLOGICAL CONSIDERATIONS IN THE
TREATMENT OF BREAST CANCER

ABOVE
AND
BELOW

A Journey Through Our National Underwater Parks

by

HELGA SANDBURG
and
GEORGE CRILE, JR.

M c G R A W - H I L L B O O K C O M P A N Y
NEW YORK   ST. LOUIS   SAN FRANCISCO   TORONTO

ST. PHILIPS COLLEGE LIBRARY

574.92
S 2 13 a

Copyright © 1969 by Helga Sandburg and George Crile, Jr.
All rights reserved.
Printed in the United States of America.
No part of this publication may be reproduced,
stored in a retrieval system, or transmitted, in any form
or by any means, electronic, mechanical,
photocopying, recording or otherwise, without
the prior written permission
of the publisher.

Library of Congress Catalog Card Number: 76-98489

FIRST EDITION   54606

For
Lilian Steichen Sandburg

and the memory of
Carl Sandburg,
Grace McBride Crile
and George Crile

16674

Introduction

Shortly after the world's tallest mountain was climbed by Edmund Hillary, a book was published entitled *An Innocent on Everest*. The author, Ralph Izzard, was a *Daily Mail* reporter stationed in the Far East. He had never dreamed of climbing a mountain until he received a telegram from his home office ordering him to cover the Everest expedition. Slogging along in his tennis shoes, Izzard tried valiantly to overtake the professional climbers and finally succeeded in doing so. In fact, he climbed with them almost as high as most previous expeditions had reached.

Impressed by the vivid account that Izzard wrote of his adventures, it occurred to me that I might try the same tactics with my new wife, sending her down instead of up. Therefore, when a McGraw-Hill editor suggested to Helga that she write a book for Justice Douglas' Wilderness series, I bullied her into accepting the assignment of writing on the Underwater Parks, an area that at the time the contract was signed she had not even glimpsed. It is thus through the eyes of an innocent that in this book the ocean is seen. It has been my function only to guide Helga into the areas where she could learn the most, both under the water and in the literature of the sea.

July 1968

George Crile, Jr.

Acknowledgments

WE ARE GRATEFUL to Secretary Stewart Udall for helping us contact the people in charge of the National Parks we visited, to John and Lauri DeWeese for detailed information about the wildlife of the Dry Tortugas, and to the Rangers in the Virgin Islands and the Channel Islands who guided us through their underwater and adjoining domains. We are indebted to the writers we have consulted from Aristotle to the present day, and wish particularly to thank Carleton Ray and Elgin Ciampi for their reference book *The Underwater Guide to Marine Life*.

Contents

*So is this great and wide
sea, wherein are things
creeping innumerable, both
small and great beasts.*

—Psalm 104:25

CHAPTER ONE

The Beginnings

Oh! if I were a sailor lad, or even a bombardier.
I'd hire a boat and go afloat,
And straight to my true love steer;
And straight to my true love steer, my boys,
Where the dancing dolphins play,
And the whales and sharks kick up their larks,
Ten thousand miles away!

—Carl Sandburg: *The American Songbag*

MY husband George is known as Barney to his family and friends. When I met him for the first time a few years ago, I had never worn a faceplate or flippers. Reared as a child on an inland lake, I had never seen snorkeling equipment. He, on the contrary, had known the sea bottom since a child. It is not that I was unaccustomed to water. I swam as well as any. When we were invited before our marriage to visit Ed Link on his *Sea Diver,* a boat especially built for underwater work, I startled those on board by plunging on the first afternoon into the sea with no more equipment than my bikini. The others went their own way, Barney borrowing the customary gear and speeding far under to examine the bottom and searching for wreck remains, Johnny Margetis, the Greek cook, collecting conchs for salad that evening. I had always loved ships and clambered back on board to watch the divers from the deck.

ST. PHILIPS COLLEGE LIBRARY

They bobbed to the surface and shouted that they had an octopus. Barney swam it back, twisting about his arm, and brought it on board. Its flabby head was the size of a baseball and the tentacles dragged on the deck. Everyone declared that we would have some for an *hors d'oeuvre*. Johnny knew what to do with it, and I watched amazed as he took the head in one hand and the tentacles in the other and bit the creature in the narrow part below the head; it went limp and he removed the stomach so the ink would not flow out and then proceeded to hurl the octopus onto the deck repeatedly to tenderize it before taking it to the galley. Barney said that the octopus was a member of one of the truly blue-blooded families of the world, for the oxygen-carrying capacity of its blood was augmented not by a union of protein and iron in the form of blood-red hemoglobin as in most creatures, but by a combination with copper which tinted its blood. The blue color was not discernible in the creature which turned brick-red in Johnny's pot, as it simmered and steamed for two hours in red wine and olive oil with some vinegar and onions and cloves, celery and bay leaves and peppercorns; it would cool in the sauce and be served with it later. The only seagoing people I had known until that trip had been stewards and chambermaids and captains and porters upon large ocean ships or tourist liners on small seas, engaged in their passengers' comfort; it was the first of my encounters with these self-sufficient enthusiastic perennial voyagers.

My childhood had been passed in the dune country of Lake Michigan. We lived in a tall house my mother had designed on a bare sand hill beside the inland sea. From its terrace we witnessed a procession of brilliant sunsets because beyond the western sky was Chicago's smog. The red ball would blaze through it while multi-hued banners ran about the horizon. The house in time was threatened by the undermining movement of the sand. In many ways it was a violent land and we children were turned loose upon it. If there were a darkening sky and thunder roared before an approaching summer storm, we hurried into our swim suits and rushed through the hot sand to plunge into the water as the first rain began to sting our heads and shoulders. If ice floes were on the lake in early spring, we took swift dips, beating by days the proud Polar Bear Club people from Chicago. We swam in the dark or moonlit nights, the water so still one could not be sure which direction was horizon and which beach. In the scorching afternoons the sand burned our feet and the shore water was tepid. There were no lifeguards or teachers and each of us worked out strokes to suit himself, individual. We clutched our noses going under at first, later held our breath, and in time were able to walk the bottom competently.

When the water was wild and the waves towered, the children of the community would link hands in order to get through the heavy undertow and out to the first sandbar. Sometimes one of us would nearly drown, gasping, swallowing water, clutching at the hands of others. Our only experience at diving was from the low platform of the community raft, which was supported underneath by rusted oil barrels. We were accustomed to swim with our eyes open, for the water was clear unless there had been a storm to stir up the lake floor. I was near-sighted and it had not been until I was nine or ten and the teachers reported to my mother that I would ask permission to go up to the blackboard to read the test questions that glasses were obtained. Then I met the stars and moon for the first time intimately. However, had I the finest vision there would have been little to see under the inshore lake water but shoals of tiny grey minnows above the white-gold sand of the bottom.

There was an ancient lifeboat on the beach, and if one of the men took it out, children were sometimes allowed to go along to fish. If the water were rocky, we got seasick and waited patiently to be returned to shore and a firm footing. The fish life was abundant then; within the sandbar were immature sunfish, shad, whitefish, trout, bass, yellow perch. The far-out fish, seldom caught by our local fishermen, were pickerel and blue pike and occasionally a predatory muskellunge, the fierce bony-jawed barracuda of freshwater lakes, the largest of the Pike family, weighing as much as sixty pounds and reaching near six feet.

We had been told of gigantic sturgeons, ten feet or more in

length, and how a few were still out there. Once in a long while
one would be pulled up from the bottom and a photograph would
appear in the local paper of an enigmatic-faced fisherman in laced
high-leather boots reaching his hand up to touch the snout of the
horny-hided specimen strung up beside him. In front of the sturgeon's small toothless mouth are four barbels used to locate the
small organisms along the lake bottom on which it feeds, straining
the mud with its protractile mouth, as it cruises lethargically along.
We knew the sturgeon was termed a living fossil, along with the
oyster and the horseshoe crab and a few others and that it was the
only existing example of primitive bony fish; its subclass *Chon-
drostei* means cartilage-bone, for although its ancient forebears
possessed a bony skeleton, the sturgeon's has evolved into a cartilaginous one. We were told in our classes at school, where we
learned of local history, how in 1821 the first steamship, the *Walk-
in-the-water,* came upon Lake Michigan and the Red Men were
told that the boat was drawn through the rivers and lakes by a pair
of trained sturgeons. The Indians had believed, hooting and cheer-
ing from the shore when they saw it move.

Occasionally we tramped some miles up the beach to Pikes Peak,
the tallest dune around. Hunting in the sand below it, we uncovered relics of a not too distant Stone Age, arrowheads and spear
points left by the Potawatomi or others of the Algonquin Indian
tribes. Not so many years before, the Potawatomi had pitched
their tents in camp sites along our shore. That was before the Red
Men lost their land through a series of treaties and most were
deported to Kansas and elsewhere. We brought the weapon tips
back with us to put them on shelves and in drawers about the
house. They joined our collections of relics of an even more primitive time: fossils of crinoids and tiny marine creatures, which we
sometimes strung into necklaces or bracelets.

I roamed unchaperoned most of the year about the shore and
woods and dunes. The summer people arrived in June and left two
or three months later. There were no close neighbors and the
school bus picked us up at Highway 12, a mile's walk from home.

My mother had a scientific bent and encouraged me from the first to make a definitive collection of the Lepidoptera of the area. With her we studied the insect life and examined the stars through a second-hand telescope. Aware of conservation, she explained that one did not net a butterfly indiscriminately, but only for the specimen one needed, an upper and under side, and if the sexes differed, one of each. We pressed flowers in our Riker botanical presses and taped them and the leaves and needles from trees into notebooks and labeled them with their Latin and common names. We made lists of birds observed; in the spring and fall we listened to the scream of the loon on the chilly lake at dawn and hung out of windows while ∨s of Canada geese went by sounding like a distant pack of dogs.

Occasionally one of the creatures of the dunes—a raccoon or possum, an owl or crow, would be found as a baby and become a family pet. I had a collection of white and piebald mice and rats. Now and then in the fall, one of the white-footed deer mice would come into the house and be captured and put in with the tame ones to interbreed and in time become quiet to the touch.

In my late teens, my mother and I established a herd of dairy goats, as well as flocks of chickens, ducks, geese, and pens of domestic rabbits on the acre of land behind our sand dune. A three-year-old buckskin mare called Nancy was brought there; tractable, she learned to rear and kneel and paw the ground upon request. I looped a strip of rawhide about her lower jaw, Indian fashion, and rode her bareback over the sand hills down to the lake. She liked the water and would swim far out; holding to her black mane, borne slowly along, it seemed she was a sea creature, not of the land, but an old-time monster that one had tamed.

Along the shore were pieces of driftwood of various sizes and shapes, some resembling gigantic fish, porpoises, or the drowned body of some prehistoric beast. They had been molded by the force of the inland sea when lashed by heavy storms, in combination with the grinding power of the sand. Sometimes the debris was driven a hundred feet and more by the high waves to the foot of our sand hill. During the beginning or ending of storms, we would walk along the shore, the sand whirled by the violent wind stinging the face and hands. One went barefoot in the warm season and when it was cold one's shoes would be filled with sand. We were instructed to dump them out at the door before coming in, but still the linoleum and wood floors always had a gritting of the grains on them.

The south shore of Lake Michigan was formed at the close of the glacial age. The sand was made by the grinding millstone-like action between the stony matter at the bottom of a glacier and the rock bed over which it moved. The particles were bits of silica, which did not adhere but always remained separate and incoherent and in a state of unstable equilibrium. At a distance the beach appeared white or golden, but if the grains were looked at closely they were pink, black, yellow, red, depending on the quartz or granite rock from which they came. Their high polish was due to the glacial grinding as well as the rolling and sliding of the grains upon each other.

In the winter, icebergs formed off the shore; and in the thaws and freezes of the season, a second line of ice hills would rear twenty or thirty yards past the first. Another line might be repeated past that later. The waves beat caves into the icebergs, forming half-igloos. We would speculate on January mornings, gazing at the frigid scene, upon whether the lake would freeze across, which had been known to happen. In my adolescent years I trained the family's four or five dogs to pull a sled tandem, and wandered with them about the icebergs, the wind whistling in our ears, the surf pounding in the distance, Jack London's tales which I had read the night before impressed upon my romantic mind. During a thaw, if the sand were uncovered, it whirled out to film the white hills of ice with a brown layer of grains. By late March, there would be intimations of the approaching gentle season; the wild country would become still; the ice would break off in floes and drift. Sometimes in later years, one would come upon newspaper reports of a group of deer spotted on a drifting floe, forced by the expanding human population in the north down to the country from which formerly the whitetail had been driven. As the season advanced, the ice floes would melt, the water would lisp again upon the quiet shore, the sun would set in a pool of red, and summer would be upon us.

Once upon a time, in the dunes and surrounding country there roamed large animals—the mastodon, mammoths, the giant beaver, saber-toothed cats, sloths and tapirs, the dire wolf, shrub oxen, antelope, early relatives of horses and camels, and others totaling more than a hundred species. Then, at a time which coincided with the glaciers' retreat into Canada and primitive man's subsequent movement southward, most of the large mammals of North America disappeared. This loss took place about ten thousand years ago. The fossil record shows no similar casualties among plants, small vertebrates or marine life. There has been some argument about the mysterious overkill, but it seems to have dogged the footsteps of migrating primitive man. It has been suggested by scientists that in the years since then, man may have learned and forgot a number of times the lesson of sustained yields and the preservation of fauna.

In 1300 a book was published in Italy by a traveler from Venice, *The Book of Marco Polo*. Another Italian, a Genoese in the service of Spain, Christopher Columbus, was stirred by it to search for a shorter route to the Indies. He sailed across the Sea of Darkness which lapped upon the western coast of Europe. Explorers who succeeded him continued the westerly search and came in 1634 to Lake Michigan. The population of the Red Man in the Great Lakes region then was so small that they had made no notable changes in the natural conditions. But from that point on, the pattern of destruction to the dunelands began which was to continue for a century and a half.

The forests were largely removed; the Galien Woods of beech and maple which bordered the dune country were wiped out. As swamps were drained, the enormous flocks of wild geese and ducks, deprived of their feeding grounds, were reduced. The last wild turkeys were seen in the late 1800s; partridge and quail became scarce. Because their natural nesting grounds were destroyed the Passenger Pigeons disappeared; they had seemed abundant and were clubbed from their roosts or caught in nets as well as shot at random or struck down with long poles as the apparently endless flocks flew low. Their last great flight in the region was reported in 1880. The dunes had been the northern fringe of the American Bison's feeding grounds; the estimated herd of fifty million dwindled to less than two dozen in the span of a century. Deer were hunted until near extinction. The plentiful beaver, mink and muskrat because of the fur trade were almost wiped out. The prairie wolf, black bear and puma were casualties. Reptiles were slaughtered by the thousands; the rattlesnake, called the Massasauga by the Potawatomi tribe, smaller and not as deadly as the western ones, was nearly killed off.

There were no laws to protect any creature from the curious hunting lust which far exceeded any requirements of food and clothing. Against the judgment of many the Red Men too were driven away or deported, having lost all rights to the land where they had been setting up their camp sites through the years. White man's firearms and steel and whiskey had induced profound changes in the mode of life as well as the character of the Indian, who had been leading a well-organized life at the time that Jean Nicolet, hunting for the fabulous Indies, first saw the waters of Lake Michigan.

When the giant sturgeons came up the streams in the spring spawning run, men would gather in crowds to net them, hauling them away by the wagon load often to be fed to hogs in the same fashion as the Passenger Pigeons had been. Fish, an important source of food for the early settlers, were netted and speared the year around. As children we heard in our local history class of a party of men who had taken five thousand whitefish in a day with a seine at New Buffalo, two miles up the beach from our house. In those day there was as yet no problem with water pollution and the dumpage of wastes, which in time would change the number and species of fish able to exist.

Attempts to enforce conservation laws were resisted consistently by the public. All creatures were assumed to be unlimited in the new land. When game and fish wardens were appointed, they became the most disliked of all law enforcement officers. As the dune country became popular as a resort in the latter part of the nineteenth century, thousands of visitors arrived by car or the South Shore Line rail to pick or to pluck up by the roots the various swamp and dune flowers. Many of the rare species disappeared subsequently. The Lepidoptera were collected indiscriminately, with faith in their inextinguishable supply. Of late, one will occasionally see certain familiar butterflies, the Camberwell Beauty and the Tiger Swallowtail, but others like the black-striped avocado-colored Zebra Swallowtail appear to be gone. The moths are suffering too. Perhaps due to the general use of insecticides, as well as the common legalized patio traps used outside homes and restaurants, the pale green, long-tailed Luna and the huge golden Imperial, the brown Cecropias and Cynthias, spectacular with four half-moons on their bordered wings, seem to be only memories in the minds of the older residents of the area.

Efforts are being made through organizations like Save The Dunes, to whose council I belong, to lobby for conservation in Washington. Land areas in the duneland are being set aside, where climax forests and natural fauna and flora may live unmolested. The welfare of the great freshwater lake itself is not at all assured. Powerful private interests stand against efforts to contain pollution of the water, and the planners of the cities along its shores are in a quandary over the increasing smog. It is said that as the air and water smother the life about the Great Lakes, the sun's rising and setting will become more brilliant and even the day-sun will outdo its present beauty.

Barney, like myself, spent most of his childhood on one of the Great Lakes. His father was one of the more vigorous citizens of Cleveland, then a flourishing port on Lake Erie's shore. Old Dr. Crile had come from an Ohio farm family, one of eight children, and was a surgeon, philosopher, traveler and author of books in those fields. Before the first world war, in 1915, he purchased a country place thirty miles out of Cleveland for a holiday and week-end camp for his family. He wrote later that it was his feeling "that we would get away from formal living to one of adventure and doing for ourselves." The place was called The Knob and proved a success. It contained two hundred acres, and was named for a rocky wooded hill on it, which looks off to Lake Erie, seven miles distant. There also are woods, pastures, and unique rock formations and caves, called Devil's Kitchen and considered haunted by the Indians who once lived nearby. On long weekends the Criles rode and fished and hiked; they dammed the streams and made lakes and pools and waterfalls. Barney's father planted lilies and iris about the ponds, flowering crab apples in the meadow and hemlock and rhododendron on the hill. A well was sunk, a filtration plant was built, and a garage and a pump house. A shack was put up with a fireplace and two bathrooms, about it tents were raised to house the family and their guests. The children wandered in the woods where dogwoods were blooming, crab apples and hawthorns budded and trillium carpeted the forest floor, as did various violets—white, yellow and blue.

Today the buildings on top still stand, although in need of repair and without electricity. Barney and I own the lower half of The Knob, and have graded a new road so that it is accessible the year round, and have built on it a one-room house called The Unicorn's Lair, thirty feet square, with a balcony and complete with freezer and washing machine. We have established on the hundred acres a small preserve and are attempting to build up wild flocks of ducks and geese looking for refuge, as well as maintaining imprinted vultures and crows, fallow deer, swans, a woodchuck, capybaras and various other creatures for our mutual pleasure.

Barney became acquainted with a salt sea early in life. When he was four or five years old, he had a persistent and unexplained fever, which his family treated by sending him with a nurse to the sea shore of Atlantic City. There he actually did throw off the illness in a few weeks, and he has a vague memory of a wide sandy beach and tall grey waves. Someone told him about a treasure occasionally cast upon the shore—ambergris, vomited by whales and worth more than its weight in gold. As he walked the shore in the fruitless search, he came upon less rare treasures—horseshoe crabs, conchs, starfish, jellyfish, snails. After storms there would be long necklaces of conch eggs, torn free from some undersea attachment, the twenty or so egg containers resembling potato chips and connected by a tough cord; when dried each one rattled and when opened there were dozens of minuscule conch shells. As Barney built his castles and walls of sand, which were promptly and regularly destroyed by the tide, he came to find the ways and secrets of the sea irresistible.

When he was older, though not yet in his teens, he met the sea life in a new way, not spewed upon the shore or discovered in the close waters, but away from civilization and within the sea itself. It was at Sombrero Light on a reef off Lower Matecumbe in the Florida Keys. The Crile family were on Christmas holiday and had chartered a seagoing houseboat. With them were two naturalists, for Barney's father was a representative from the Cleveland Museum of Natural History and one purpose of the trip was to collect bird and marine life from the mangrove swamps about the Keys for preservation in the museum. At that time Key West was almost unpopulated. The overseas motor road had not been built yet and Miami was but an overgrown village. There was little commercial fishing, and since the Keys were out of range of the smaller sport-fishing boats, the waters were in a natural state and the sea life was unspoiled. The only depredation upon the reefs was when the anchors of the larger fishing boats would tear at the coral. It was not considered generally safe to dive on the reefs, which were notable for their plentiful barracuda and sharks, but the Criles had for their captain an experienced diver, who also was co-inventor of the *Dunn Divinhood,* one of the earliest successful underwater helmets. Captain Dunn placed the heavy hood over Barney's head and shoulders, which were almost not wide enough to support it. There were lead weights on the front and back designed to keep the apparatus from floating off and a squeaky handpump was used to supply the air blown through a fifty-foot hose. Barney was told to breathe normally and was lowered under the surface.

The fish, in their virgin territory, were curious and unafraid. About him in a circle swam a school of opalescent jacks, each near eighteen inches long. Level with his eyes ten feet off were sword-like barracudas suspended, opening and shutting their massive jaws. A grouper rose from the crevice in the coral and hung before him fanning its dark fins. The water was close to twenty feet deep as Barney descended. The reef was composed of dark red coral with purple and yellow waving gorgonians, and everywhere tiny reef fish flickered in and out against the constant blue of the sea.

The *Dunn Divinhood,* heavy before going under, became weightless as Barney touched bottom. All about was the new world, not dark but dazzling, and, bending over and pushing, Barney moved forward until he reached the coral edge of the reef where the sea began. Conchs crawled along it and a dozen lobsters were waving their antennae. Out of the branching staghorn coral below moved a monstrous spotted jewfish, twice Barney's length and eight times his weight; it came up to eye level, gaped slowly and then descended again to its lair. Barney had been told to give a signal when ready to be pulled up, but after fifteen minutes or so as he meandered about the reef, stooping to examine a sea fan and wandering through the schools of fish, he was finally hauled up on deck by Captain Dunn so that the next member of the family could take his turn with the hood.

From Barney's earliest days, even when the camp on The Knob had been completed and was being used, the Crile family took camping excursions of ten days or more at a time, packing their own tents and if necessary employing guides. Old Dr. Crile was a member of the Winous Point Shooting Club, west on the lake about seventy miles from Cleveland, near the head of Sandusky Bay. There the family would migrate now and then during the summers. They punted through the marshes and swales, pushing their poles through the narrow ditches and cutting through reeds and rushes four or five feet over everyone's head; the children pursued butterflies and toads and snakes and remained constantly wet. The Shooting Club marshes were where Barney's maternal grandfather, John Harris McBride, had also hunted at the turn of the century. Then it was not uncommon for the log to show as many as fifty ducks brought down by a hunter in a day, and the record had been set by Grandfather McBride himself on the twelfth of November 1901, when he shot on the wing 167 Mallards, 31 Black Ducks, 2 Widgeons, 6 Pintails, 1 Shoveller, 2 Gadwalls and 4 Blue-winged Teals. That was the year before a daily limit of 25 ducks to a hunter was placed by the federal government. Barney remembers the strings of game hanging by their legs from windows on the shady side of the McBride house, ageing until the bodies were ready to drop. In the days before electric refrigeration, a duck was not thought fit to eat until it had acquired the flavor of decay called "a gamey taste" by gourmets.

In the days spent at Mud Creek Bay, Barney grew to know the marsh birds: the gallinules, the coots which were called "mud hens," the bald eagles, white heads and tails glistening, nesting high; the black-crowned night herons, the green herons and the great blue herons with huge black-tipped wings in their rookery on Graveyard Island, once an Indian burial ground. The family walked the beaches of Squaw Island and on the rocky shoreline and in the close water, they hunted and brought home arrow and axe heads, peace pipes, Egyptian-looking stone figures of ducks with holes drilled in them, thought to be ornaments to attach to canoes. Sometimes at night the children went along with the local carp fishermen to watch them draw their nets and haul in the huge silver-scaled fish. On winter vacations, as Barney came into his teens, he would go to Peach Island to live with trappers in a shanty that was warmed by a round coal stove. Muskrats were speared through the ice as they swam through their passageways, which they kept open to their reed-built houses. Those were the years of the first world war and the pelts brought as much as eight dollars apiece, the carcasses being sold in the market as Marsh

Rabbits. Barney learned to place decoys and shot mallards and black ducks as they set their wings to light in the open water of a swirl of the river. He skated for miles over open ice, unbuttoning his coat and holding it out to let the wind blow him back to the shanty again.

Later in life, when he was married and his children came along, Barney continued the pattern of camping out, exploring the sea and traveling whenever possible. By the time the second world war was over, he and his wife Jane had three daughters and a son and spent their vacations exploring ancient shipwrecks, digging in sunken cities, studying marine life, and writing about as well as photographing all these adventures with still and movie film. They experienced, in the weightlessness of the underwater world, the three-dimensional freedom of faceplates and flippers and the excitement of finding silver and ivory and ancient artifacts from the days of pirates and buccaneers. They found that while at first they hunted fish and crustaceans and molluscs with spear and knife as well as line, they began soon to respect the sea life so that their pleasures were rather in photography and as amateur naturalists.

During one of their diving trips, the Criles visited the same reef off Matecumbe in the Florida Keys where Barney had gone down as a child using the *Dunn Divinhood*. Now, wearing faceplates and flippers, all six went under to see the underwater area as he had remembered and described it. There were no barracuda or jacks, no groupers or jewfish; the sport and commercial fishing boats from above and the spearfishermen below had taken them or driven them off. There were a few wary reef fish who at once took shelter in the cracks of the dead and eroded coral. The branch coral and gorgonians had long since been gathered and sold in the souvenir shops after the Overseas Highway was built. There was a lone conch and no lobsters to be seen; they had been fished out or had deserted the reef, which is their way when one of them returns disabled or dying to the colony.

Later, when the Criles traveled, they found that depredation was associated with human habitation. They visited the Ocho Rios coast of Jamaica, planning to dive in the coral gardens there, famous for their abundant and varied sea life, and were told that the natives' wicker traps had depleted the reefs of practically all fish. On another trip, they met Ed and Marion Link and shipped out on *Sea Diver* into the open sea, ninety miles off Jamaica to lonely Banner Reef to explore the wreck of the *Genevesa*, a Spanish galleon that had been worked on by turtle fishermen based on Grand Cayman Island, who were said to have found gold bars and coins on her. They found Banner Reef as populated by sea life as the reef off the Florida Keys where Barney first went under fifty years ago. As they worked the wreck, Barney was surrounded continually with the gentle and curious hog snappers and groupers that came to eat Toredo worms from his hands.

After Jane died, Barney did not want to return to the sea for a while. Then, when we were married, we visited the Costa Brava of Spain on our honeymoon. Barney borrowed a faceplate from someone at the pension and showed me the underwater life around an old pier. I was intrigued and the next year when we traveled to Andros Island in the Bahamas, in our bags were Barney's old underwater gear; and for me new long yellow flippers and a faceplate, into which Barney had fixed an extra pair of my glasses with the earpieces removed. He had a Bahamian friend at Staniard Creek whom he had known for years, Captain Joseph Johnson, who welcomed me with Andros Island enthusiasm. For a modest fee, the entire family turned their house over to us and went to stay with relatives. They assembled a Johnny Canoe band to play all night for and with us, and in the long golden days Captain Joe ferried us in his leaky stalwart boat from reef to reef in the seemingly trackless green-blue Bahamian banks. Large ships are unable to enter because of the dangerous reef and beyond is the mile-deep trough called Tongue of the Ocean. We spent hours diving on the Red Reef through forests of branching elkhorn coral. During my first views of the delicate and colorful reef fish, they seemed like the lost butterflies I had known in the dune country as a child. By the time we returned to Cleveland, I was under the ocean's spell and under Barney's urging, as an innocent with him for a guide, I wanted to write about it.

Before his next vacation came around, when we planned to travel to one of the National Underwater Parks, we drove over to the Sandusky Bay area where Barney had spent much of his childhood. Here we observed an enigma: in this area where wildlife was abundant at the turn of the century, there was none of the usual evidence of the American man's overkill of flora and fauna. We rented a small boat and rowed down Green Creek, which flows into Sandusky Bay. We visited Squaw Island and punted through the marshes. Here the carp still run in the shallow waters; in the pools of Green Creek the small-mouth bass still jump; the heronry is maintained; the bald eagles are seen soaring high; and muskrats, coots and ducks persist in nesting.

The seeming paradox of the Winous Point Shooting Club is explained by the fact that this club and similar ones which adjoin it, also run by a select group of sportsmen, control thousands of acres of marshland and have systematically protected the feeding grounds of the waterfowl and preserved their natural environ. The membership of the clubs is small and the toll of game birds kept low. Many of the members have become knowledgeable and schooled amateur naturalists. Thoreau said the young man goes to the forest "first as a hunter and fisher, until at last, if he has the seeds of a better life in him, he distinguishes his proper objects, as a poet or naturalist it may be, and leaves the gun and fishpole behind."

It was not until mid-life that Barney found himself more interested in observing and photographing wildlife than in hunting it. He says he still likes to catch a good fish, but if the water is clear, would prefer to put on a faceplate and swim with it. He can still shoot a duck on the wing and thrill to the sight and sound of the dead weight splash in the soggy marsh, but he would rather sit in the evening and watch the wild mallards and wood ducks at The Unicorn's Lair circle and set their wings against the pink of sky and alight in the cold dark water of the pond below.

The hunter and fisherman have always been aware of conservation, in order that their pleasure in their sport be uninterrupted. While many of the small wildlife refuges are sponsored either by or for them, others have been developed by breeders of migratory and fancy wild birds for sale to sportsmen, bird lovers and other breeders. One of the latter is a friend of ours, whose thirty-eight-acre farm is a paradise for every kind of waterfowl, domestic and foreign, as well as a variety of deer and small animals. His place has become a haunt for naturalists and schoolchildren. One day it was charged by game officials that our friend had sold wood ducks to a person not licensed to purchase them and that his records were not accurately kept. He was prosecuted and his fine was to include not only revoking of his permit, but the capture and transfer of four hundred wild ducks and geese from his farm to another area. Alarmed local naturalists called us up about the trouble, for since it was the middle of the post-nuptial molt when neither the old nor the young birds could fly, the disturbance would be such that mortality would be high. We had no interest in whether our friend were guilty or not, but we felt that conservation officials should realize the obvious danger when these creatures, who had their nests and mates and territories established, were invaded and captured and released in a foreign situation. The affair culminated in a pseudo-comedy atmosphere when the alerted local bird people—watchers, hunters, and admirers—banded together and appeared on our friend's farm on the morning the federals were due, armed with every sort of motion picture and still camera and prepared to record the event as their next step of protest. The fifteen game officials from the State Wildlife Division and the U.S. Department of the Interior's Bureau of Sport Fisheries and Wildlife gazed at the scene, turned about face and went home. By the time they had organized themselves again, most of our friend's young birds were able to fly and escape the human predators. Later many of the older transported birds found their way back one by one to their homeland.

The role of the official is quite clearly defined, but it would seem that punishments for law-breaking in the field of conservation should be slanted so that if possible man and not wildlife suffers. A neighbor of ours brought us a cardinal that had had its wing chewed off by a cat. They had called the wildlife office and were told to release it and that they were disobeying the law by housing a protected songbird. We sheltered the wounded creature, because we had a permit to investigate imprinting in various songbirds and could use the cardinal in our program. It remained our unwilling guest until it finally settled down and tamed. If released it would have been instant prey for neighborhood cats who patrol our yard nightly for loose latches on cages of newly hatched baby wildlife.

As Barney and I talked of our coming trips, we felt curious as to the laws set up in the Federal Underwater Parks and adjacent land areas to protect the creatures who had been holding those territories for all these years before the great Underwater Invasion of man during the past half century. We were curious about the Department of the Interior's plans for the future. We were assured by Secretary Stewart Udall that we would be supplied with naturalists, biologists and rangers to help whenever possible, to let us use their boats and to give us bibliographies and published information.

We looked ahead to the adventure into the sea. We realized that we were a species of larger land mammals. We knew that back in the phylogenetic scale, our far ancestors were of the water. We knew too that hidden in the flesh of certain intelligent water mammals were vestigial leg bones and that anciently their predecessors walked on land. We believed that in the future man would become increasingly dependent upon the sea as a source of food, fresh water and materials for his comfort. We felt that the oceans of the earth might be the last frontier of beauty, majesty and if one wished it, seclusion and quiet.

CHAPTER TWO

We Are on Our Way

"Yes," he said, as he poured the hot water from the kettle into the tea-pot, "if a man could only manage to get right down to the bottom of the sea, and live there a while, he would discover some wonderful things—things that people have never dreamed of."

—Hugh Lofting: *The Voyages of Doctor Doolittle*

IT was nearly mid-June; the sweet warm evening air swept through the open windows of the Red Room of our house where we were discussing the projected trip. Our duffle bags were packed: two yellow ones for my daughter Paula, whom we had asked to come along as Chief Photographer, four green ones for Barney and me, and a red one carrying books for reference and pleasure, our journal, notepads and miscellany. In a few days we would be in the Dry Tortugas. We planned to fly to Miami where we would visit the *Sea Diver* again, and then drive down to look at the Everglades, and on to Pennekamp, a state underwater park that Barney knew of off Key Largo, and take the Overseas Highway to Key West. The Park Service people had written us that in order to get to Fort Jefferson we could either charter a boat out of Key West or take advantage of the National Park Service boat which left the town every two weeks on a Saturday and returned in twelve days. They said that Everglades National Park and Fort

Jefferson National Monument were jointly under the supervision of the National Park Service in Homestead, Florida. They had written too that the tern-nesting area of the Dry Tortugas was closed to visitors until mid-June in order not to disturb the birds, and that although there was a room ready for us, it was not a service which they were prepared to offer a casual visitor and "since we do not have formal guest accommodations as yet, you may find the room a bit rustic, but adequate." Wary, I told Barney and Paula that I felt that we should bring along plenty of rough clothes, and heavy ones too, because I knew we would sleep in the dungeons that quartered the prisoners in those old days. Barney assured me one sweater would do for land, but said we should pack cotton jerseys to wear in the water and on extended trips in small open boats as a protection against coral scratches, jellyfish stings and sunburn. In my bag with the swim gear was a new underwater mask; Barney had sent it to an Optician for Divers with my prescription. The makeshift one that we had used in the Bahamas had not been a great success; the relationship of the lenses to the eyes was abnormal and it was difficult to clean under the glasses and keep them from fogging up. The optician had precision-ground extra large, wide angle, safety lenses and bonded them directly to the plate; I was looking forward to trying out the mask.

Barney had been to the Dry Tortugas a number of times, had written about it, and had produced a 16-mm. movie on it for television many years ago. He also knew the Everglades well and Cape Sable and the Florida reefs, rich in the treasure wrecks he had been interested in. I had been to Florida but once, twenty years ago, traveling by train to judge a South Florida Goat Show. The most astonishing event of the whole trip to me then, an untraveled Midwesterner, had been the first sight of the palm trees. It had reminded me of the little old lady who told her sailor grandson, "I believe in mermaids, because everyone knows there are mermaids, but don't tell me stories about flying fish. I'm not daffy yet!"

About the room in which we sat and talked were red chairs and a red sofa; an ancient polar bear rug, complete with head, covered the floor. In a bookcase were the two dozen books written by old Dr. Crile, and in the shelves over the fireplace and about on tables and the sideboard were odds and ends Barney's parents had picked up in their travels from the Arctic Circle to the Tanganyika territory. There were walrus tusks with scrimshaws by Eskimos on them, African ebony figures, whale baleen, decorative trumpets carved from elephants' tusks, a foot-long petrified piece of the tusk of a woolly mammoth. On the wall was a fossil herring, *Diplomystus Dentatus,* from the shale formation in Green River, Wyoming; under the table was a wastebasket made from the hind foot of an elephant and beside it a standing lamp, its stem the foreleg tibia of a giraffe, both beasts having been shot by Barney's father on one of his scientific expeditions to study the energy system of animals, which was subsequently written up in one of Barney's mother's books, *Skyways to a Jungle Laboratory,* also on the shelf. When I had first come to this house, I had been somewhat overwhelmed by all of these museum-like effects, and while covering the furniture with red, had hung my two Sioux Indian masks upon the wall and on the fireplace shelf set my ivory netsukes. In the same way that I expect visitors now accept our varied birds and animals, I came to accept and grow attached to these odd Red Room objects.

Certain of our birds fly free in the house at times, the white pigeon in the kitchen, the crow and the parrot in my study. Most live in their cages; in the kitchen are finches and a cockatiel, and in the Sun Room are ringneck doves. In a pen in the Sun Room, ceiling-high and large enough to house a fallow deer as once was necessary when one of ours was hurt by dogs, are kept the Gambel Quail, the bantam rooster who was raised with them, and our Turkey Vulture, Lenore—affectionate, imprinted on us, and allowed too to roam through the house now and then.

On the walls of the Sun Room are a polished sixty-five-inch-long tusk from old Dr. Crile's same Tanganyika elephant, shot at Lake Manyara in 1935, as well as four sea-damaged tusks, salvaged by

Barney from the wreck of an eighteenth-century slave ship off the Florida Keys; on the floor is a ship's cannon recovered there also. A long table with a built-in glass case runs the length of the room, eight inches deep, lighted from within and with a sandy bottom. In there are the artifacts that Barney and Jane brought back from their travels—amphoras from the waters off Crete, copper ore from King Solomon's Mines, blackened pieces of eight from the Silver Plate wreck off Plantation Key, Roman coins, potsherds from Caesarea, ballast stones from the reef at Silver Shoals off Haiti, bricks and rum bottles from the Sunken City of Port Royal that he visited with Ed Link on his *Sea Diver,* and other relics from ancient cities and from the bottoms of oceans. In the sand too when I married Barney had been Jane's footprints, stepped in there before her illness. These were left untouched until, as the months went by, the natural movement of the silical grains erased them. Then, with the same feeling of territoriality which had stirred my changes in the rest of the house, I placed in the case a few odd specimens from my collection of Michigan Lepidoptera, as well as crinoids and Potawatomi arrowheads from my childhood lake shore.

Territoriality is the naturalistic principle which caused Barney's daughters to mourn at first when I moved an accustomed lamp from an old position and substituted one of my own; and his son to write from Europe on learning of our engagement, requesting that his grandfather's elephant tusk remain over the fireplace. It is the urge which impels Polynesia, our parrot, free-winged, to remain in her cage; and the hybrid Canada goose, Pogliani, to consistently attack the amiable hired man who comes to clean his pond and dishes; and our dog, Gustav, to roar at the mailman and drive him off daily after he has dropped the mail through the door slot. It is what prompts certain reef fish, like the jeweled Demoiselles, to defend a particular cave or rock hole successfully against fish ten times their size; and why, when fish like these are dispossessed because their homes are destroyed or invaded, they become ready prey to predators.

That night we sat up late in the spring breeze, talking about the coming days and *Sea Diver,* where we would have supper the next evening. Barney said he had always felt a certain responsibility for *Sea Diver's* captain's undersea activities, because he had started Ed out on that course twenty years ago. Edwin Link had been an industrialist and flyer, noted for inventing the Link Trainer; he was a yachtsman too and with his wife, Marion, had sailed their sloop, *Blue Heron,* in the oceanic races. Barney claims that the lives of the Links were all sunshine, sparkling waves and beauty before the day he persuaded them to come diving on the wreck of HMS *Looe,* which the Criles were salvaging. In no time at all, Ed had traded his *Blue Heron* for a shrimp trawler, the first *Sea Diver,* filled it with underwater equipment and was going down into the silt of the Sunken City of Port Royal. Barney ran off films for us of later years when they dived with the Links on Silver Shoals, in the Mediterranean, the Bahamas and off the Florida Keys.

Ed's original trawler had been replaced in a few years by the present *Sea Diver,* ninety feet long, designed by Ed and the world's first boat to be constructed expressly for oceanographic work. She was equipped with everything a scientist could wish for, including a colony of white mice for testing decompression chambers. We felt that all *Sea Diver* lacked was a mascot and had made arrangements with a Miami dealer in various animals from about the world to have a baby capybara ready for us to bring as a gift to our hostess. The capybara is a web-footed aquatic animal, a vegetarian, the largest rodent in the world, weighing up to a hundred pounds, one of the few survivors of that age ten thousand years ago when the mysterious overkill of primitive man decimated the larger animal life. The capybara retreated into the Brazilian jungle and has changed little over succeeding centuries. We wanted to give Marion a capybara because we had had a few ourselves and considered them ideal companions. At present there was one at The Unicorn's Lair called Helen of Troy. Her voice was a high soft neigh; her eyes were gentle; stroking her bristle-like hair while she pushed against one, there was a feeling of a communion with another, a pre-man age. When Helen of Troy was a baby, we had kept her in the town kitchen and she would come into the Red Room when there were visitors and sit on the sofa with them, singing her song. She swam now and then in the duck pond in the town yard. Then she grew so large that we took her to live with the deer and other creatures on the pastures and woods of the country with two ponds for her use. When she dived under, she darted about like a seal, her webbed hind feet outstretched behind, staying down for long moments. When she moved along the surface, only her nose, eyes and ears protruded and like a hippopotamus or crocodile, she was hardly to be noticed. Her nostrils had inner valves which closed when she descended and opened when she surfaced with a snort. Our water birds took her presence matter-of-factly and even when she bobbed up under them, nudging, remained undisturbed.

When we landed in Miami the next afternoon, we picked up our rented car and drove to the Pet Farm. We were pleased with Little Sea Diver, which we christened him at once; he was timid, the size of a rabbit and happy to be held. After a few inquiries, we found *Sea Diver* tied to the wharf of a shipyard in the Miami River. It was hot and muggy and the air had a brackish scent. Barney looked at the veritable slum and protested that a ship of her power, who had sailed the high seas, crossed the Atlantic and weathered the dread mistral of the Mediterranean, deserved a happier fate! On one side of her was the rotting hulk of a seemingly abandoned vessel; on the other, as we passed, was a rusted flat creation being attacked with rivet hammers, air compressors, and other screaming instruments to scrape her clean. Saline muddy water lapped *Sea Diver*'s sides, garbage floated by, and we could see the dark humps of a family of manatees, sea cows, docile and sluggish along the bank. Sea cows are vegetarians, mammals, and gather their food with their whiskered upper lip. Their nostrils, like our capybara baby's, were able to shut out water, the manatees' valves being more conspicuous; they are reported to be able to whistle too. They are thought, in the animal kingdom, to have a distant relationship with the elephant. Their dugs, like the elephant's, are situated up between the front limbs. It is thought that the manatees, who are often about the size of human beings, first gave rise to tales of mermaids; they have a way of holding themselves halfway out of the water sometimes, and do this when suckling their babies, held in one flipper. They belong to the order *Sirenia*, named after the temptors of Ulysses. We had read Pliny the Elder: "As for the mermaids . . . it is no fabulous tale that goeth of them: for . . . such a mermaid was seen and beheld plainly upon the coast near to the shore: and the inhabitants dwelling near, heard it afar off when it was dying, to make piteous moan, crying and chattering very heavily." Manatees are easily caught and have been hunted for their oil and meat; now the Florida law protects them from molestation.

We were met on the deck by Johnny, the ship's Greek cook, who took Little Sea Diver in his arms with equanimity and said, "Missus and Captain coming right back. You like conch salad, doctor? I take some from the freezer. No conch here." He gazed sadly at the sea cows in the sluggish water.

Marion was hailing us, running along the dock, "I'm so glad you're here!"

"This looks like a long way from the days of the *Blue Heron*, Marion," Barney said.

"I still dream about her sails set in the rolling sea," Marion sighed. "What on earth is that, Johnny?"

"Little Sea Diver, Missus," he said. "I like."

We told her, "He's yours, Marion!"

"Well," she said as Johnny handed her the animal, "he sounds like a canary."

"He's a mascot," we explained.

Marion and Little Sea Diver got on together at once. When the capybara was shown a newspaper in the lounge, he recognized its purpose and in all his days on board remained housebroken. We settled our duffle bags and while Barney and Johnny found a bottle that belonged to Johnny's baby son in Miami, and heated

milk for Little Sea Diver, Marion took Paula and myself on a tour
of the ship. There were booms and winches for hauling up
weighty objects from the sea's floor, thick glass plates deep in the
bow, an air lift to remove silt and gravel from the bottom, twin
diesel motors, an eighteen-foot launch called *Reef Diver;* the
wheelhouse included radar and an automatic pilot; the tool shop
could make and repair all parts; there was a freezer compartment
under the deck, and the cabins had accommodations for twelve.
Marion was in charge of commissary, often feeding the ship's full
capacity of passengers for two or three weeks. She told us that Ed
was Chief Engineer as well as Captain, and ran the ship himself as
a rule.

When we were going through the dining area by the galley,
Marion showed us a painting of old Port Royal, once the capital
of the Caribbean pirates and center of trade between Old and
New World. Barney had gone there with the Links in 1956 on the
first *Sea Diver*. They had used an air lift to suck up the four-foot
layer of empty bottles and bricks and muck covering the ruins.
The fireplace in the ship's lounge was made with bricks they had
retrieved. It was there that Ed had begun to consider designing the
present *Sea Diver* in order to return and properly work the under-
seas ruin. Three years later, in June 1959, the Links set out with an
expedition of twelve and stayed through the summer, joined by
various divers, including a group from the U.S. Navy. Among the
artifacts recovered had been an elaborate brass pocket watch,
which they later presented with everything else of any worth to the
Kingston Museum in Jamaica. The watch had stopped when an
earthquake struck at seventeen minutes before noon in June
1692. In ten seconds the waterfront and most of the city of Port
Royal slipped a quarter of a mile into the channel while, as a
spectator at the time remarked in a letter, "the whole was attended
with . . . the noise of falling mountains at a distance, while the
sky . . . was turned dull and reddish, like a glowing oven." It was
said there today that the buildings still stood beneath the sea and

in stormy weather when the surf ran high the church bell could be heard tolling.

In the ship's lounge, Little Sea Diver on Barney's lap was taking his bottle. Beside the fireplace was a tall Greek amphora, on one wall was a replica of Agamemnon's golden death mask from the grave circle at Mycenae and on another a sea-washed elephant tusk from the same ivory wreck as those in our Sun Room. And then Ed arrived, energetic, and began talking of his plans. *Sea Diver* would shove off from the shipyard in a few days, carrying on board a newly built miniature yellow submarine, *Deep Diver*, designed for search and exploration in the ocean depths and on the bottom.

"Look, Barney," Ed said, "we have a hydraulic crane so we can launch or retrieve her in any kind of weather, even without dropping anchor. She's built to hold four passengers, and we can load and unload them at will, even if they are inexperienced, and they can wear only face masks if they don't want to use an Aqua-lung. And we can maneuver her like a helicopter."

"How about decompression on the *Deep Diver*?" Barney asked.

"We'll park her on the bottom and build up the pressure in the divers' compartment until it equals the water pressure outside, then out they go. When they get in again, they'll close the hatch which locks the pressure in with them and they'll come up. We'll swing them aboard, the crane will set *Deep Diver* in her cradle in the stern, we'll haul up anchor and off we can go if we like, while the divers are decompressing in their compartment."

"Is decompression a long business?" I asked.

"It's according to the depth and the time spent down there. A four-hundred-foot dive with return in fifteen minutes might take three hours or so. A thousand-foot dive, which we aren't ready for yet, although *Deep Diver* is—and say two or three weeks on the bottom, well, that might take days. We'll need to work out a decompression chamber on the deck that's more comfortable. This one will be pretty hot and humid."

"Where are you heading first?" we asked.

"The Caribbean," Marion said, "with our capybara!" And she took Little Sea Diver to her lap, where he settled to doze.

"Do you go down, Mrs. Link?" Paula asked.

"Yes, but I'm not a very good swimmer. I try to look outwardly calm. Why don't you three come along?"

"Marion's a great swimmer, and why don't you come aboard with us?" Ed urged. "Helga might take to it, Barney."

"Not me," I declared. "I'm just getting used to a faceplate!"

"Sorry," Barney said. "We're committed to this trip."

"We're going to try to set some records," Ed lured him.

"Will you ask us again?" Barney said.

"Tomorrow we go to see the trained dolphins at the Seaquarium," I announced.

"Porpoises," Barney said.

"You can call them either," I argued. "Even Aristotle said, 'Many people are of the opinion that the porpoise is a variety of the dolphin.' "

"Then why not call them little whales? Technically, that's what they are," Barney said. "A dolphin is a bright-colored fish that doesn't play around boats the way porpoises do. It likes deep water and they say it can go fifty miles an hour in the open sea, which no porpoise can."

Paula said, "Isn't the dying dolphin supposed to be ten times as colorful as a living one?"

"Fable," Barney said. "A living one changes its iridescent shades constantly—blue, yellow, green. A dying one is nothing—grey. I've caught them. They're a good-eating fish, aren't they, Marion?"

"They are, Barney," Marion said and added firmly, "and those porpoises at the Seaquarium that are used in most of the acts are called Bottle-nosed Dolphins by everybody, you know."

"The Greeks started the confusion," Barney declared, "and for the sake of clarity, I'll stick with what the biologists call them—porpoises."

"Don't they push dead and drowning people ashore too?" Paula said. "And rescue children who are hurt and drive sharks away from shipwrecked men?"

"And I've heard fishermen tell about porpoises driving fish into their nets too," Barney said. "They have a way of nudging swimmers and boats, so those stories are surely based on fact. They're docile as manatees and friendly as Little Sea Diver."

"But as bright or brighter than man, some say," Ed said.

"The Greeks thought porpoises were men turned into creatures of the sea," I said.

And in some ways I knew it was the truth, for it is known that porpoises descended from land mammals. Like ourselves, originally of course, long before that, they came from the sea. It is likely that the porpoise, like the capybara, sought a retreat from some threatened danger to the species and readapted gradually to the sea. In their flippers are vestigial limb-bones, and their blowhole was originally one of the nostrils. The porpoise, being a re-entrant and a mammal, must breathe. It would drown if it inhaled water, therefore its breathing is not automatic like that of land creatures, but a conscious act. It can stay under water for five minutes without breathing, but usually surfaces once a minute or so. Its lungs, like other diving animals' such as the sea turtle, are much smaller than man's, but the volume of its blood is much greater, so it can store oxygen chemically in the hemoglobin of the red cells. It has also been shown that in long dives of air-breathing vertebrates, the heart rate slows and the peripheral arteries which shunt the blood to the vital organs constrict, enabling them to require but little oxygen. The porpoise sleeps in brief snatches if at all—it is not established yet whether it actually ever does sleep. If it is anesthetized, a respirator must pump air to its lungs or it will die. When the baby porpoise, three feet long and weighing twenty-five pounds, is born after a twelve-month gestation, it emerges tail first, for else it might drown. One or more friends of the mother stay about at the time to nudge the young mammal to the surface and remain to guard it as it grows to adolescence. New babies are swift swimmers and keep at their mothers' flanks. They are not

weaned until a year and a half of age. The mammary glands are
concealed within two flaps of skin; the baby nudges the vent and
the mother opens it enough for the young one to grasp the teat;
instantly she squirts milk into the baby's mouth so that the highly
concentrated fluid reaches it without any salt water. Porpoises
form close family groups and in the same way that Canada geese
will come together in huge bands but will fly off in small related
flocks, the porpoise maintains a strong family tie.

The next day we drove along the Rickenbacker Causeway to
Virginia Key, where the Seaquarium is set upon its fifty-seven acres,
and the vast collection of marine life is housed and maintained
behind glass and steel and concrete walls, in tanks, on islands, and
the sharks are kept in a special 750-foot channel. We were informed that the transplanted whales, giant squid, iguanas, turtles,
rays, sea cows, as well as shrimp, sea horses and worms, required a
million gallons of freshly filtered salt water. A special team collected the exhibits and a laboratory was conducted for their study,
the aquarium working with scientists and the facilities of the University of Miami School of Medicine and Institute of Marine Science.

We watched the Circus of the Sea, where the creatures performed smoothly under the direction of their trainer. We knew
that the porpoise was the only living creature whose brain was
larger in proportion to body size than man's, and that in some ways
it appeared to be more complex. The porpoise, it would seem,
learns faster than the brightest of primates. We had read of the
intensive research being done with them, usually using the species
Tursiops truncatus, the Atlantic Bottlenose, the one Marion had
mentioned, with the built-in smile. This silk-skinned grey species,
weighing three hundred to eight hundred pounds, has ninety-six
conical teeth with which it grasps and holds the fish it catches and
swallows whole. Its weapon of offense is the hard nose, and many
of them will gather together to ram at approaching predators.
They hunt and feed in packs and when a number of them attack
a large shark, they can easily kill it, butting it from below and

rupturing the huge liver and internal organs of the cartilaginous creature and rolling it over the surface and even knocking it into the air. The name porpoise is from the French *porc-poisson*, pig-fish, given by early mariners, for a pod of porpoises fishing in the shallows might remind homesick sailors of a flock of truffle-hunting pigs. The porpoise, adapted to the buoyancy of salt water, will exhaust itself if placed in fresh, trying to keep near the surface.

The crowd about us cheered when one of the creatures surfaced and made a part-squeaking, part-whistling, part-grunting sound. When it dived under, the sounds it would make were different and unheard by the audience. Those were the ones that particularly interest the scientists of today—clicks, which are thought to be the result of air being forced from two sacs near its blowhole. Each click lasts a split second and the frequency of each varies from 20 cycles per second to 170,00 cycles or more per second, about ten times higher than a man can hear. The porpoise apparently has a sonar or echolocating ability which is remarkable.

About twenty years ago, it was noted that these mammals seemed to be able to see where nets were placed, even in murky water and at night. It has long been known that bats echolocate flying insects, and the Navy and ships at sea have adapted the principle for their purposes. The porpoise employs his sonar to locate his food, and many think also to communicate with his kind. It has been calculated that the range of frequencies of the sounds he emits, and the fact that his body is in motion while he emits them and receives the echo, allow the porpoise to form a three-dimensional sound image, called a sonogram and equal in accuracy and detail to a visual image that a human perceives. Of late the porpoise has been communicating with man who, using words, whistles, gestures and a variety of electronic equipment to give cues, seems to gain extraordinary results. Scientists working for the Navy have perfected an electronic device to translate words into a pattern of sounds that the porpoise learns to understand, and it is thought that the language barrier between man and porpoise may be initially punctured.

Scientists and naturalists have always been studying living creatures to learn about man. Certain of them, such as the porpoise, have stirred writers in the humanities as well as the sciences, by their beauty and mystery. It may be that if the code of the creature's language is broken, through an understanding of his sonar ability, we would find that he is capable of feats of communication, orientation and intelligence which earthbound man has not dreamed possible. Beloved of ancient seafarers for his fun-loving and amiable nature, the porpoise has been the subject of myth, fable and story. Aristotle, studying marine biology from 344 to 342 B.C. on the island of Lesbos, said they had the most gentle and kindly nature and would assist their companions when young or when hurt, and even attempt to keep their dead from being devoured by predaceous fish.

He said too that he had heard stories of their passionate attachment to boys. Pliny the Elder, the Roman naturalist, wrote of a porpoise "which loved wondrous well a certain boy, a poor man's son," and how the boy would go at noon and call the creature and feed him bread. In time, the porpoise responded at once to the child's call, and "offered him his back to mount upon, and then down went the sharp pointed prickles of his fins." When he had the boy on his back, he would carry him over the sea to school and again home in the afternoon. So long as the human lived this continued and when he fell sick and died, still the porpoise "gave not over his haunt, but usually came to the wonted place, & missing the lad, seemed to be heavy and mourn again, until for very grief and sorrow he also was found dead upon the shore." It would seem that if it is true that the porpoise is at least as intelligent as man, then he has directed his nature toward a more tranquil beneficent life.

Barney, Paula and I gazed at the shimmering bodies as on cue the porpoises slipped out of sight into their pens adjoining the pool. Once it had been thought that the supply of all of the creatures of the sea was inexhaustible. We knew the curious history of certain of the species of re-entrants when attacked by man. The sea elephant, the largest of living Carnivora, weighing up to two tons, was almost exterminated by man over the last century and a half for the sake of its blubber. The methods of capture seem so brutal and the animals' reactions so mild that we were reminded of reports about the attitude of porpoises when captured, submitting without struggle and seldom even biting or exhibiting anger. When the sea-otter was first discovered in the mid-seventeen-hundreds, its fur became at once the most esteemed of any, the price of a pelt by the turn of the following century rising from six dollars to close to two thousand. The creatures fed in the sea and would come upon land to rest in droves and to bear their young. The massacre was carried out easily, the men walking up to the otters and hitting them with a club. When struck, the otter lay down, covered its eyes with its forepaws, whimpering or crying and making no resistance. A mother otter never left her young, and if fleeing on the water, held the cub cradled in her arm. In a century the sea-otter was almost exterminated; it has adapted now to feeding, resting and even bearing its young in kelp beds near shore, rarely approaching land.

As poignant a story is that of the walrus, a creature weighing three thousand pounds, almost as large as an elephant seal and, in addition to its hide and oil, having much-sought-after two-foot-long ivory tusks. The common fashion employed by many hunters was to catch a calf and then club until it began to wail. The mother and all other adults, which helped as porpoise nursemaids do to raise the young, would come to the rescue. They would be struck down as they approached, seemingly with no fear. The walrus now is about extinct—a few herds roam about in the Arctic wastes and Greenland. Their story resembles that of the bison massacred in the eighteen-hundreds by those who thought of their extermination as part of the conquering of the country, along with cutting the forests and plowing the plains. At the ending of their pursuit, fires were ringed about their watering places; when the curly-headed monsters met the fires, they galloped off to other ponds, where other fires in turn had been set. In time they either deliberately moved through the flames to the water and death or turned back exhausted to the dry prairie where they were killed with ease. We had been brought up with the story of the flightless bird of the same order as the Passenger Pigeon, *Columbae*. The dodo lived without natural enemies on islands in the Indian Ocean, till discovered by man in 1598. An odd-appearing creature, it attracted instant attention—large as a swan and heavy-boned, with stout legs, a huge hooked beak, a short curly tail and rudimental wings. It was easy prey to sailors who roamed inland, clubbing it. The dogs who followed the sailors, and the pigs they brought to the islands, did their part and in less than a century the dodo was extinct. The word *dodo* had come to mean a dunce, since the creature did not escape attack.

The porpoise, the sea-otter and the elephant seal all carried vestigial forelimbs, complete with hands and even fingers in the flesh of their flippers. All but the porpoise had vestigial hind legs and toes. We felt a bond with these re-entrants, as we left the Seaquarium. They were so gentle-dispositioned and unused to malice that we wondered if it was this very genetic trait which made them unable to compete with land animals and caused them to re-enter the sheltering sea. There, with their herd instinct for cooperation, their only battles were for survival when attacked by sharks or whales who fed on them; and their natural prey were fish and invertebrates.

We knew that many anthropologists and naturalists believe that since animals of both lower and higher species do not make war against their own kind and rarely do serious harm to individuals even in the violence of the mating season, and since they employ symbols of aggression such as snarling, roaring, posturing or butting their heads together in place of actual mortal violence, it seems unlikely that the cause of war is carried in the human's genes. It seems more probable that it has arisen in societies as a result of man's ability to symbolize in words and in the subsequent perversion of his language. Before man will kill one of his own kind, he persuades himself by means of his language that the victim is a danger to humanity, is subhuman and therefore not of his species, or because of his religion, color, race or customs, is different from himself and should be dealt with as a threatening predator.

As we turned down Route 1, toward the Sea of Grass, Barney said, "Maybe the porpoises are the Quakers of the sea and prefer peace to war."

And we agreed.

CHAPTER THREE

The Sea of Grass

And God blessed Noah and his sons, and said unto them, Be fruitful and multiply and replenish the earth. And the fear of you and the dread of you shall be upon every beast of the earth, and upon every fowl of the air, upon all that moveth upon the earth, and upon all the fishes of the sea; into your hand are they delivered.

—Genesis 9 : 2

IT was hot and dusty as we drove through Miami and down toward its outskirts. In open places and vacant lots we saw what we had remarked when we landed at the airport, white birds flecking the landscape. When we had mentioned them to the Links, they said the birds were common in droves all through the state and especially where there were pastures of farm animals. We knew the species, for a few had been seen as far north as Cleveland in the past few years: the Cattle Egret, smaller than our American Egret, with long legs and beak and curved neck. Of the same family as the heron, *Ardeidae,* they stood erect and usually motionless. The first of them had been blown over to the coast of Florida in a hurricane two or three decades ago and in the way of many birds introduced into a strange country, they had prospered.

Some think egrets may become as numerous as starlings and English sparrows. The starling was introduced around the latter

part of the nineteenth century and spread in a phenomenal manner, a menace to bluebirds and woodpeckers. They will watch a
flicker excavating a nest hole and as soon as the size seems to suit
them, the starling drives off the other bird and takes over. As the
flicker goes to make a new hole another starling posts himself to
wait. The tale of the English sparrow is well known and it is hoped
that the egret will adapt more gracefully to its new environment.

When we heard how egrets attended cattle and how they plucked
insects from the air around them, we discussed the idea of each
of us imprinting an egret for himself, Imprinting is the principle by which a baby animal or bird accepts as its mother and its
own kind who or whatever happens to be with it at the critical
period at which imprinting takes place. With precocial birds
able to run after the parents shortly after hatching, like goslings,
or with baby animals born able to follow, like fawns, the imprinting takes place at once. If a baby animal, born helpless like a
puppy, is taken at the moment of flight; or if altricial birds,
hatched naked and blind and too weak to stand, like robins and
crows and our egrets, are taken just before they leave the nest, they
are then imprintable. We thought that on warm Ohio nights when
the mosquitoes were plentiful, each one's egret would perch on the
back of his chair and pluck the insects from about him.

At the southern end of Miami, across from Key Biscayne, we
turned off Route 1, for Barney insisted that we see the Parrot
Jungle, since it was so close by and proved, he said, that imprinting could be an aid to conservation and the education and pleasure of the people. At home in The Unicorn's Lair we had many
imprinted animals and had even entertained our patient guests
and occasionally a professional audience here and there with a song
we had written about it, while I played a guitar:

The crow is black and the rabbit's white and

in the wil - der -ness they'd fight or

run with all their might!   But

because they've been raised together, you see,

they be-have most   am-i - a - bly,   am-i - a - bly!

The silky's white and the vulture's black
And it doesn't matter if you turn your back
*   and that's a fact!*
And this as we'll explain, you see,
Is the imprintation theory, theory.

If you take a goose when he leaves the egg
And the first thing he sees is Barney's leg,
*   is Barney's leg,*
He'll love that leg the rest of his life
Even when it comes to selecting a wife,
*   Barney's leg's his wife!*

Helga took a squirrel before he left his nest
And he thought a baby bottle was the swingingest
*   and the very best;*
And he grew up quite confidant
That Helga was his sister and his cousin and his aunt,
*   and his uncle and his aunt.*

The imprintation is stronger still
If you make a baby duck climb up the hill,
 he'll get a thrill;
And he'll love you better if you step on his toes,
For that's the way imprintation goes,
 smash his toes!

Now, the imprintation experience
Was first discovered by Konrad Lorenz,
 by Konrad Z. Lorenz!

The Parrot Jungle lies in twenty acres of hammock land and contains a cypress swamp, which has been preserved and augmented by plantings of exotic trees, vines, orchids and water plants. Pheasants, peacocks and cranes live in a half-acre of beach and lake, and in the mossy pools, free-winged wood ducks float and set their eggs nearby, unperturbed by passersby who stop to peer into their nests as they follow the winding paths and go over the bridges and under the gigantic cypress limbs which meet overhead in a tangle. We purchased peanuts and sunflower seeds to feed the birds and monkeys which we found in cages at the turns of bends. Overhead, screaming occasionally, flew parrots—the macaws being rainbow-hued and wide-winged with sweeping tailfeathers. At regular intervals during the day, these uncaged birds came down at their trainers' calls to perform various complex tricks. Most impressive and touching, we thought, was the flock of a hundred flamingos kept in pink color with a diet of fresh shrimp. The birds are not seen in a natural surrounding in America any more. In the time of Audubon they were abundant in southern Florida, but by 1850, naturally shy and constantly pursued, they were confined to the extreme southern portion, Cape Sable and nearby keys. When molting and unable to fly, native and visiting hunters would chase and capture or kill great quantities of them. Once the colors of the huge flocks were said to be remarkable, as they mounted to the sky, their flame-like rose-pink resembling a sunset. Watching the fearless delicate creatures, we felt that without displays such as the Parrot Jungle fostered, the species would be forgotten.

As we drove back to continue on Route 1, we talked of how the adaptation of wild creatures to areas where they become accustomed to man is only half the problem. The other is to rear man to accept the presence of wild creatures with respect. Many children from our neighborhood in Cleveland come to our kitchen and the Sun Room and the garden to see the animals. There are certain rules. One small first-time visitor looked at our baby Brown Thrasher called William Butler Yeats sitting on the chairback and pointing his finger, said "Bang!" I told him that he must leave and that he might return the next day and that everyone had to remember that the place belonged to the birds and the animals and not to the company who came to visit. When he was gone, the others went out into the garden. In a few minutes, two children came to me, hand-in-hand, the larger spokesman for the smaller. "Billy wants to use the swing. Does the swing belong to the birds too, Mrs. Cwile?" I said that it did but that Billy might use it sometimes.

We have found that seldom will these children on their first visit be content to observe the animals or birds or let them come to them. The smaller ones want to bang on the cages and the larger ones to get their hands on the creatures. On occasion, a group will come to the other side of stone wall of the garden, armed with toy guns which they aim shouting at the fawn or swan. A friend of ours who has a pond of Canada geese in the country has a problem with boys who come with bows and arrows to wound some, often fatally.

These of course are American urban children. One of our neighbors escorts flocks of schoolchildren through his farm, rich in all wildfowl but also having examples of farm and forest creatures. He has a Holstein calf that comes rushing to the fence for a pail of milk; he asks the children what the calf, when grown into a cow, will give us and the answers vary from orange juice to pork chops to eggs. Among our friends are several farmers and gamekeepers and waterfowl breeders. Their children, accustomed to birds and animals, do not see them as something bizarre or remarkable and move quietly when with them, seldom running from Odysseus our aggressive male turkey and usually settling down to some game unrelated to the animals. On occasion, Barney has invited the families of English physicians to visit our town and country places. We have noted that these foreign children are more respectful of the creatures. The last little English boy allowed our crow Smokey to peck his bare toes and stood with tears in his eyes, saying, "What shall I do now, Dr. Cwile?" We gave him a stick, which kept Smokey somewhat at bay shouting, "Baw, baw," at the top of his arrogant voice.

It seems that the English were the first of the western world's conservationists. Centuries ago by royal decree they protected the Mute Swan which covers their lakes and rivers. The Danes dubbed them royal birds too and their swans occasionally joined the English herds, so that as early as the mid-1700s, they were discovered there, wearing golden or silver crowns about their necks inscribed with the king's coat of arms and designating them "Royal Fishpond Dwellers." Barney has often visited Green Park in London, famous for its waterfowl which are hatched and reared in an area where they live in confidence and close association with man. And he is familiar with the Slimbridge Wildfowl Trust, known over the world by ornithologists interested in the preservation of species, the study of disease, migration, feeding habits and other problems, and which covers nearly fifty acres. It was established in 1946 by Peter Scott, and has been built into one of the world's most complete reference collections of waterfowl.

It was evening when we turned onto State Route 27 at Florida City, soon reaching Everglades National Park Headquarters. The DeWeeses, our hosts in the Everglades and to be our guides in the Dry Tortugas, lived just inside the park, in the pineland region. It was evening and cool; the wind sighed in the long Caribbean Pine needles; a woodpecker rattled above and Lauri DeWeese, binoculars in hand, was stalking him. Barney had known the DeWeeses for twenty years, since he spent a week with his family in the Dry Tortugas where he was making a film. John De-

Weese had been General Mechanic for a while until he was appointed Superintendent of Fort Jefferson National Monument. He and Lauri were inveterate bird watchers and had made regular counts there, as well as collecting and classifying sea shells, another of their naturalistic passions. They had handled the maintenance of the Fort, run the ancient sixty-foot boat back to Key West for supplies every few weeks, operated their two-way radio, acted as electricians, plumbers, carpenters, masons, fishermen, customs officials, guides and diplomats in aiding visitors to the site. John's official position now was personal representative of the Superintendent of Everglades National Park. Lauri was beckoning us while at the same time motioning us to silence. It was a Pileated Woodpecker, big as a crow with a blazing red crest. It flew off chattering, and Lauri said, "Come on in. Do you want to see my shell collection? John will be back soon. He's worried about another drought this year. There's been one every year now for four years and it gets pretty tragic."

Barney said, "Have you had to move any of the animals?"

"Some of the alligator holes in the Sawgrass country went dry and the rangers have been roping them and trucking them to deeper holes. Sometimes they've even dynamited new holes but that's not the answer."

"I've been reading about it, Lauri," I said. "What do you think is the answer?'

"I've got my ideas but they sound rather revolutionary," she laughed. "You'd better talk to John. He's the practical one, and besides he might give an official opinion."

We knew of the ecology of the Everglades, how fifty thousand years ago there was a warm shallow sea covering the area and how the ocean currents rounding the tip of Florida had piled and pushed the sedimentary rock made of soft lime particles, called oölite, into a flat bank. When the climate cooled and the seas receded the region was formed. It is scarcely over sea level now; we were five feet above at the DeWeeses'. The Everglades are literally a sea of grass, the Seminoles called it "Pay-hay-okee"—

Grassy Water. Sixty-six miles to the north lies Lake Okeechobee and due to its spillover and the seasonal rains, the land was a moving spoon-shaped shallow freshwater lake, supporting varied wildlife. Since the rim of the Everglades basin was only a little above sea level and tides would spill over into the spoon's bowl, it was salty at the edges always, although the water in the center was sweet.

That night we sat up late with the DeWeeses; Lauri's shell collection contained seventy-one different species collected in the waters around the Dry Tortugas. We made plans for meeting them shortly in Key West and asked if we might see the birds and sea life and mammals of the Everglades. They had already arranged to guide us down the thirty-eight-mile Park Road to Flamingo where we would lunch. Barney and John talked of the complex problems of the Everglades. The original violation occurred in the first decade of this century when the limestone ledges which formed the rapids of the Miami River were dynamited to make the river navigable. This breech of the natural dam between salt and fresh water caused the Miami River to become the saline muddy canal where the Links' *Sea Diver* was presently tied. Succeeding violations took place when proposals were made to convert south Florida into farms and pastures. Below Lake Okeechobee and far south canals were dredged, the fresh water was run off to the sea, the inner water level fell, salt water rushed in, vegetation died, and often there were long-lived fires. The dried muck of the swamp was like a peat bed and if ignited would continue to burn almost without cessation; in 1933 its smoke alarmed the citizens of Miami as the smog alarms them now. Conservationists tried to persuade the people of the state that the canals should be filled and natural vegetation allowed to renew itself. By then, however, the area around the lake was heavily populated and the wealthy owners of the farms were politically influential and nothing was done. A natural event occurred in 1928 which stunned the nation—a hurricane roared through and hit Lake Okeechobee, the resulting flood costing the lives of an estimated twenty-five hundred people. Work was started by the federal government on a series of dams and dikes and levees and canals which extended down into the Everglades National Park. The program of construction is still under way and because of this complication of man-made control, the interests of the agricultural element, and the demands of the towns and cities dependent upon the system, there had been an appalling loss to the Everglades flora and fauna. The regulation specifies that when the water level of Lake Okeechobee stands at twelve feet above sea level, water may be directed to the Everglades. In time of drought, water is therefore withheld although the order has on occasion been superseded by direction of the governor of the state. As a rule, during a drought nothing can prevent the dried mud flats which occur everywhere and the subsequent vast death toll.

We argued with John far into the night regarding the fostering of wild creatures. John took the stand of most of the Rangers of the Department of the Interior, that wildlife should not be dependent upon man and should live as if man were not there. He told us of forest creatures back in the wild country—bobcats, cougar, black bear, white-tailed deer and gray foxes, possums and raccoons. Lauri pointed out the window—a family of raccoons were working on the garbage-can lid in the back yard where the porch light shone.

"They'll have it off soon," she said. "They're bright. I admire them, but down on Cape Sable they've had a time with them. They eat turtle eggs and have nearly decimated the loggerheads. We began a trapping program to send them off to other parts of the park and then the egg destruction dropped to normal."

"That's what I'm talking about," Barney stated. "Control of predators. If there were not a deprivation in the area due to drought and subsequent uncontrolled multiplication of predators, the life would have persisted in its original abundance and there would have been plenty of alligators to keep the coons down."

It seems that when the balance of nature is disturbed by man, it has little chance of re-establishing itself without help. We felt

that perhaps it was time for a compromise between the rigid gov-
ernment-sponsored hands-off policy of management in which each
species, predator and prey, worked out its own destiny; and the
system of protected predator-free breeding areas like those we knew
of in the United States and abroad, so successfully maintained
by private enterprise.

Barney argued with John that man, with his unique ability to
use the symbolism of language, has always measured the intellec-
tual attainments of animals in terms of his own abilities. Because
of this, he has consistently underestimated the ability of other
creatures to learn and adapt to their specific environments. In
regard to the situation in the national parks, Barney said, the
government has been slow in learning from those who rear and
manage animals either as hobbies or commercial enterprises, and
tends to disregard and even legislate against their successful methods of conservation and propagation. Flamingo, where we would
go the next day, the center of the Everglades Park, no longer
harbors the once-indigenous birds for which it was named, although not many miles away a commercial outdoor aviary, the
Parrot Jungle, attracts thousands of tourists to its well-managed
flock.

John said quietly in return that in the morning he would demonstrate his points and the validity of his policy. We set out early,
the DeWeeses leading the way in their car and Barney and Paula
and myself trailing in ours. The Everglades National Park was
created in June 1947 and contains over two thousand square miles
of land and water. It reaches south into Florida Bay and from
the keys west to the Gulf of Mexico and as far north as the tiny
Ten Thousand Islands. Over the centuries, marine life has come
in on the Caribbean ocean currents and seeds of plants and
varieties of birds on the West Indies wind tides.

As we followed the Park road, we stopped now and then to go
down some of the trails maintained for visitors, the Gumbo Limbo
Trail and the Anhinga Trail, the latter named for the long-
necked bird that streaks underwater after fish, which it brings

to the surface, flings into the air, and swallows head first; it lacks the large oil glands common to most waterbirds and when it dives, gets soaked and must climb to a limb and spread its wings out to dry. We admired the signs placed regularly along the trail or on bridge railings, occasionally hinged to open to an illustration, and always explicit about the Latin and common names and habits of the creatures. Sometimes there was dried cracked mud in areas where John said the water-dependent birds and mammals and fish had flourished. We heard of how the starving alligators would eat the young ones of their kind and how they were depleting the otters hunting the remaining fish. We saw dead gars in a shrunken pool, unable to live because of the oxygen depletion; John said they were a hardy fish and other species had perished days ago. Farther along, we came on a healthy stream spanned by a bridge that was tourist-crowded. There were anhingas, egrets, alligators, fish, water snakes, cormorants, coots, little blue herons and the wood ibis which is truly a stork and the only representative of that family that we have in the United States, *Mycteria americana.*

After a while we returned to our cars, driving slowly, stopping when the DeWeeses did. We felt that the trip would have had much less value without them to guide us. We took one trail to an observation platform where we could observe the panorama of the open Everglades, the scene reminding me of Kansas prairies I had seen on my way to Colorado from a train window. The Everglades contain the greatest expanse of Jamaica sawgrass in the world, often taller than the tallest man, truly a sedge, *Cladium effusum,* and not a grass, its thin leaves triple-edged with rough sharp teeth.

Barney said, "It may be that Jamaica sawgrass rather than legislation is what's saved the wildlife of the Everglades from earlier depredation by mankind."

"Look," Lauri pointed overhead where in the blue two birds were soaring, black with white head and underparts and long forked tails.

"My favorite bird," John said. "I'd spend all day watching them if I had time."

"Are they Man-o'-war birds?" Barney said. "We'll see a lot of them in the Dry Tortugas."

"We have Man-o'-wars here," John said, "but they're bigger. These are Swallow-tailed Kites. I met them here for the first time, and I think they're magnificent. They're marked something like female Man-o'-wars and immature ones, though there's more white on the wings. The species are easily confused."

We asked the DeWeeses about the Everglade Kite, which we knew was one of the country's doomed birds, and if they ever saw any. John said seldom and it was a pity. They were smaller than the kites we were viewing and without forked tails and resembling rather a hawk or vulture. Their sickle-shaped bills were adapted to eating one food—the large freshwater marsh snail, *Pomacea*. As the Everglades were drained and dried, the snail became scarce and the species of kite therefore, too, seldom seen beyond the immediate environs of Lake Okeechobee.

As we came down from the tower, Paula asked, "Do you think we'll see a spoonbill, Lauri?"

"I know where a flock usually feed," she said and told us that one of the happier events recently had been the increase of the Roseate Spoonbill; nearly two hundred nesting pairs had been sighted of late at a nearby rookery. Once the spoonbills, like the flamingo and the egret, were slaughtered wholesale for plumes to put on hats and fans. Now, protected, they were making a comeback. We came on a group of fifteen or so in the sunlight, white and bright pink, with a carmine accent on their shoulders, their stilted legs half as high as the flamingos at Parrot Jungle, swinging their spatulate bills from side to side, feeding on fish, crustaceans and insects.

We paused at a deserted spot and John sighted his binoculars into a distant grove of Caribbean pines. "She's there. Take a look."

I saw a gigantic white-headed bird, the bald eagle on her nest. While we took turns at the glasses the male was seen approaching

with a fish in his talons. The female left the nest at once and
soared off screaming; we could see the two fluffy fledglings as he
lit on a branch beside the rough nest.

"We'd never have seen that without you two and your field
glasses," I told the DeWeeses.

"We'd never have seen anything at all," Paula said.

The character of the country was changing, for we were dropping a few more feet toward sea level as the road went south toward the mangrove coast. We had seen the typical bald cypress
everywhere and the hammocks, which are clusters of trees that
form islands of dense vegetation in open areas. We knew of the
Manchineel tree, called Death Apple or Tree of Death, small,
its fresh sap able to produce severe skin irritation and its crab
apple-like fruit providing unpleasant experiences for early travelers here who tasted it. There were mahogany trees, the largest in
the United States, palms and air plants—one of the latter, the
strangler fig, begins life as an air plant in a tree, sends down
roots and in time, parasitic, destroys its host tree. We had observed it in the Parrot Jungle's collection of subtropical flora. If
the tendrils are cut, it resumes life as an air plant until its roots
become established again.

Then we were passing the line of transition between fresh and
salt water and were in the mangrove swamp, interlaced by mazes
of winding waterways and extending far up the coast to the west.
We got out of the car and walked to where mangroves stood
in the brackish water. Barney pointed and we saw the long hump
of an alligator, near eight feet long; on another log a group of
youngsters were humped, twelve to eighteen inches, almost indistinguishable from their background. We knew the alligator
could be considered a living fossil, since a hundred million years
ago there were many species of *Lorincata,* mailed reptiles which
generally resembled these at which we gazed. The American
Alligator has a broadly rounded snout and is common in the
swamps, lakes, marshes and bayous of the land adjoining the Gulf.
There are perhaps three hundred thousand in its total range.

John said that only two states had open season on them, Louisiana and Georgia, and that the take ran to about fifty thousand of them reported annually, which didn't include those killed by what John called "Nature's noblemen who wanted to have an outdoor experience." In the Everglades, the alligator population has shifted from the tidal rivers to the open glades. Once they avoided the open, where airboats and glade buggies hunted them commonly; with the establishment of the Park, the use of the vehicles was halted and a slow recovery began. At the same time, the price of the hides increased due to a change in fashion, and they were hunted illegally from small boats all about the tidal rivers which are practically impossible to police; the poaching continues and the alligators are disappearing. John believed a bill should outlaw the use of alligator and other native reptiles in manufactured goods; this would make the poaching of the creatures no longer profitable; the bill might be patterned after the one at the turn of the century that saved the egret and other native plume birds of this country.

The American Crocodile may be distinguished from the alligator by its pointed narrow snout and the prominent teeth visible when its jaws are closed. John said that it was probably in more danger of extinction than any other creature in the Park. The highest concentration of the reptile remaining in the United States is probably in the Everglades and does not exceed a hundred. The crocodile once inhabited the Keys for it prefers brackish or salt marshes or even the sea, while the alligator likes fresh water. The development and destruction of its original habitat have forced the crocodile into the protection of the Park and there is a poaching problem with this species too.

It was a primeval scene before us, the quiet armored monsters amid the stilted mangrove trees which are said to walk. In the water the mangroves stood on their long curved legs, their prop roots. It is because of these trees that land becomes nailed down, for the mud clings to the exposed roots and thus the banks are built. I thought of nature's way and the sand dunes of my childhood country which were called "the walking hills." We returned to our cars, and soon reached Flamingo. We followed the De-Weeses through the parking lot into the crowded but comfortable restaurant overlooking Joe Kemp Key and Snake Bight. In the distance were Oyster Key and Catfish Key of Florida Bay. Brown and White Pelicans and shore birds lined themselves on the sandy bars or flew here and there in squadrons. We were aware that the pelican had been around in practically its present form for about forty million years; it was used as a heraldic device in the Middle Ages; and its distensible gular pouch was not for storing food or water but for catching fish. We watched a Brown Pelican dive from thirty feet above, entering the water with a splash and coming up with a fish.

"Is it true," Paula asked, "that White Pelicans band together and wade in a cordon to drive fish into the shallows to feed on them?"

"That's right," Lauri said. "They don't dive like the brown ones and if the water's too deep to wade, they flap along the surface in a line."

"Have you heard of our Green Turtle program on Cape Cable, Barney?" John asked.

"Do we have time to go over there?" Lauri said.

"I've heard about Operation Green Turtle and the Brotherhood of the Green Turtle," I said. I knew certain scientific groups wanted to save the species and also to settle the riddles of their migration and where they live and lay their eggs. The subject was still in question. Celestial navigation, chemical gradients, Coriolis force, continental drift, as well as imprinting all seemed to contribute to the final answer not yet in sight. We hoped to see Green Turtles in our journeys to the various underwater parks.

John said, "Over a three-year period we've released four thousand baby Greens on Cape Sable. And the program involves liberating about eight hundred on the Dry Tortugas this year."

Man until now seemed bent on destroying the turtle. In its earliest form, over two hundred million years ago, it had teeth and the beginnings of a shell. Conservative and long-lived, it spread over the earth through the millions of years since, in fresh water, deserts and the salt sea where, like the porpoise, it was a re-entrant. The sea turtle reveals its beginnings by breathing air and coming on the land to spawn. Its feet have turned into flippers with which it speeds under water.

Tales are told of the turtles' destruction. Even when there are laws to protect them, poachers lured by the cash work at night to destroy them. The calipee is the cartilaginous part of the under shell which is the important ingredient of English green turtle soup, and calipee hunters slaughter the creatures by cutting off the under shell and leaving the beasts to die on the beach. Turtle-leather skins are at an increasing premium on the fashion market, as alligator and crocodile skins are and as the plumed birds' feathers were. Harried poachers have not the time to permit a laying turtle, digging her hole upon land, to deposit her eggs, but slaughter her as soon as she comes in from the sea. Others, more thoughtful, will attach a buoy to her foreflipper as she is spotted on the beach so that when she returns to the sea she can be hauled on board a collecting boat in the morning. If a female turtle is unmolested, she will lay every thirteen days for up to seven times from July to November, often as many as a hundred at a time of the leathery golf-ball-size eggs. The Green Turtle program involves the collection of eggs and replanting of the harvest in government hatcheries. After two months' incubation the babies wriggle to the surface, are tagged, and over one hundred thousand have been airborne to various localities in South America, Mexico, the West Indies, Florida, the Bahamas and various keys. Nesting families are tagged by the program scientists also and the tags have been returned from thousands of miles away. The turtle has an accurate navigational ability and homing urge; it is thought that smells of certain areas may be borne upon ocean currents and that a sun-compass sense of some sort may guide them.

We knew about the decline of the Galapagos Tortoise and how

when Charles Darwin visited that island in the middle of the eighteenth century, the creatures were plentiful and when American sailors discovered the island a hundred years later, they took one hundred thousand tortoises within thirty years. The American, brought up with the pioneer philosophy of unlimited supply, carried this feeling with him about the world. The giant tortoise, more than eight feet in circumference, may weigh a quarter of a ton and its shell be over a yard across. Two circumstances contributed to its demise—the meat is excellent and, like the dodo, it was defenseless against outside predators. It could compete with natural enemies, but when new ones were introduced upon the island—escaping rats from ships, dogs and cats that turned wild when left behind, and pigs or cattle released for future use—destruction was rife. Pigs and rats relished the eggs, dogs and cats ate the babies as they hatched, and the cattle destroyed the flora and water supply. The Galapagos Tortoise had another quality—it could live for months without water; passing ships would put in to the island before crossing the Pacific and fill their holds with tons of the living larder to be used when needed, placing them in rows on their backs.

"In my opinion the turtle has an innate sadness," Barney said, sipping the beer which the waitress brought us while we waited for our fish to be broiled. "Haven't they been driven by predators who relish their savory meat to undertake the Herculean task of carrying their fortresses upon their backs? It seems to me that, alienated from the land from which she came, the turtle of the sea returns there only to deposit her eggs and her eyes fill with tears, weeping for her racial memories."

"Goodness," Lauri said. "All creatures that drink sea water have to excrete the excess salt somehow."

"Maybe they're just washing the sand out of their eyes," Paula offered.

We knew that the sea once was not so salty as now. And from the wearing down of mountains and the washing to the oceans, over the millions of years there had been a constant increase of the sea's salinity, which was why the body cells of all creatures, including fish, had a lower salt content than sea water. And while the kidneys excreted a measure of salt, they could never take care of the reptile or bird who drank only ocean water. Their kidneys were adapted to the past and were unable to change over the eons. We knew that the salt gland of a turtle was just behind the eyeball—a special organ whose function was to eliminate salt. Gulls and terns and pelicans had the same type of glands but their excess dripped from their beaks.

"Would you folks mind," John said drily, "if we just discussed the problems of the Park—and unemotionally?"

"Not at all," said Barney. "The problem of the Everglades is contained in the word *water*. When the voice of the northern Florida counties is heard too loudly in the State Senate, the Everglades will dry up and the Sea of Grass become stubble and chaff. When the conservationists speak clearly again, it will bloom and what wildlife is left will return. The balance of nature here is at the mercy of the balance of political power, and the creatures fulfill Genesis that puts them dependent upon man's mercy and command."

"Hear, hear," said Lauri.

"John," I told him, "it seems to me your problem is one of musical chairs that you play with your predators, moving them about and unable to bring yourself to destroy one."

"You have to define the terms, Helga," Lauri said. "What's a predator? It seems to me the big fish eat the little and down the line till you get to shrimp."

"What do shrimp eat?" Paula said.

Our meal had arrived and as Barney boned the mackerel, he said, "Perhaps it is unfair to condemn the situation in the Everglades. In generations past the resources of nature have appeared to be infinite and man has acted accordingly."

"I'll never agree that man has any right to take over the earth," I said. "I'm constantly ashamed of my species!"

Barney continued, "I wonder what we may be doing today with

the best of intentions which may have similar results in the future. I'm thinking of the effect of sonic boom on animals as well as man, frightening birds off their nests, jolting the incubating eggs and if too frequent rendering the creatures as neurotic as men."

"I've read," I told them, "in Aristotle's *History of Animals,* 'If it thunders while a hen-bird is brooding, the eggs get addled.' "

Barney said, "In medicine, I've seen examples of treatments devised with the best of intentions which have resulted in disaster. Today the long-range results of appendectomy are being questioned; with antibiotics many cases can be controlled and studies of late suggest that removal of the supposedly vestigial organ, filled with lymphoid tissue, which is known to have immunological significance, in some cases increases the susceptibility to certain kinds of cancer. Even in immunization against infection, as when it was tried against the hemolytic streptococcus, the patients developed a serious and even fatal disease, *lupus erythematosus.* We don't know what final effect major intervention in the various cells of a man's body, as well as in the ecology of nature, may cause."

"Now you sound as if you're talking about park preservation," John grinned.

Barney said, "We can see immediate gains in the field of medicine when we control certain infectious and viral diseases. However, it is just possible that the price will be an increase in the incidence of auto-immune diseases which result perhaps from sensitization of the person not only to the vaccine but to himself. This is the crux also when the ecology of natural areas are tampered with. A well-meant change can result in a series of changes and the end can never be foretold."

"That sounds like the international situation," Paula said, "and the basis for wars."

"A small move is made," Barney said, "and it's impossible to predict the ultimate result. The initial move often seems for the

best. Man has to be plastic enough, in his ideas of what is good
or bad for himself and his world, to admit his mistakes when con-
fronted with the ultimate interrelationship of all things, and to
follow the cause that is best for all."

It was well into the afternoon when we at last left the restaurant
in Flamingo and headed back up the Park Road. We waved
goodbye to the DeWeeses, who would meet us the next evening
at Key West where the government's sixty-five-foot diesel boat,
Bush Key, was due to put in for supplies and would take the five
of us the near seventy miles across the sea to the Dry Tortugas
in the Gulf of Mexico. Now we wanted to get back onto Route
1 and reach the Overseas Highway and make Key West by
nightfall.

The afternoon sun blazed hotly as we skimmed over the brittle
road. We were still oppressed by the plight of certain of the creatures we had seen and somewhat discouraged about the future of
the great national park that seemed forgotten by much of the country. We had read statistics that showed that since the twentieth
century one mammalian form a year had become extinct due to
man's activities. We knew that over a thousand species of birds,
mammals, reptiles and fish were in danger of the same fate. Paula
and I listened to Barney, still on the same theme, as the hot breeze
blew through the dust-covered car:

"Within a lifetime I've seen what had appeared to be the almost
infinite resources of the land ravaged not so much by man himself
but by a third person neither organic nor inorganic, which is technology, and which uses the accumulated energy of eons of organic
evolution, fossil fuels and their degradation products, to lay waste
a country which man alone could not easily despoil. This third
person, neither man nor nature but the child of both, the hy-
bridization of science and natural resources, has in one generation
made much of our land unlivable. Will this happen to the sea
too?"

We had no answers.

CHAPTER FOUR

The Carpet of Gold

A ship I have got in the North Country,
And she goes by the name of THE GOLDEN VANITY:
O, I fear she will be taken by a Spanish gallalee
As she sails by the Lowland, lowland!
        —Old Ballad: "The Golden Vanity"

T HE wind was rising and the salt air swept through the car windows as we neared the Florida Keys, refreshing us after the heated inland trip. We crossed the bridge over the sound and came to the narrow strip of island called Key Largo, the northern-most of the long strand of coral reefs which continued over two hundred miles to the Dry Tortugas. Barney talked of how twenty years ago he had come to the Keys, struck with gold fever, to search for wrecks of the Spanish Plate Fleet of 1715. Ten of the eleven galleons with deep square sails, batteries of guns, two thou-sand men aboard and laden with close to twenty million in silver and gold, jewels and other treasures plundered from Montezuma and Atahualpa had gone down in a hurricane off these keys. A certain amount of the riches had been recovered back then by Spanish divers and indentured native Indians but the rest lay under the sea. It has been estimated that perhaps one-eighth of all the gold and silver shipped during the time when Philip V reigned in Spain and pirates and buccaneers hunted the Caribbean lies still on the floor of the waters of the Florida Gulf. Barney had come upon a coral-crusted anchor off Key Largo, ten feet long and bearing no crossbar, signifying that it was from an ancient ship. Finding no sign of other wreckage, the Criles had moved down the coast to Marathon where they took a boat to Delta Shoals. There they came on the remains of a slave ship and retrieved many sea-damaged African elephant tusks, four of which hang on Sun Room wall. Barney and his family spent their vacations, often with other divers, working in sometimes storm-driven seas, threading their way through the reefs and coral heads by bright sun and starlight, hoping to be the ones to find the treasure upon the bottom.

In those early days, divers were not interested in archaeology as a rule, and it seldom occurred to them to preserve wreck sites as historic monuments. One of the few and first to recognize the romance and pleasure to visitors of intact wreck sites was a man who had dived with the Criles on the ivory wreck where the elephant tusks were found; he was called "Silver-bar" McKee after he found three seventy-pound silver ingots at Cay Gorda in the Bahamas, sending one bar to the Smithsonian in Washington. Art McKee had a museum of his recovered treasure in Tavernier just below Key Largo, and we hoped to meet him shortly. Barney said he and most of the divers he knew had never dreamed of how millions of people over the world would be buying faceplates and flippers and taking to the sea. Barney himself had been responsible for dynamiting the ivory wreck of the slave ship to shake a cannon loose from the coral and bring it home where it now stood in a corner of the Sun Room.

To our east, three miles from shore in the waters off Key Largo, was the world's first park to be completely under the water—John Pennekamp Coral Reef State Park. In this seventy-five-square-mile area, shipwrecks are now protected and glass-bottom boats carry tourists to view and dive on them. We knew there was a nine-foot submerged bronze statue somewhere there, cast in Italy and called "Christ of the Deep," a duplicate of one in the waters off Genoa. We wanted to stop and visit the park, but the winds which swept through our car were beating the sea into tall waves and we were advised that the boats would not be going out. We talked with the park biologist and were told that over two hundred and fifty species of marine fishes were found in the area, thirty-two different starfish, six species of sea anemones. Forty of fifty-two species of Atlantic Reef coral have been observed here, where the system of both lagoon and barrier reefs comprises an enormous nursery for reef and pelagic fish.

The John Pennekamp Coral Reef State Park was established in 1960, when it was on the way to total depredation. Acres of the coral forest had been broken off and carted away by souvenir hunters and curio vendors from the shops along the Overseas Highway. Spearfishermen had come in droves to target practice on the fish, killing thousands. Now coral harvesting and spearfishing have been prohibited and the underwater flora and fauna are slowly coming back. The fish are becoming tame and will eat from visitors' hands if approached quietly. Tourists may inspect the wrecks of galleons as well as more modern ships that have sunk off the violent coast. The most famous wreck in the park in the HMS *Winchester,* which went down in 1695 and from which cannons and ballast rocks have been brought up. Gold and silver coins, anchors, pottery and various artifacts have been recovered from the park's waters over the years. The birth of the underwater diver and the popularity of the sport, the discovery of offshore oil and the recovery of treasure from the bottom, all have altered the public's concept of the sea. In Barney's day, when he first started diving for treasure, the only person he had ever heard of who had found anything was "Silver-bar" McKee, using a hood since neither faceplates with air attachments nor scuba gear had been invented yet. McKee had been one of those who dived on the *Winchester* wreck, which touched off the first frenetic hunt for Florida treasure. Since then he had raised a few gold and silver coins, pieces of jewelry and the artifacts, but nothing except the silver bars of great intrinsic value.

McKee was a small conservationist in the sense that Barney's grandfather McBride was in belonging to the Winous Point Shooting Club, which fostered wild birds. After McKee obtained a lease from the State of Florida, giving him exclusive salvage rights on wrecks he had located on the offshore reefs, he placed an underwater sign on his favorite wreck, stating that he had the right to work it. Then he set about to make the site attractive; he piled up the scattered ballast stones in the shape of a ship hull, rearranged the cannons and the anchor. He tamed and hand-fed fifty-pound groupers and big hog snappers which soared through the clouds of minnows that clung to the wreck. He filled his glass-bottom boat with tourists whom he let dive on the wreck and photograph it. One day he arrived to find that some ambitious treasure-seeker had dynamited the site, scattering it, burying it in sand and killing off the fish.

A few miles below Tavernier we came to McKee's museum, a dusty home-like building, marked by a huge coral-covered anchor outside. McKee's father, a little man bowed with age, was showing a group of visitors through the museum, pointing his gnarled finger at artifacts and in a quavering voice telling of his son's exploits—how in 1948 Art McKee had located most of the nineteen vessels of a 1733 fleet that vanished in a hurricane with near seventy million in silver. It was from the wrecks of that storm that McKee's Museum was largely stocked.

Then "Silver-bar" McKee himself appeared and over Coca-Colas informed us that he was still searching and salvaging, but had had hard luck. Barney told him he was not surprised, for McKee somehow managed consistently through his life to be misunderstood and to become embroiled in semi-serious trouble. When he went to New York to appear on television with some of his treasures, he was waylaid, beaten and robbed; he had been captured by Cubans, had vessels burned under him at sea, nearly died of inhaling oil fumes from a leaking air compressor; and had driven off the Overseas Highway once, plunging car and all into the swift tide which flows between the keys, and when he regained consciousness, finding the tide sweeping him back to shore. When he decided to settle on an exotic island to learn the secrets of shipwrecks from the natives, he fell in love with a girl there and even that incident had its tragic ending, Barney said, because it was the end of McKee's sea-going freedom when he married her.

We went outside the museum to look at the piles of salvage stacked about in a fenced yard, which McKee intended some-time to examine closely. Then we visited his sturdy unhandsome diving vessel, with its diesel engines and cranes, air lifts, jetting equipment and electronic metal detection gear. He told us that he was working on a new wreck whose whereabouts would remain a secret, and had already come on a few gold coins. When we told him that the glass-bottom boats at Pennekamp were not going out due to the high sea, he at once offered to take us up to the park in his boat. Barney became alert and interested, but Paula and I, recalling the legends of disaster which dogged "Silver-bar" Mc-Kee, were wary. Before leaving, we accompanied a fresh group of tourists about the museum, down to the double-locked vault in the cellar where jewelry on velvet pillows and gold doubloons and pieces-of-eight from Vera Cruz and Porto Bello and huge bars of Spanish silver bullion were displayed in lighted cases.

Barney and Art talked continually and enthusiastically about the old days. When the Criles had first come upon the ivory wreck, they were skin-diving with no more equipment than faceplates and flippers. On their second day out, they were told that a famous treasure hunter had arrived in Marathon and was trying to rent a boat. They were sure that he was after their wreck and they were right. No sooner had they anchored over the cannons than a boat came chugging out bearing Art McKee. They stifled their jealousy and decided they were lucky to be working with a professional. They spent a week salvaging the wreck and raising stacks of brass dishes and pewter plates, knives, forks, spoons, muskets, musket balls, clay pipes, pottery, glass, stacks of cannon balls, two cannon, and twenty-six elephant tusks. Throughout our house are some of the items, including pieces-of-eight found scattered in the sand, so oxidized that they have trebled their original thickness and the silver salt has made them unrecognizable as metal. Barney has another silver coin which he got off the same wreck, but it was attached to a cannon ball and the electrolytic action of the iron protected it so that although the coin is more than two hundred years old, it is as bright as when first struck. It is only when silver is next to iron or in the form of ingots or when quantities of coins are piled together as in a chest that the metal is spared from the chemical destruction of the salt sea.

Twenty years ago, when Barney became interested in searching for treasure in the shipwrecks which litter the reefs of Florida and the Bahamas, there were only a handful of people who took it seriously. Few appreciated that for the first time since the galleons sank, technology had advanced so that their location and salvage was not only feasible but might be monetarily rewarding. The history of the huge losses of treasure was often reported in maps and accounts and copies of shipping manifests in the Spanish archives. In addition there were hundreds of unreported sunken pirate vessels and privateers laden with captured spoils. Recently divers set out from the same dock at Marathon where Barney had and going down in waters only a few hundred yards from the ivory wreck, recovered a fortune in silver coins, the largest haul yet made in the Keys and estimated at two million dollars.

An indication of treasure is the spotting of coral-encrusted ballast stones, which are smooth round Spanish river rocks carried in the bilges of the galleons to keep them upright. When the wooden ships rot and disappear, the mounds of stones remain to mark the spot. This treasure of silver came from the Silver Plate Fleet, the *Plata Flota*, which went down on the coral rocks near Sombrero Light in July 1773, bound for Seville with ingots of silver from Mexico and Colombia, chests of coins, barrels of pieces-of-eight, precious stones, ivory, and varied riches, valued at twenty million. After the ships broke up one by one, a lone survivor returned to note on now-ancient maps where the wrecks occurred.

The divers who salvaged the silver fortune were a fishing guide and a salesman, energetic weekend divers with the information from the Spanish archives in their hands. After weeks of harassment by storm, ship breakdowns, trouble with crewmen and a variety of problems, they came upon twenty pieces-of-eight, some dated 1732, odd-shaped coins, oxidized in the sea water so that the coating hid the silver with its stamped design beneath. The work was not easy and they spent eight hours a day under water. It was weeks later in a surging sea when they came up with a record find one day of close to four hundred silver coins, with a collector's value of near a hundred dollars each. Since then small planes may be seen searching for outlines of ballast along the reefs and boats ply the water with casual and professional hunters aboard; on the beaches men move with mine detectors looking for coins washed ashore, and in towns up and down the Florida coasts con men and realists encourage the hordes who are migrating there seeking the grail—treasure. Barney at home is often heard to groan as he reads the latest report of a find: "I was only a hundred feet from that one" or "I was right there; if I'd only been able to stay a few weeks or months instead of a few days, I'd have had the treasure!"

One of the most dramatic finds in recent treasure hunting was made by Kip Wagner, originally a Florida construction man, and his associates in the Real Eight Corporation, farther up the coast near Fort Pierce. After a long time at the grueling work, they recovered thousands of silver pieces-of-eight as well as gold doubloons, silver bars and bullion, gold ingots, gold rings and artifacts, Chinese porcelain, a golden necklace over eleven feet long with a dragon pendant appraised at fifty thousand dollars. In New York we had seen the exhibition in a gallery, where the original model of the ship was reconstructed complete with parrot and where a movie of a ship tossed at sea was projected with the screams and prayers of the Spanish seamen filling the room. The wreck was that of the Spanish Plate Fleet of 1715 and one day as the Real Eight men cut a hole in the overlying sand with their blaster, a propeller-driven jet stream of water, "they were blinded by a bright-yellow glow," writes Kip Wagner. "There, in all its magnificent splendor, was a veritable carpet of gold, the likes of which modern man had probably never seen before. The divers burned up almost a full tank of air just staring in awe at the sight." By the day's end they had over a thousand pieces of gold and were beginning to worry that if they continued the pace they would ruin the world market for rare coin specimens. Their find to date is valued at more than five million dollars and only two of the ten galleons have been explored.

The lost treasures of the sea, over the centuries believed irretrievable, are slowly being fished out. In the frigid waters off Scotland, after three years of diving, a barnacle-crusted chest containing $168,000 in silver coins was brought up. Off Nova Scotia, French gold that has laid there for over two centuries, churned in the erratic currents of the cold waters, has been retrieved after three divers gave their lives in trying. Off the coast of western England in a subterranean cave, gold and silver coins were found strewn on the bottom, thought to come from the flagship of a Mediterranean fleet which sank in 1707 with over two million worth of treasure aboard. In the soft mud a hundred feet below the surface of Tokyo Bay lies the lost treasure of the shoguns, who were being demoted from their dynastic rule and were fleeing Japan and heading for Shanghai with perhaps ten million in gold and treasure. And in the Indian Ocean, not far from the shores of the coast of Africa is the Peacock Throne of an Indian potentate, made of gold and studded with jewels and worth thirty-five million dollars, which went down with all aboard in 1792 along with more millions in gold and silver and jewels. The richest treasures that the sea holds are probably those spilled into her from the sixteenth to the eighteenth centuries by Spanish ships filled with plunder from the Inca and Aztec empires. The uneasy galleons sailing up the eastern coast of Florida and across the Bahama Bank were caught in fierce hurricanes and dumped the bodies of thousands of Spaniards, along with the riches, into the reefs.

Casting a last glance at "Silver-bar" McKee's vault where a gold earring lay with a tear-drop emerald dangling from it, which had been recovered from one of those very galleons, Paula and I went upstairs to join Barney and Art, who were still reminiscing. It was late in the afternoon as we left the museum to continue down the Overseas Highway. Once the Keys had been isolated and sur- rounded by water, Key West itself over a hundred miles from the mainland. In the early 1900s a railroad was built, employing Grecian deep-sea divers, immigrant laborers from New York, Cubans and Bahamans, all by the thousands. The sections of shallow water between the keys were to be filled and bridges were to span the deep-water channels, all of this against the advice of authorities, who felt it would interfere with the flow of water between the Bay of Florida and lower Biscayne Bay in case a hurricane came roaring in and an escape valve was necessary. In 1906, the hurricane arrived as predicted and at the beginning during the first lull, it was said that the local settlers, called "Conchs," lashed themselves to palm trees and called "Go back!" to the workers who felt the storm was past. When the lull ended, those in the open were washed into the sea, the death toll coming to two hundred. The railroad took seven years to rebuild.

The Overseas Highway was begun in 1934, using twenty-five thousand CCC workers under President Roosevelt's orders. In the following September the men, many from the north and few of whom understood the ways of hurricanes or the Bahamian saying "September remember," paid no heed to the blowing wind; by the time they understood what was occurring it was too late. A hur- ricane is a swirling doughnut of power, the lull its hole. The pat- tern of the storm is to hit powerfully from one direction, followed by the lull, and then to lash in from the other side. Walls of water and a furious wind swept men, women and children out to sea; as usual the survivors of the first wind emerged from their houses to survey the damage and search for the lost and while out there were caught by the second wind. The loss was difficult to estimate; in the hot weather the known and unknown dead were cremated in a Labor Day Hurricane Funeral Pyre; officially it was judged an Act of God and no blame was leveled. The tidal waves had been set off by the solid fill which interfered with the sweep of water between the bays. The railway was nearly demolished and sold its right-of-way to the Overseas Highway builders. In 1938 the ribbon of road on which we traveled, costing over a thousand lives, became a part of U.S. 1.

We passed from island to island: Big Pine Key, Cudjoe Key, Sugarloaf Key, Saddlebunch Keys, Boca Chica Key. The road was a string of towns, motels, fishing camps, restaurants, bars. The atmosphere was of transiency, the people concerned with the sea in some way and the encouragement of tourists. Spanking yachts with white-clad crews were moored in ports alongside disreputable hulks manned by bearded ragged fellows. The sun had set when we reached Key West. The bougainvillea was in bloom and gleamed everywhere in the dusk of the crowded little town. Horns honked. Neon lights winked and blazed. The Key West Naval Air Station was nearby and everywhere were white-jacketed sailors, some with girls on their arms. Barney wanted us to visit Sloppy Joe's, Hemingway's old hangout, and we went through the swinging doors to the long counters, the brass rail beneath; it was so dark one could scarcely see. Sailors were sipping beers at the circular bar and the jukebox was tinkling away.

Barney was disappointed and complained about the ravages of time, as Paula and I took our places at the bar on either side of him. The colorful atmosphere he remembered was drab now, he claimed. The vigorous bartender had been replaced by a young woman, the sailors were engendering no riots, the authentic quality of the customers was no longer, not a man with a salty beard was to be seen, resting from his labors on the sea! Paula was delighted with the scene nonetheless, and promptly ordered a key lime pie, the speciality of the area, on the recommendation of two sailors up the bar and they joined her to discuss the state of the Navy. Barney sadly ordered beers for us. The girl behind the bar demanded of me, "Let's see your identification."

"Identification for what!" Barney roared.

"Her age," she said sharply. "Where's her driving license?"

I was wearing slacks as Lauri DeWeese had advised me was the custom of the Keys, and a loose white gondolier shirt which I had got in Italy; in the dim light I did not measure up to my forty-odd years. Fishing through my pockets, I came up with membership cards in The Poetry Society of America and the American Milk Goat Record Association and The Author's Guild, but not the license. As I was deciding that it might be in the car, Barney began growling again.

"This girl beside me that you gave the pie to is her daughter."

"You can't be too careful." The barkeep nodded her head. "Everything's going to the dogs these days."

Barney agreed. "It's the ravages of time," he repeated.

But then a crab fisherman came along and sat on my left. I recognized his profession by the odor of his clothes. He drank a tall draft beer straight down, slammed it on the bar with a meaningful look at our barkeep, who at once hurried to refill it. I saw that the end of his ring finger and his thumb were missing, as he turned to me, breathed out contentedly and said, "First time here, dear?"

By the end of the evening a few hours later, as we wound our way to a shabby unpainted motel for the night, Barney was happy once more. He liked the crab fisherman very much and found out that he was a stone crabber and that that was the only commercial crab around. Barney had thought the stone crabs were all fished out long ago, but the man said they were coming back. The claws were the only parts of the stone crab that were good to eat, so instead of taking the whole creature, the fishermen broke off the big claws and threw it back. It wasn't hurt and grew other claws right away and could be caught again. Stone crabs were plentiful now that they had learned how to harvest them. The crabber said they still had to look out for the claws and that was how he'd lost the end of his finger and thumb.

Barney and he argued about how many other creatures might be farmed that way. Amphibia like salamanders are famous for their ability to regenerate missing parts and Barney thought lobsters might grow new tails if you broke them off and threw the body back. The crabber didn't agree, but said it might work with their claws up in the north; here the lobsters didn't have claws. Barney told him about the Japanese Hanging Oyster farms, where a dozen or so oyster shells containing spat, which is the larvae, are strung along short wires attached to wood racks that are set into water deep enough so that none of the shells ever touch bottom. The method is successful because it protects the young oysters not only from creeping predators like starfish but from competition from other creatures of the sea floor; the survival rate is eighty per cent rather than the usual twenty; they are also ready to harvest in eighteen months instead of the usual three years. The stone crabber said he had a Spanish friend from Ria de Vigo in northwest Spain, who used to work in the mussel industry there. They reared them like the Japanese oysters, fastening them on ropes of esparto grass which were hung from the outriggers of big rafts anchored in the mouths of rivers.

As we fell asleep we were talking of how in the morning we would meet the DeWeeses and buy our supplies and by the next night would sleep in one of the prisoner's cells of Fort Jefferson.

CHAPTER FIVE

The Ghost Fortress

If a step should sound or a word be spoken,
Would a ghost not rise at the strange guest's hand?
So long have the grey bare walls lain guestless,
Through branches and briars if a man make way,
He shall find no life but the sea-wind's, restless
      Night and day.

—Algernon Charles Swinburne:
"A Forsaken Garden"

E ARLY the next morning, we were wakened by the telephone. It was the DeWeeses, who had got in late the night before. They said that the *Bush Key* would be leaving at eleven, and we arranged to meet them shortly at the local A & P to put in supplies for twelve days at the Dry Tortugas. The sky was a clear hard blue and the air hot as we walked down the deserted street to breakfast at a tiny café. It was nice to see the DeWeeses again, and Barney and John went off to buy beer and some Scotch and rum while Lauri and Paula and I shopped for food.

Lauri had a check-list, the paper well-worn and soft, the penciled entries smudged and disappearing from long use. She had developed it over the years when they lived at Fort Jefferson. Paula and I duplicated her list and when it was filled, we piled more cans of fruit and boxes of powdered milk and a large jar of instant coffee into the shopping carts, unbelieving that her list was suf-

ficient. Lauri disdained the synthetic coffee and informed us that
the DeWeeses carried their own coffeepot and special grind of
coffee everywhere they went if there was an electric line in.

The men returned and we loaded the boxes into the DeWeeses'
station wagon along with our seven vari-colored duffle bags of gear
and books and camera equipment. After checking in our rented
car, we headed for the Naval Station, where we would board the
boat. The sentry at the gate glanced at John's credentials and
passed us through into a maze of driveways lined with ancient
drab-looking buildings. The station had been a submarine and
destroyer base during World War II and one of the East Coast's
centers for anti-U-Boat patrol. Now it looked like a deserted
mining town. John and Barney remembered that it was back in
1948 that they last met here in Key West to make this journey,
John being Fort Jefferson's Boat Captain, when the Criles arrived
with cameras and equipment to record the Dry Tortugas on film.

"Remember the old Park Service boat, the *Fort Jefferson?*"
Lauri said.

"When the engine nearly burned up," Barney said, "we thought
the boat would catch fire."

"And the week after you left the engine did, and the *Jeff* had to
be towed in by the Coast Guard," John said.

"Never a dull moment," Lauri said.

"Have Helga and Paula heard about your first time in the Dry
Tortugas?" John asked.

"Wasn't that in the thirties?" Lauri said. "We hadn't met yet."

"It was December of thirty-six," Barney said, "the year after the
area became a national park."

And as our car laced its way toward the dock, he told about that
reckless trip. The young Criles had gone in a small single-motor
boat, captained by a local conch fisherman and loaned by someone
whom Barney had at first considered to be a grateful patient. The
trip to the Fort was quiet enough, but after they arrived a norther
blew up, which lasted for five days unabated, making life on the
boat even in the shelter of Fort Jefferson difficult. The swells beat

them against the pilings of the dock all night so that the Criles finally carried their mattresses into the shelter of the Fort where rats ran about and over them making sleep a disturbing affair.

During the days they explored the Fort, unable to take to the sea or even to dive and swim, since the norther had churned the ocean up and it was frigid. They confined their water activities to shelling in the Fort's moat. The only alleviating factor was that the custodian had a goodly supply of demijohns of untaxed Cuban rum which he received from Cuban fishermen in return for the use of his docks to ride out storms. When Barney pleaded with the old conch fisherman to try to make the run back to Key West, he shook his head, muttering about the sucking quicksands of Rebecca Shoals. And so for five evenings they sat in the Fort drinking rum and listening to the visitor-hungry custodian talk on and on. When at last they did ship off for Key West they got windbound in the shallows past the lee of the islands, where the tide and the wind opposed one another and raised monstrous waves that came close together in a sequence perfectly timed to beat the bottom out of a little boat. The fisherman said it was impossible to turn back, as they would capsize in the trough and must head into the open sea. The planks of the boat began to spring and all took turns at bailing. After nearly twenty-four hours they swung into the Key West harbor, at which point the propeller shaft broke. Barney said that if it had happened over Rebecca Shoals there would have been another small wreck buried in the treacherous shifting sands, graveyard of ships, and that anyone diving off the wreck of the little boat would have found no pieces-of-eight but only a minor treasure of interesting shells.

"Is there any chance of a norther now, John?" I asked.

"We have a nice supply of taxed rum, if there is," Lauri said gently, "besides our coffeepot, so there's no cause for worry."

"I love a calm sea," Paula said. "I get seasick at the drop of a hat."

"She's been warned," I told everybody, "that when you travel with Barney you have to keep on your toes. You don't ever complain."

"I'm determined to travel," Paula said. "And I'll put up with any stipulations. The first trip I made with them was to Mexico, and Helga told me before we left that anyone following Barney might as well wear track shoes."

"Before I met him, Lauri," I said, "my idea of travel was to sun on the Côte d'Azur. Barney never deliberately sunned in his life; he says tanning is bad for your skin. He likes to go as far as modern transportation will take you, and then move off into the wild; that's when his vacation begins."

"I draw the line where the coffeepot can't go," Lauri said. "I'll follow John anywhere we can take our coffeepot."

When we reached the dock, we found the *Bush Key* all set to go. Mr. Gallagher, one of the maintenance men from the Fort, was the Acting Captain and with the help of another crewman and John, if necessary, would manage the boat. They had been laying in supplies and had just completed loading them on. The *Bush Key* was not quite what I expected. Somehow, after the tales I had heard of former expeditions to the Dry Tortugas, I was prepared for a trim modern vessel to replace those troublesome ones. There she was, a great hulk, her name unmistakable in block letters on her prow, rusting quietly alongside the worn dock, a few working boats and coal and sand barges not far off; she was sixty-five feet long, steel-hulled, diesel-engined, with nothing but a pilot house on her ancient but clean deck.

"Is she safe, John?" I asked.

"She needs a little shining up," he said briskly, "but she's a good boat." And he began to unload the station wagon, which would remain locked in the parking lot by the dock, waiting for their return.

Mr. Gallagher and his mate joined us and we formed a safari line and carried on our gear and supplies. Lauri supervised the stowing of the perishables in the hold. John descended the little ladder and the boxes were handed down to him. John DeWeese has an almost unnoticeable limp; he has an artificial limb, having lost one leg below the knee in a shipboard accident when he was in the Navy in World War II. This disability does not stop him from swimming, at which time he removes the contraption. He is not particularly shy about the situation, but he doesn't throw it around either.

Mr. Gallagher started the engines, and John came up to fasten on the hatch and Barney undid the lines which held us to the dock. The *Bush Key* backed into the channel and began the sixty-eight-mile trip, following the buoys out of the harbor. White-winged Herring Gulls, Ringed-billed Gulls, Royal Terns and Laughing Gulls circled over the stern begging for garbage, their shrill cries audible above the noisy engines. We passed sandbars, some gleaming white in the sun, and then felt the roll of the Gulf Stream swell. We began to settle down for the journey which would take a minimum of six and a half hours. There were no chairs and we sat or stretched out on the hatch, using the blankets that the experienced DeWeeses had provided. The sea odor was in the air and somehow it seemed more fragrant than on land, a subtlety to it. The green-blue sea of the harbor grew darker until it was a deep blue in the open ocean. We caught the glisten of a flying fish and then there seemed to be a hundred of them, like a flock of silver sparrows iridescent-winged, continually rising and skimming the surface in the hot sun—eighty, a hundred, a hundred and fifty feet before splashing again into a wave. Some remained in the air while we counted ten.

Flying fish are found over very deep water; before taking off the tail may beat as many as fifty times a second in order to attain the forty miles an hour needed to put it into the air. The wings are folded against the sides until the fish starts from the water, when they are at once spread. As the fish slows in its glide it may either re-enter the water or dip its long lower tail in for another push and another sail. We knew that the blue flying fish built nests for their eggs by binding together the floating sargasso weed and that the young were brown while they lived in the weed and were one of the sea's examples of color protection. We knew too that during the adaptation of the species to leaving water and returning, the cornea of the flying fish had altered. Instead of being a segment of a sphere like the cornea of other fish, a property which makes them near-sighted when they are in the air, the flying fish's cornea is a low three-sided pyramid, the corneal material having nearly the same refractive index as water. Because the light is not bent sharply, the flying fish has a long focal range in air.

High above in the sultry blue a few Man-o'-war or Frigate birds circled, their wings motionless as they tilted and turned in the trade breeze. There would be many of these birds where we were going; we knew that they were scavengers and also pirates, stealing much of their food from gulls and terns and even their own kind. They had longer wings in proportion to their body than any other sea bird. Arthur Cleveland Bent, in his *Life Histories of Birds,* had said, "The flight of the Man-o'-war bird is an inspiration; the admiring observer is spellbound with wonder as he beholds it and longs for the eloquence to describe it; but words are powerless to convey the impression that it creates. It is the most marvellous and most perfect flying machine that has ever been produced, with seven or eight feet of alar expanse . . . steered by a long scissor-like tail." During World War I the German Fokker plane, speedy and effective, had been designed upon this particular bird.

It was still and hot and I was drowsy, lulled by the steady motion of the boat and the sound of the motors, muted now that we were under way. John and Barney were talking about the people from the Florida Audubon Society who had been staying at the Fort on their annual bird-banding visit, living in the quarters that would be assigned to us. They were using mist nets and worked in collaboration with the National Park Service and the University of Florida. They were concerned with the Sooty Tern and the Noddy which they had been banding regularly since 1937, and which assembled between May and September every year for their nesting season on Bush Key, the small island for which our boat was named. Lauri called out from the bow of the ship that there were porpoises. We came to lean over the rail and watch four of them riding the bow wave the way a bird will use an updraft to coast without effort and seemingly also with pleasure in mind.

Barney and I looked for others, recalling a herd of hundreds which came to accompany *Sea Diver* once for half an hour as we went through the Yucatan Channel heading for British Honduras. The sea had been choppy, the sun bright, and certain of the creatures leaped continually out of the water in a high arc. After a while they suddenly disappeared, as our four were doing now into the expanse of blue where in the distance could be seen the low outline of the Marquesas Keys.

The Continental Shelf, from which the Florida Keys, the Marquesas and the Dry Tortugas emerge as tiny coral islands, bends due west from Key Largo. The Marquesas Keys are in the formation of an atoll, which is a ring-shaped coral island almost or completely surrounding a lagoon. Barney, who had visited there, said it was doubtful if the Marquesas were a true atoll. Large colonies of Man-o'-war birds and various herons frequented the place and in the lagoon sawfish, ten to twenty feet long, came to spawn. The sawfish is a shark-like ray that uses its extended saw-toothed snout to stun and attack fish and to locate invertebrates which it also eats; when the living young are born a protective sheath, soon to be discarded, covers the tiny saw of the two-foot-long baby. Barney said that in the days when he was as intent on spearing fish as he now was on photographing them, he used to chase the Marquesas sawfish in an outboard motor boat and try to get a tow on his harpoon line.

"Were you successful?" we demanded.

"No, but I kept trying," he shrugged. "And I've never forgotten the time in the Florida Keys when I was ten and my father speared one and it gave the boat such a jerk that I fell off the stern and they had to cut the line and go back and retrieve me."

A few miles past the Marquesas was Rebecca Shoals, the waters greenish and unlike the blue deep sea. In those shallow quicksands hundreds of shipwrecks are said to be buried. John told us that Rebecca Light had been damaged in a hurricane which had roared a path through here three weeks ago, battering lighthouses and wreaking damage among the nesting terns at the Dry Tortugas. The Audubon people reported that during the storm the chicks had made their way to the center of Bush Key above the water and all the adults had flown away. When the hurricane was over and the water subsided, the surviving chicks came back to the nesting sites and the adults returned to care for them; chicks that were discovered buried in sand and twigs recovered, seemingly unhurt, when the debris was removed. Barney said that on Matecumbe Key, which he had revisited after the great hurricane of 1935, a human baby had been found in a palm thicket, unidentified, wailing and unharmed.

Lauri and Paula and I were trying to recite Lord Byron's canto which seemed so appropriate for the scene and its potential; we were doing pretty well with our combined memories:

> *Roll on, thou deep and dark blue Ocean—roll!*
> *Ten thousand fleets sweep over thee in vain;*
> *Man marks the earth with ruin—his control*
> *Stops with the shore;—upon the watery plain*
> *The wrecks are all thy deed, nor doth remain*
> *A shadow of man's ravage, save his own,*
> *When, for a moment, like a drop of rain,*
> *He sinks into thy depths with bubbling groan—*
> *Without a grave—unknelled, uncoffined, and unknown.*

It was one o'clock when we assembled, standing about the hatch, for a lunch of "submarine" sandwiches and soft drinks that Lauri had brought, and hot coffee for the hardy DeWeeses from their thermos bottles. Then I was drowsy again and napped on the hatch cover. John was occupied with some engine problem on which he was being consulted. Lauri, binoculars beside her, was perched in the prow. Barney was reading a paperback, and Paula was skimming a book she had brought along, *You and Your Congressman*, since she would be working for one in Washington on our return. Rocking in the boat's motion, my thoughts wandered by themselves.

Long ago it was believed that the world was dirt and rocks and about it ran a body of water, relatively narrow. Now it is known that water covers seventy per cent of the earth's surface. There is no other planet like it in the solar system; some lack sufficient gravity to hold water or its vapor, others have icy patches but no ocean, being too cold and too far from the sun. The sea in places is deeper than the land is high. Mount Everest, the tallest peak, 29,028 feet, could be submerged with room to spare in the ocean's deepest area, the Mariana Trench in the Western Pacific, 35,800 feet down. It is believed that in the deep layers of the ocean may lie the early history of the planet Earth. In the soft mud of the bottom, undisturbed by violent sun or storm, may be preserved the skeletons and shells of earliest life. For centuries the deepest a diver could go was a hundred feet; now with special gear they are going a thousand and doubtless will go deeper. Submarines have descended near seven miles in the Mariana Trench. Every animal found on land is basically represented in the ocean. Every year a new species is discovered in the sea as man explores it more closely. In 1938 the coelacanth, a fish thought to be extinct for sixty million years, turned up off the coast of South Africa; of late, in the Indian Ocean off the Comoro Islands a specimen was photographed in its own habitat about a hundred and thirty feet down. It was four feet long with the heavy appendages which demonstrate its relation to the species that crawled out of the sea once and made it my ancient relative. The French photographer had reported: "Its huge phosphorescent eyes glowed at me, and its wide-spaced teeth looked like a dog's canines. . . . Then the coelacanth swam off, disappearing into the depths again."

I must have slept for Barney was calling. "We're nearly there. Come, you can just see her."

On the horizon, like a mirage, was the outline of something large and dark. Closer, the red castellated walls with their casemates and corner bastions became clear, and we thought of prisoners nearing this place and wondering what the life would be like. Seven sandy keys now compose the cluster called the Dry Tortugas and along with the surrounding shoals and waters covering sev-

enty-five square miles of land and sea make up Fort Jefferson National Monument, the first area of the sea to come under federal
protection. Over four hundred and fifty years ago in 1513, coming in June as we were, Ponce de León found the tiny islands and
called them *Islas de las Tortugas,* after "the great amount of turtles
which there do breed." He said that "In one short time in the
night, they took . . . one hundred and sixty tortoises." Now turtles
are seldom seen and live on only in the name of the place. In time
the name became Dry Tortugas as a warning to passing ships that
no fresh water was to be had there.

The dark red ruins we were approaching seemed to resemble
some crumbling medieval castle with the decorative high cornice
work, the enigmatic casemates with their jagged openings and no
life to be seen. John pointed out some of the tiny keys, scarcely discernible sandy strands—East Key, Middle Key, Hospital Key. As
we neared the Fort we passed the larger Bush Key with its flat
white sandy beach where the Sooty Terns nested and we could see
the brush beyond where the Noddies were being raised. Then we
observed the phenomenon of Bush Key—the great funnel of constantly chirping and calling terns rising in a column to the sky. We
could make out Long Key lying beyond. But our amazed eyes were
drawn back to the sight of the birds—thirty thousand in the air
at a time.

We had read the report of the naturalist, painter and orni-
thologist John James Audubon, visiting here before the Fort had
been planned, in May 1832: "On landing, I felt for a moment
as if the birds would raise me from the ground, so thick were they
all round, and so quick the motion of their wings, Their cries were
indeed deafening, yet not more than half of them took to wing
on our arrival. . . . Some of the sailors, who had more than once
been there before, had provided themselves with sticks, with which
they knocked down the birds as they flew thick around and over
them. In less than half an hour, more than a hundred terns lay
dead in a heap, and a number of baskets were filled to the brim
with eggs. . . . The sailors told me that the birds were excellent eat-

ing, but on this point I cannot say much, although I can safely recommend the eggs, for I considered them delicious, in whatever way cooked, and during our stay at the Tortugas we never passed a day without providing ourselves with a good quantity of them." As we chugged past Bush Key, we noted the stern sign on the sand close to shore: KEEP OFF / BIRD SANCTUARY.

A Brown Pelican was floating upon the water as the engine cut and we tied up alongside the ramshackle wooden dock on the east side of Garden Key. A few people had gathered to watch the landing, among them our captain's wife, Mrs. Gallagher, waiting for her supplies; the Fort's Management Assistant, who was responsible for its maintenance and activity; and his wife and two little boys. The men came to help Barney and John unload our cargo, which was piled into a trailer behind a small tractor which puttered off past a sign stating that this was Fort Jefferson National Monument and across the drawbridge which led into the heavy walls of the Fort itself.

With our cameras across our shoulders in the late afternoon sun we followed, our footsteps echoing on the wood planks over the moat of the once-prison Fort, and under the American flag, through the gateway of the ruin, the sally port, its only formal entrance, framed by massive smooth granite. Once there was a heavy iron gate and the drawbridge was kept pulled up and overhead were the cells of prisoners. We were subdued as we took the path across the stubble of the parade ground, whispering rather than talking, past clumps of Spanish bayonet and prickly pear and organ cactus, surrounded by the serried vaulted arches, sixteen or so to each of the fifty-foot-high walls that composed the hexagonal fort. The Assistant's house, with its screened veranda and shrubbery, was at the end of the parade ground path and past it were seven arches in the second tier which had been bricked up and beneath them two boarded in to make quarters for visitors—the Florida Audubon group, naturalists, government people, and semi-official guests like ourselves. There were clotheslines strung along the lower archway. The DeWeeses would have their quarters on the upper story in the casemates and we would live and sleep in the

enclosed rooms below. As our whispers sounded through the archways, a special delegation of black Salt Marsh Mosquitoes that had
not yet had supper met us in full force. Lauri and John, parting
at the stairway and heading up, assured us that as soon as the evening wind blew, the delegation would disappear.

At the doorway to our quarters, I halted and endeavored to appear unconcerned about their stark spareness. I remembered the
letter from the Park Service people: "You may find the room a bit
rustic." Openings for windows had been left in the enclosed archways and wooden frames set in the screens. Someone had laid white
paint upon the old red-yellow bricks and it was flecked about. Ill-
sorted furniture was scattered here and there and we put our
cameras on the linoleum-covered table and gazed at the four bare
Army cots, on three of which the cordial Assistant's wife had folded
the sheets she had washed after the Audubon people left a day or so
ago, and dried on the lines outside. I began to unpack our perishables from the A & P boxes which had been set inside our door
along with our duffle bags. Paula made up the cots, while I put
the meat and eggs and juices in the two ancient and unmatched,
creaking-doored and musty refrigerators where the Audubon
people had left a few withered oranges and a half-filled carton of
cream.

"This is great," Barney cried. "Hasn't changed a bit in twenty
years. I was afraid someone might have modernized it. As soon as
you and Paula finish that, could we inspect our new home?"

"My gosh." I slapped at the soft, filled body of a large mosquito.
"Home sweet home."

"I'll sweep next," Paula said, cheerful.

"Don't overdo it," I told her, rubbing the welts rising on my
bare arms and examining the collection of cast-off pots and pans,
the plastic dishes, the rusty flatware. "I wonder if the rats still run
as freely as they used to, Barney?"

"Come on," he urged. "The sun will be setting and it will be a
stunning evening. I want to show you everything. Let's walk
around the top of the walls."

And so we climbed the long circular granite staircase, up and up, that wound through one of the bastions and led to the top and began to walk the massive forty-foot-wide half-mile-long battlements of the six-sided Fort. Barney was talking about man's incorrigible tendency to try to buy security by building walls instead of diffusing information—Hadrian's Wall, the Great Wall of China, the Maginot Line.

"Perhaps the time has come," he said, "when the power of our modern weapons has made war itself obsolete, so that we must start rearing a new generation free of the necessity of defending archaic ideas with outdated techniques."

We felt the offshore breeze rise and the salt air cool; the mosquitoes has disappeared. It became golden and beautiful up there and also rather terrifying. There were large open holes into airvents and incinerators and ancient drains designed to carry the rainwater down from the parapets through filters of sand and brick and into an elaborate maze of cisterns which were under the gunrooms and which underlaid all of the Fort, even the parade ground. There were jagged spots where bricks had broken and tumbled and mortar crumbled; quantities of sand had been blown up there, making mounds and little dunes, where prickly pear cactus flourished and desert-like grasses, vines, and burr-plants had found a foothold. A scorpion slithered away, and we glimpsed the Tree Rat or Black Rat, *Rattus rattus Alexandrus,* occasionally seen on all these keys, the DeWeeses had said, fond of ships and climbing trees. Southward stretched the ocean's expanse, the blue of the water lightening or varying into greenish shades where the underwater reefs reared and becoming dark blue again over the channels. To the east beyond the tiny dock where the *Bush Key* was moored, along with a few shrimp trawlers and fishing boats of varied sizes and states of repair, was Bush Key itself, where the terns' chatter now was muffled as they nested for the night. In the distance stretched the sandy banks of Long Key. A black lighthouse of rusting iron, unused now and with many-faceted turret windows, stood on the angle of wall which overlooked the dock at the top of one of the spiral staircases. To the northeast and southwest were battered ruins of pilings that Barney said were Navy coaling rigs which had been damaged by a hurricane in 1904, repaired and then wrecked again in 1910 and abandoned. To the west half a mile was Loggerhead Key with its 150-foot-high light, that had long ago replaced Fort Jefferson's little black one. Within the Fort below us sprawled the darkening parade ground where the coconut palms had suffered in the recent hurricane and there were old ruins of buildings—the dynamited soldiers' barracks, the slabs where the officers' quarters had been, razed now to the ground, the two unfinished round-topped powder magazines, the little rough outline of the hot-shot furnace. As we clambered and walked along, we came upon ancient cannon, rusting in the sand; some were 10-inch Columbiads, six having been installed on the ramparts in 1863, one in each bastion; some were 15-inch Rodman cannon which replaced the Columbiads in 1874, heavy iron smooth-bore weighing close to 25 tons and firing a 450-pound projectile. A self-guiding trail had been set up here for visitors by the Park Service, winding about the Fort. Everywhere we saw arches in all conceivable spots, fanciful, decorative and with purpose.

I was reminded of the Colosseum in Rome where I had tried to comprehend the past in that place which swarmed with tourists. I had climbed higher and higher, apparently alone at last, feeling the drama and terror of the gigantic arena and those strange times. Then from somewhere unseen below me, a visitor from my country had piped up to her little boy, explaining, "You see there, Johnny, that's where the lion comes out and that's where the Christian!" I had given up, amused, and returned to my pension. Here I was grateful that no tourist but the three of us, whispering, was on the battlements, and I returned in time to former dramatic days.

Juan Ponce de León, first coming upon the group of ten or more keys with their cover of tropical growth—palms, mangrove, button-wood, bay cedar, sea-lavender, cactus, seagrape, purslane, sea oats—had remarked upon the great turtles and the fantastic horde of birds. The Dry Tortugas were indicated on navigators' maps henceforth, and fifty-odd years later, in 1565, Sir John Hawkins, who had a reputation in England as a slave trader, landed on Bird Key for supplies of birds and eggs. He reported that in half an hour he had loaded his pinnace down with terns, and that if there had "beene ten boats more, they might have done the like." Pirates continually used the Tortugas for a base in the three hundred years between their discovery and the pirates' final ousting. Silver was uncovered on East Key in the late 1800s and Loggerhead Key was reputed to contain Spanish gold underneath its sand and coral.

Garden Key, which Fort Jefferson covers, contains sixteen acres; when the United States Corps of Engineers came in December 1846 to plan the building of the Fort, they reported that the key was oval-shaped, scarcely three feet above sea level and had a stagnant pond in its middle. There was a small lighthouse which had been built in 1825 and a keeper's house and a dock. The Dry Tortugas had for years been termed The Key to the Mexican Gulf by Mexican Gulf by naval strategists who worried about the protection of that water area with its important ports—Galveston, New Orleans, Mobile, Pensacola. When the decision was made to arm the Tortugas, the gigantic fort-to-be was named The American Gibraltar and its plans, under the supervision of the Army's Chief Engineer, Joseph G. Totten, were drawn by Lieutenant Montgomery C. Meigs. Slaves began digging the foundations for the officers' quarters in the fall of 1847, the work for it directed by a young officer, Horatio Governeur Wright. Two years later the wall to enclose the moat was begun, the twofold purpose of the latter being to protect the Fort walls from heavy seas and to hold off enemy landing craft.

The moat wall had been breached to the west, the side opposite the sally port, where a gate had once let small boats into the moat. There the sand had drifted in and the water now was shallow. Barney said the Crile children had done most of their swimming in that part of the moat when they had visited here, the youngest seven. Fort Jefferson was given its official name in November 1850; until then it had been known as The Fort at Garden Kay. The work was slow; the foundations, to be fourteen feet wide and two feet thick, had to be poured five feet below the surface and were protected by a temporary coffer-dam. Enormous quantities of materials were needed from the mainland far away as the Fort grew: iron from Mobile for gun-ports and traverses; slate from New York for gunroom floors as well as roofing; Vermont granite for gun platforms, stairways and coping; lumber from Portsmouth, Savannah, Mobile, New Orleans; sixteen million bricks from Maine, Charleston, Savannah, Pensacola, Mobile, New Orleans. Mortar was made from cement and lime from New York, mixed with sand and coral debris brought from nearby keys; it was quarried by the ton, and decimated numerous coral reefs; shells and skeletons of sea creatures and pieces of coral were visible in the floors of the Fort everywhere.

After ten years of temperamental sea, fear of yellow fever from passing fishermen and wreckers, and problems with the labor, hired and forced—Irishmen and rented slaves particularly—who managed to keep the officers in continual dismay over their escapes, thievery, sabotage, illegal use of liquor and various illnesses, the walls of the Fort were scarcely above water. Now that the foundations were laid, Wright left and later distinguished himself in the defense of Washington when the Confederates tried to take the Capital. His successor, Captain Daniel Phineas Woodbury, was assigned to continue his work on the walls, to build the hundreds of complicated gunrooms and to finish the inner structure of the Fort; an authority on arch construction, he would remain at the Dry Tortugas until most of the masonry work was completed.

On the eve of the Civil War, the Fort was still halfway completed; about Garden Key were scattered a blacksmith shop, lime house, bakery, lumber shed, cattle pens, carpenter shop, cement house, a hospital of sorts, as well as barracks for workers and quarters for the officers and men. It was estimated that a million and a quarter dollars had been spent. Then it was noted by the engineers that gigantic cracks were appearing in the eight-foot-thick brick walls; measurements were taken and it was determined that certain foundations had sunk three inches in six months. It had been believed that the key was a solid coral reef; now it was apparent that it was but a heap of coral debris—shells and sand cast up by ocean currents; there was no solid rock within eighty feet of the surface.

There were other problems. Fort Jefferson's eight-foot-thick brick walls were designed to stop round shot from smooth-bore guns, not shells from the new rifled cannons. Before long in 1862, it would be proven at Fort Pulaski that this fort was obsolete. There in two days, 110,643 pounds of metal, which would be fired from thirty-six guns and mortars placed on a nearby island and maneuvered by federal gunboats, would breach Pulaski's brick fortress and cause its surrender; thereafter the South would need to defend its forts with sand or some yielding material which might not be breached irreparably and which would slow down or stop heavy shells and if displaced might be shoveled back.

Despite all arguments it was decided that Fort Jefferson should be completed. There was fear of civil war, and most of the Gulf of Mexico's shipping passed through these channels; it was necessary to protect them. A drawbridge across the sally port was installed, gaps in the outer moat wall used for bringing in materials were closed and artillerymen were shipped over. Seventy-five guns were put on their wooden carriages: six of the ten-inch Columbiads we had seen rusting by their barbettes on the wall tops; six heavy James rifles and two Siege guns in the second tier to rake the moat with crossfire; and in the first tier thirty-seven eight inch Columbiads and twenty-four Howitzers. By the time of General Robert E. Lee's surrender at Appomattox, over a thousand men would be stationed in the Dry Tortugas and eighty-nine guns would be mounted. The wood platforms on which many stood would rot in a short time; a cannon being tried out one day would capsize at the third shot. The guns were never used, except for occasional warning salvos aimed at Confederate privateers sailing close. Before the guns were workable, it happened one afternoon that an armed Confederate schooner had sailed up and anchored and sent a messenger ashore demanding surrender to the State of Florida. The Commander, Major Lewis Arnold, had hollered through the embrasure over the sally port that he'd blow the blazes out of the ship if it weren't gone in ten minutes and he might sooner! The bluffed ship had retreated.

Various garrisons served during the country's conflict—Regulars, Zouaves who were forced to burn their colorful uniforms and wear regulation ones, Volunteers, Negro troops. The morale of the soldiers was aided by drills, band concerts, organized fishing expeditions, egg-collecting parties at Bird Key, and catching of the great sea tortoises, identifying them with tags and holding them in the moat until ready to be eaten.

Building continued during the war; by the end of 1862, most of the walls had reached their full height of fifty feet. Yellow hand-made bricks faced the outsides of the walls, ten feet thick at their base and tapering to eight feet just above the foundation. The officers' quarters stood three stories high and four hundred feet long, with billiard rooms, library and offices; there were arched hallways and handsome finishings—glass silvered doorknobs, carved granite window sills and lintels, and verandas outside the rooms with iron-grilled balconies. The soldiers' barracks could handle six companies and ten were planned; they contained storerooms and mess-rooms; the hospital and chapel were completed. Two powder magazines were begun, which were to supplement the several small magazines next to the gunrooms, and which were to house equipment for hundreds of guns; their unfinished remains were below us now.

A hot-shot furnace was installed, where a round iron shot was to be heated at its high end for half an hour until white-hot; then it would be rolled down, removed with tongs, the scale taken off with a rasp and it would be carried in a ladle to one of the cannon. There it would be placed between the powder bag and dry and wet wads made of clay or damp straw; a light charge would be used to propel it, because if a ball went too deeply into the wood of an enemy ship, there would not be enough air for a fire to start. We knew that hot shot had been used before gunpowder in our culture; in 54 B.C. heated clay balls were hurled by the Britons into the tents of Roman invaders. We gazed on the brick arches, the roofless mazes of the power magazines, the buildings in rubble, revealing the former life of the Fort.

By the end of the war slaves, under the impending proclamation of emancipation, had been gradually replaced by war prisoners, and the Fort, now a military prison, was beginning to be referred to as The Terrible Dry Tortugas. A variety of inmates were sent there, as many as a thousand at a time could be housed in the cells—political prisoners, deserters, bounty-jumpers, thieves and murderers. Originally the Fort was designed to contain the prisoners in the Guard House, but when it overflowed, casemates and bastions were enclosed and served. Guards were placed about to prevent the continual slipping away of escapees. Sharks were caught and turned into the moat, seventy-five feet across, to the terror of many inmates; the largest, a ten-footer, was dubbed The Provost Marshal.

In July of 1865, a famous prisoner arrived—the young country doctor from Maryland who had treated John Wilkes Booth when his shinbone was broken above the instep as he leaped from Abraham Lincoln's box at Ford's Theatre in Washington. Dr. Samuel A. Mudd had heard him pounding at his farmhouse door, removed his boot, set the bone and sheltered the assassin for a few hours, not knowing of the event. Later, suspecting the truth, he informed the authorities at Bryantown of the incident. He was taken into custody and the tenor of the country was such that he was shortly convicted of full knowledge of the conspiracy and sentenced to life imprisonment at hard labor. Along with him were three others, the group being called the "Lincoln Conspirators." One, Edward Spangler, got eight years; and Michael O'Laughlin and Samuel Arnold received life terms.

Dr. Mudd was quartered in a cell in Bastion "D" on the ground floor; from one window across the moat he could see distant Loggerhead Key and from the other the drawbridge which would be sometimes lowered and again raised. He was to write his wife, "I am beginning to realize the saying of the Psalmist—*I have grown old in my youth,* etc. Imagine one loaded down with heavy chains, locked up in a wet, damp room, twelve hours out of every twenty-four during working days and all day on Sunday and holidays. No exercise allowed except in the limited space of a small room, and with irons on. . . . My legs and ankles are swollen and sore, pains in my shoulders and back are frequent. . . . With all this, imagine my gait with a bucket and broom, and a guard, walking around from one corner of the fort to another, sweeping and sanding down the bastions. This has been our treatment for the last three months, coupled with bad diet and water and every inconvenience."

By midsummer of 1867, about three hundred people were on Fort Jefferson: fifty prisoners, and four companies of the 5th Artillery, besides the engineer force which was still working on the barracks. On the eighteenth of August, yellow fever struck. The post surgeon, Major Joseph Sim Smith, died on September 8, his tiny son following him; they were buried on the key, and the Fort was thrown into panic. Dr. Mudd's chains were struck and he was pressed into service along with old Dr. Daniel Whitehurst who came hastily from Key West to take charge. The pair worked day and night, as the list of patients steadily increased—yellow-skinned, burning with fever, having the "black vomit" in fatal cases. Dr. Mudd, who could have escaped now, wrote home, "By the hand of Providence my fetters have been broken, but I run not, preferring the fate of those around me, and to lend what aid is in my power to break down the burning fever."

In an attempt to control the spread of the disease, one company was sent to Bird Key and a hospital was erected on Sand Key, since called Hospital Key, a mile and a half away. Five of the six officers became victims while for three months Yellow Jack reigned. Dr. Mudd himself had a touch of it. Many of the soldiers sent to Bird Key died, an officer's wife at the time writing, "It is a rugged little island where our dead rest, the white headboards distinct in the fading light of evening." Mudd in a letter to his wife told her, "The burial party are allowed a drink of whiskey both before and after the burying, which infuses a little more life in them. They move quickly, and in half an hour after a man dies, he is put in a coffin, nailed down, rowed a mile to an adjacent island, the grave dug, covered up, and the party returned, in the best of humor, for their drinks."

Before the epidemic was over, there had been 270 cases and of them thirty-eight deaths. It was thought the cause of the fever was the miasma, or poisonous vapor, supposed to rise from the moat. No one heeded the mosquito, *Aedes aegypti,* who was considered a nuisance and no more. Since then it has been determined that mosquitoes transmit, besides this fever, malaria, encephalitis and other diseases, and have most likely caused more fatalities to the human race than any other insect. In recent attempts to eradicate the mosquito, the biological method seems most hopeful. If its ability to reproduce can be destroyed, as has been done with other insects, the species could be controlled. An examination of the yellow-fever mosquito's sexual life shows an elaborate behavior. When the male and female forms emerge from the pupa, the male feeds on plant nectar and water; the female, equipped with the proper cutting tools, searches for animal blood. The male, at this point, undergoes a rotation of his abdomen, the last two segments pivoting on the membrane between the seventh and eighth segment; in twenty hours the rear abdomen makes a full 180-degree turn and is upside down; the male is now able to copulate with the female, whose abdomen remains unchanged. The genital apparatus of both sexes is complex; the female is unable to develop eggs until she had had a meal of blood by piercing the skin of an animal with her proboscis; she lays her white eggs in the daylight between two and three in the afternoon; shortly after, they swell and turn black and in two days the larvae hatch, their hearts begin to beat and they begin to feed; they shed their skin four times and then transform into the pupal state, looking at this time to the unaided eye like commas; the pupa sheds its skin as the insect emerges in about two days and the cycle is again under way.

The garrison at Fort Jefferson, grateful to Dr. Samuel A. Mudd, petitioned for his release. It is said that their testimonial paper never reached President Andrew Johnson's hand. Dr. Mudd was again incarcerated in his dank cell, writing his wife that his bed was of "moss gathered from trees," and his quarters were boarded up, making them more unpleasant than ever. Again in chains and under guard, he was put to his former menial tasks. It was almost two years later, in March 1869, that Dr. Mudd was pardoned by President Johnson along with Spangler and Arnold, O'Loughlin having died of the fever. The release of the "Lincoln Conspirators" is said to have been due to the persistence of Mrs. Mudd, who continually besieged the White House and Capitol Hill, rather than to the efforts of anyone at Fort Jefferson. The doctor was permitted to return to his neglected Maryland farm, dying fourteen years later of pneumonia contracted while out one stormy night to attend a patient.

Six years after that yellow fever epidemic, another one struck. The Fort's Commander Bell, who would die himself shortly, ordered all the well over to Loggerhead Key to wait out the disaster, camping in tents. The death toll was heavy. A month later, a raging hurricane hit. The Army ordered all troops to leave in the following January, the commandant stating that there was no possibility of the Fort being completed even within fifty years. Fort Jefferson was on its way to ruin. The stacks of cannonballs in the parade ground sank gradually and the guns rusted; the wharf rotted and a hurricane finally destroyed it, as well as whirling away the galvanized iron roofs of the soldiers' barracks; the platforms under the guns gave way totally, and to top it all a steamer arrived at the dock with a smallpox patient sent from Key West who was deposited with a male nurse upon the dock. Although it was not official and there were bitter protests, the Treasury Department was busy turning Fort Jefferson into a Quarantine Station to be complete with sulphur fumigation and steam disinfecting equipment. Funds were allocated to build a new dock and warehouse.

Very soon, however, the War Department requested that the Dry Tortugas again be a military post, and when the second-class battleship, the *Maine,* carrying three hundred and fifty-five men, on its way to Cuba, put in there in January 1898 and was subsequently blown up in Havana Harbor on the fifteenth of February with a loss of two hundred and sixty officers and men, they had their way and Fort Jefferson was no longer a quarantine site. In April the United States recognized Cuban independence and its fleet set out from Key West for Cuba; Spain declared war and it was not until December that peace was agreed upon.

Both my father and Barney's had gone off to that strange little war; mine, a private sworn into Company C, Sixth Infantry Regiment of the Illinois Volunteers, within two months after the *Maine* settled on the bottom of the harbor; his, a major commissioned as a Brigade Surgeon in the First Division of the Second Army Corps. Both had written autobiographically about the event, old Dr. Crile saying what seemed most poignant to us, and dangerous in retrospect since we had not been yet conceived: "The detachment of the Sixth Illinois Volunteers was firing supposedly over our heads at the enemy, but the spent bullets [from the old Springfield type rifles] were continually falling among our men, occasionally wounding them."

Fort Jefferson was again officially sheltering ships; the Navy began dredging the harbor channels deeper and building coaling docks of steel and concrete off the southwest and the northeast ends of Garden Key, each to be capable of handling the largest battleship and to hold 10,000 tons of coal. By now the total cost of Fort Jefferson was nearing three and a half million. The Navy was to be in charge of her and negotiations were under way for her transfer from the Army officially. Contracts were let to salvagers by the War Department and they were taking everything that was movable which vandals, who had been looting the Fort over the years,

had left behind. The embrasure irons and gun traverses were removed, and the lighter cannons and guns, and much of the slate
floors. In 1901 the lighthouse near us on the wall caught fire and
was rendered useless, supplanted by the Dry Tortugas Light on
Loggerhead Key.

By 1904 the Dry Tortugas Coaling Station was finished, as well
as a tank storing two million gallons of distilled water for warships.
As the Navy was accepting the sheds and docks from the contrac-
tors, a hurricane arrived; the steel girders were tangled, the trans-
porters were twisted about, and perhaps a million dollars of destruction resulted. The Navy set about some repair work, but before long decided to abandon the post. In 1908 the Dry Tortugas
were assigned to the Department of Agriculture as a Bird Preserve.
Two years later, in 1910, another hurricane slammed into the area
and wrecked the coal conveyors beyond repair besides damaging
the Fort. The parade ground became overgrown; looters still
prowled—doors from the officers' quarters were removed in one
piece, and windows; the delicate silvered doorknobs were lifted.
The soldiers' barracks were dynamited for the wrought iron they
contained; finally in 1912 a fire broke out, gutting them along
with the lighthouse-keeper's house. In 1914 the Boston Iron and
Metal Company began salvage work but abandoned it. In 1917 a
wireless station which the Navy had set up in 1904 was re-installed;
a few Marines were sent for a year or so and then it too was given
up. In the 1920s rum runners began to base on the abandoned key
which was on the direct route between Havana and Tampa. The
Cuban boats left their loads at Fort Jefferson to be picked up by
Florida transfer vessels. In 1927 the head of the Key West Army
post, Captain Rice, discouraged by the wanton destruction, set fire
to the remains of the officers' quarters, declaring that he would
leave nothing for vandals further to pilfer. The harbor was closed
for official navigation and was used only by the Cubans and by
passing ships to ride out storms.

Fort Jefferson was now The Ghost Fortress. It would not be

until eight years later, on the fourth of January 1935, that President Franklin Delano Roosevelt would declare it a National Monument and a.part of the National Park Service. Later in that same year in a violent hurricane, Bird Key, the established rookery of the terns, would sink into the sea with a heavy loss to the nesting birds. For a few years the confused terns would scatter, some nesting on Garden Key beneath the walls, some around the coaling docks and some within the Fort itself. In time they would transfer to Bush Key where we had seen them. During World War II, the Dry Tortugas would again be employed strategically by the Navy as an emergency mooring for Inshore Patrol and minesweepers and convoy escort vessels.

We watched the blaze of sunset as we stood on the precarious walls, feeling the history of the Fort, hearing the noises—the groans of prisoners, the cries of the fevered, the shouts of the workers, the crackling of fire; and always the tropical heat, the ever-repeated hurricane wind and storm, the continual calling of the terns in season. Overhead a squadron of Man-o'-war birds circled effortless on the thermal updrafts while the ball of sun dropped and the color spread until we were surrounded.

As we descended the circular granite staircases after a while, the scent of insecticide met us. The DeWeeses had told the Management Assistant about the Salt Marsh Mosquito delegation and a fog of bug spray was enveloping our quarters, ejected from a machine drawn by the little tractor outside our windows. Choking, we welcomed it. John told us that we were invited to the Gallaghers for dinner and that he had accepted for us. We went to visit the DeWeeses first, turning left at the top of the stairway, where their quarters were above ours in three bricked-up arches, their rooms ample with a dividing wall, which impressed us. There was a huge kitchen, a combined sitting room-bedroom, and Paula and I noted that their bathroom was rather roomier than ours, the shower fully three feet square.

Lauri declared she was in heaven, and looked up from a huge book, *American Sea Shells,* from the New Illustrated Naturalist

Series. "John and I want to make a good representative-shell list for Fort Jefferson this year," she sighed.

"I used to collect butterflies when I was little," I told her.

"This is different," she declared. "You don't wait for them to come along. You never can tell what is behind the next bit of coral. Did you ever see a *Cyphoma signatum,* the Fingerprint Cyphoma—it's rare?"

"Did you ever see a *Papilio Marcellus?*" I retorted, "with long tails and striped green and called the Zebra Swallowtail and you never see them anymore!"

"Have some legal rum, girls," John said gently.

Later, before knocking on the Gallaghers' door, which was on the other side of the stairhead, we roamed along the broad casemates past the southwest bastion. The vista of arches stretched one within the next, disappearing in the distance, telescoping into blackness. Examining the construction of the arches, we saw how each was fashioned with the mortar clean and the bricks beveled. The cool breeze blew in the dusk. All along the heavy walls were the rows of gun ports that opened upon the sea, an iron semicircle built into the stones of the floor at each where the traverse had been placed. Returning, we entered the gloom of the seaward side of the bastion, where three series of arches led to a window over the water. John pointed with his flashlight beam to a small inscription in the overhead arched brickwork: *Jno Nolan 1859.*

"One of the master masons," he said.

On the other side of the bastion was the circular stairwell to ascend to the ramparts or descend to the parade ground. Along the narrow way leading to the stairs, we stopped and John opened a door into a large chamber and snapped on the electric light. Once a gun supply room, it was now a hurricane hideout for people of the Fort. We saw the candles and radio and comfortable chairs and table that the Gallaghers had provided in the style of the midwest where cyclones are not unexpected.

In the midwest fashion too, a picture window had been built

into the face of the apartment of our hosts and looked upon the wide aisle and the sea beyond. Mrs. Gallagher, round and cheerful, reminding one of an Indiar.a country woman, which she at once told me she was, made us welcome. She showed us her rooms: the white kitchen with its immaculate cabinets and equipment and organdy curtains; the bedroom and living room, all in a line and disguised within the casemate so that it seemed transported from some other land. We sat in the soft-lit place and gazed at her seashells spread under the coffee table glass.

"I don't know their names, but I think they're pretty," she said. "All they're good for is to look at. You can't eat them."

And Mr. Gallagher showed us a collection of sea horses, starfish and gorgonians he had made into a design and framed upon a wall. The men helped him to pull a long metal picnic table with attached benches out into the walkway, where the sea breeze came in and the water of the moat was twenty-five feet below the railed archway and we were told the sunsets had a reputation. Mrs. Gallagher spread a checkered cloth on the table and served bowls of fresh-caught shrimp which she had just got from one of the trawlers docked outside the sally port. There were sauces for the shrimp, cole slaw, cornbread, jellies, bowls of vegetables, cold beer, fresh-baked apple pie and coffee.

When we marveled she said, "It's the freezer Mr. Gallagher bought me. And we finally got the apartment to suit us. He done every bit of the work himself—the wiring, the window, and brought all the supplies from Key West when he'd make the run every other week."

"It's a great life," Mr. Gallagher said, "all we miss is company to come over and visit. Our friends and family that's here for vacations has to leave all too soon.'

We sat in the quiet dusk which gradually turned into dark, occasionally slapping at mosquitoes which seemed less hungry than earlier. In time, we rose and thanked our kindly hosts and by the light of John's flashlight reached the stairway. We agreed to meet the DeWeeses in the morning before eight to go out in a

Parks Department boat, which John had arranged for. Then we continued on our way in the dark, hearing the wash of sea in the distance and no other sound. We groped our way down and along the wall to our screen door and put on the lights. Before long we were asleep on our hard cots as we had planned, not far from Dr. Samuel A. Mudd's quarters in a Fort Jefferson's cell.

CHAPTER SIX

Under the Water

Sand-strewn caverns, cool and deep,
Where the winds are all asleep;
Where the spent lights quiver and gleam,
Where the salt weed sways in the stream,
Where the sea-beasts, ranged all round,
Feed in the ooze of their pasture-ground;
Where the sea-snakes coil and twine,
Dry their mail and bask in the brine;
Where great whales come sailing by,
Sail and sail, with unshut eye,
Round the world for ever and aye.

—Matthew Arnold: "The Forsaken Merman"

WE woke at dawn, confused in the new surroundings, gazing at the white-paint-flecked brick ceiling and the maze of arches, aware of the scent of the musty mattresses, feeling the sea breeze coming strongly through the windows, suggestive of the day's heat ahead. Barney made the breakfast—grapefruit, bacon, folded eggs, toast, coffee; while Paula and I tidied the beds and the kitchen. We wore tennis shoes and under our slacks and tops our swim wear. We carried the cameras, binoculars and journal, and packed a duffle bag with masks and flippers, the long-sleeved jerseys that Barney recommended against the sun, towels, a book or two in case someone was bored with the sea and Royal Lyme

Suntan Lotion for all but Barney who scorned unnatural products in any form although tolerant of others' notions. When we left the Fort and crossed the moat and reached the dock at a little before eight, the DeWeeses were waiting with straw hats and dark glasses against the sun, Lauri in swim suit and John in T-shirt and slacks. They had a straw bag of underwater gear and a large freezer box.

"Let's make it all day," Lauri said. "Did you bring hats?"

"Barney did," I said. "Paula and I like the sun. Listen to those birds!"

Over all noises was the sound of the terns of Bush Key. "Let's go over and take a look at them," John said.

We walked down the worn wood pier steps and along the narrow lower dock, where a board was missing and others needed repair. The boat was white—a sixteen-foot outboard with a canvas roof and a glass bottom in the center shielded with a low wall; on its bow were the red block letters NATIONAL PARK SERVICE. John took the motor at the stern and we sat and placed our gear where he directed. Cirrus clouds were overhead, tufted and detached, and we felt it would be a clear day. Bush Key was less than a quarter-mile away, the farthest-north rookery of the Sooty Tern and the Noddy, and the only one in the United States; they were first recorded by Juan Ponce de León on Bird Key, which had lain three-quarters of a mile southwest of Fort Jefferson. Since that raging hurricane of 1935, they re-established on Bush Key, where they return every March or April, the noddies arriving first and the sooties about a week later, coming together from tropical islands in the Caribbean Sea, the west central Atlantic, from the coast of South America and other places throughout the two hemispheres. John said that it is thought they assemble from land bases within ten hours' flying time, but it is also known that they can rest upon the water and some may come from farther off. Like gulls and pelicans and the giant sea turtles, they were adapted to drinking from the sea, excreting the excess salt through their lachrymal glands.

As we neared the white sand beach through the green-blue
water, the cries and activity of the terns on the key became more
intense. We noted twenty or thirty Man-o'-war birds perched in
the scrub of mangrove bushes and grey-green bay cedars beyond
the sand, and my camera clicked steadily as we anchored in the
shallows. The surface temperature of the coral sand in the hottest
days will range from 124 to 143 degrees, hot enough to burn bare
feet; this is due to the slight elevation and the juxta-tropical location of the key. Barney, who had made movies of the Bush Key
birds, said that the sooties seemed to stand over their eggs laid
upon the sand to cool rather than heat them and protected the
young with half-spread wings in the same fashion. He said too
that he had seen parent sooties return from the sea with their
beaks full of water which they put on their eggs apparently to
cool them.

We got out of the boat and waded to the shore, keeping our
canvas shoes on as we intended going into the brush where the
noddy nests were. We knew that Louis Agassiz had come here
in 1859, when the Fort's fifty-foot walls were still not half erected,
and that the arch authority Captain Woodbury had written a
friend about the visit, "It almost repays us for our long banish-
ment to see and hear so much from the first naturalist of the
time!" Then there were hundreds of thousands of terns nesting
on Bird Key; due to decimation over the years by passing fishermen who destroyed the birds and collected their eggs as an adventure, and to semi-commercial eggers from Cuba or Key West,
the colony was reduced to ten thousand by the 1900s. The tern
eggs sold for 12½ cents a dozen in Key West and bakeries in
Florida used them in making pastry. The practice of the eggers
was to land and at once smash all eggs; the terns would promptly
re-lay and the fresh eggs were then harvested. Before long there
were less than 4000 sooties and 400 noddies, and the government
was to step in in 1907 when the area was turned over to the Department of Agriculture for the protection of wildlife.

The proportion of the Noddy to the Sooty Tern is approxi-

mately one to a hundred. The sooties, more shy of men and less
known to attack than the noddies who, we had been warned in
reports, would often swoop at the heads of visitors, were scattered
upon the beach, the young thick about us, as many of the adults
moved into the air. Before the hurricane with winds of 120 miles
an hour had hit here three weeks before, there had been on the
key, according to the report the Florida Audubon Society had
just made, 120,000 sooties and about 1200 noddies. The birds,
disturbed by our arrival, were assembling in the spiral thermal
tides, rising and falling in continual motion, the din increasing;
among them were as many as two hundred soaring Man-o'-wars.
As they grew accustomed to us, the terns became less afraid and
skimmed by and over us, screaming an arm's length from our eyes.
Scattered here and there on the beach and brush were dried
carcasses of all three species, witness to the hurricane's force.
The water had risen over the low sand spit that made up Bush
Key and when the Audubon people assessed the damage, the
population was still over 100,000, the loss sustained almost entirely among immature chicks.

The Sooty Tern is the only tern that is black above and white
below; its upper parts are a shiny black, its entire under parts
and cheeks and the patch on its forehead are white. It has been
termed the Wide-awake Tern as it seems never to sleep, day
or night. Every moment thousands flew into the air and other
thousands came to rest on the beach, the birds covering the sand
down to the waterline. Sometimes a few flew over the sea and
others were seen returning with a fish for their mates or young,
but mostly they seemed to simply stay in the air uttering their
piercing calls, as if a gigantic sort of party were taking place.
The DeWeeses said their nervous-seeming excitement had nothing
to do with intruders or disturbance but was continual. The party
would last until the first of September, when the terns would
depart in a southern migration to live in separate groups or singly
until they would congregate here again in the following spring.

The single egg of the Sooty Tern, white or creamy with varied spots and blotches, is laid directly on the sand with sometimes scarcely a depression. The birds nest close together, each pair's foot or two of beach being zealously protected by the parents, both of whom incubate the egg. The shift is made at night and the bird remaining on the nest is fed by its mate. In twenty-six days, the eggs begin to hatch and the beaches are covered with the fluffy chicks; they are fed by regurgitation, and the adults recognize their own young, who respond to the calls of the parents. Immature sooties are brown all over, lighter on their under parts, their backs spotted with white. They may be confused with mature noddies.

The Noddy is a dark brown bird with a whitish head, slightly smaller than the sooty and the only adult tern that is entirely brown; it is the only one with a rounded tail, so that when a tern is silhouetted against the sky, it is easy to distinguish the noddy from the sooty, whose tail is distinctly forked. The name noddy comes from the tern's habit of constantly bowing or nodding and its Latin name *Anous stolidus stolidus,* which translates "without reason or intellect and stolid as well," implies its fearless nature considered to indicate stupidity by early seafarers.

We had seen the report of the Audubon people who had banded 2168 adult sooties and 36 noddies. It had been found that in the handling of the 553 sooties which were previously banded birds that they recaptured, many were very old—two aged twenty-eight and twenty-nine, and that there were 111 eighteen years old or over. That was believed by the Society to be the largest number of individual birds of such advanced age known for any population of any species. They found too that banded birds were reported not only from southern and Atlantic coast areas, but from Ghana, Liberia, British Guiana, Jamaica, Trinidad, and many from Nigeria, indicating the extent of their traveling, either free-winged or on the force of hurricanes.

We went our various ways—Paula and Lauri setting out to circle the island, John remaining with the little outboard to do something with the motor, Barney and myself heading for the

interior of Bush Key. There was a lagoon there, where Barney
had once filmed the colonies of hermit crabs and he wanted me
to see them. The noddies, perched in the dead or storm-torn
branches of bay cedar, allowed us to approach to within a few
feet, while the sooties flew over and about, shrill-voiced. When
the noddies arrive in April, it is believed they are already mated;
they build their loose, shallow and unstable nests in the bay
cedars, the cactus or occasionally in ground vegetation such as
Bermuda grass. The nests are formed of twigs and dead branches
and seaweed, as well as coral and shells, which they use for lining;
old nests are returned to year after year and many by now are
enormous. After the egg, like the sooty's but less heavily spotted,
is laid, the noddy becomes aggressive and is liable to attack any
intruder including man. In about thirty-six days the eggs hatch,
and due to the longer incubation period, the noddy chicks come
out of their eggs simultaneously with the sooties.

As we made our way inland through the rough brush toward
the mangroves, we saw immature sooties in groups on the ground,
distinguished by their white-spotted brown backs. We hurried,
for the local mosquitoes with their soft black bodies were wel-
coming us with customary enthusiasm. In the marshy dank interior, we clambered over fallen branches until we finally reached
the foliage surrounding the lagoon; after the dazzling sun on the
white sand, it was like a tomb. Barney surveyed the area anxiously.

"There they are," he cried. "Can you see them?"

For a moment or two I could make out nothing but the outlines of the trees, the fallen twigs in the stagnant water and the
shapes of the noddies going in and out of their nests. Then I
caught a movement—a crab in the fork of a bush working its way
up. Then there was another and more and as my eyes accommodated and the creatures began to react to our presence, the floor
of the swampy island seemed to surge. The hermit crabs blended
into the cover of sticks and shells and coral debris, so that when
the shells themselves, of every size and shape, began to move as
their inhabitants did, the effect was startling. Still half-blinded,

we observed the shifting, scrambling, rustling horde; from each shell protruded the brick-red claws and antennae of a hermit crab.

"I wonder if Dante saw this when he dreamed of the inferno," Barney said and slapped a mosquito.

Charles Darwin in the coral gardens of the Cocos had examined the hermit among a hundred crab species and remarked upon it. Not a true crab, it is a soft-bodied crustacean which must protect its tender abdomen and arms itself with the empty shells of other reef inhabitants. It backs into the borrowed home and wedges itself there by its short rear legs. When attacked, it waves its large anterior claws, and when the danger disappears, uses them as a folding door to the adopted home. As the crab outgrows the shell, it begins to investigate new ones, retreating to the old continually to compare it, and finally making a decision. Very occasionally an aggressive large male is seen without a shell and it has been speculated that he either is unable to find one large enough or because of his temperament doesn't need one. The hermit is of the family *Coenobitidae,* meaning common-life or that of a monastery, and is found throughout the seas. The species we observed was *Coenobita clypeatus,* and it is often seen in the branches of the mangroves and scrub. They are air-breathers and must wet their gills and move in crowds at dusk to the water for this purpose. They are known to eat tern eggs and hatchlings at times and, if very hungry, their own kind. We gazed at the darkened trees and the pool of the marsh, hearing the scuttling of crackling claws and feeling transported to a primeval time when giant creatures moved.

Barney decided to push on around the lagoon to the other side of the key. I would return to the boat and meet him there. The funneling birds seemed to extend so high in their spiral that the topmost ones could be seen only with binoculars. When I came to John and asked him about it, he said that it was only in calm weather such as now that they put on so extraordinary a show; in time of storm, they were apt to hover low. Beyond, at all times on Bush Key, one saw the red Fort, seeming unreal

and as if it suddenly had loomed up from the depths. To the
south was the sandy strip of Long Key, where I knew a colony
of a few hundred Roseate Terns nested every summer. The roseate,
smaller than the Bush Key terns, was whitish with a black cap,
its tail deeply forked. I had read the beginning of Bent's discussion
of the Roseate Tern, published in 1921: "I shall never forget the
thrill of pleasure I experienced when I held in my hand, for the
first time, a freshly killed roseate tern and admired with deepest
reverence the delicate refinement of one of nature's loveliest
productions. The softest colors of the summer sky were reflected
on its back and pointed wings, while its breast flowed with the
faint blush of some rare seashell. The graceful outlines, the spot-
less purity of its delicate plumage, and the long tapering tail
feathers made it seem like some ethereal spirit of the heavens
which it was sacrilege for human hands to touch."

Once the attitude of naturalists toward the creatures they were
studying was much as Audubon's when he remarked uncritically
on the sailors' slaughter of the Tortugas terns and their gathering
of baskets of the eggs. It appeared that nature's resources were
infinite and shooting the roseate tern was the same as picking a
forest flower. It was necessary also to dissect and preserve specimens so they could be classified and the details of their bodily
structure and plumage be recorded. It was not until it became
obvious that certain species were disappearing that there was a
revolution in the approach of naturalists; they became observers
rather than collectors.

I watched the floating Man-o'-wars and how sometimes they
folded their wings and dropped through the air and then soared
up again. Highly specialized for flight, they weigh only two to
four pounds, their wingspread can reach over seven feet and their
slender legs and unwebbed toes are of little use on the ground
and of no use in water. The males are black with a metallic sheen
to their feathers and an orange throat-patch; the latter is an air-
sac that in courtship display is inflated into a balloonlike pouch,
which may turn crimson with a bluish hue at times. When court-

ing, the male stands, throws back his head, spreads his wings, protrudes the sac and shakes his head, meanwhile making a hoarse cackle. The females and immature birds are distinguished by their white breasts. After the single egg—pure white, thin-shelled, smooth and lusterless—is laid, the male no longer inflates the air-sac. The Man-o'-war, *Fregata magnificens,* also called the Frigate-bird, is piratical by nature and will persistently harass and attack smaller birds—gulls, cormorants, pelicans, boobies and terns—until they drop their catch. Man-o'-wars can be fishers too, although they never land on water; they are fond too of jellyfish, young turtles and flying fish. I watched one skim the surface, check and rise with its shining prey.

The sooties and noddies hunt by following schools of small fish, sometimes casually but often beating their wings and scream- ing, hovering over the surface and snatching the ones that leap up. If a large fish like a tuna is running the minnows, the terns will note the activity and follow to catch the fry that break water. Certain ornithologists believe the Dry Tortugas was originally adopted as a tern rookery because of the profusion of immature fish seeking the shoals and shallow waters around the keys for sanctuary from predatory open-sea fish.

The Dry Tortugas are in the pathway of one of the principal migration flyways between North and South America and during the season, waves of birds of at least two hundred and fifty species come to rest on the keys. The DeWeeses had said that the Park Biologist maintained the records of his and other qualified birders' observations when they visited Fort Jefferson. Migration is the adaptation of a creature to seasonal change and resultant diminu- tion of the food supply; two other ways of adapting are hiberna- tion and the storage of food while simultaneously building a winter nest. Bird migrations were one of the first natural phe- nomena to attract the attention of recording man who sought to account for the disappearance of great numbers of them in autumn. It was believed that they burrowed into the mud of the marshes or hid in hollows of trees; it was advanced by one student of the subject that all birds flew to the moon and spent the winter there; the Red Man understood that certain of the smaller and weaker birds were borne on the wings of large cranes and herons as they made their exodus.

Aristotle among others remarked upon it at length: "In some cases they migrate from places near at hand, in others they may be said to come from the ends of the world as in the case of the crane." He fought fable: "The story told about the stone is untrue: to wit, that the bird, so the story goes, carries in its inside a stone by way of ballast, and that the stone when vomited up is a touchstone for gold." Pliny, naturalist too, near four hundred years later, did not give up the fabulous so easily—when the cranes "mind to take a flight over the sea Pontus, they . . . ballaise themselves with stones in their feet, and sand in their throats, that they fly more steady and endure the wind. When they be half way over, down they fling those stones: but when they are come to the continent, the sand also they disgorge out of their craw." Referring to the migrating quail, Aristotle said, "And by the way, it is owing to the distress occasioned by the bulkiness of its body that the bird always screams while flying, for the labour is severe." He spoke of certain birds who "decline the trouble of migration and simply hide themselves where they are. Swallows, for instance, have been often found in holes, quite denuded of their feathers, and the kite on its first emergence from torpidity has been seen to fly from out some such hiding-place."

The mystery of migration has not yet been solved. There are various theories as to the origin of the phenomenon—one that long ago in either the Northern or the Southern hemisphere, birds successfully bred and had a plentiful food supply the year around and were not crowded and therefore retain still the powerful urge to go back to those ancestral breeding grounds. Another theory suggests that the quantity of light and the length of day are the stimulants—the Theory of Photoperiodism. Then there is the Theory of Continental Drift, proposing that the migratory pattern was determined seventy billion years ago on prehistoric

types of birds now extinct, like the *Ichthyornis,* fish-bird, with
its teeth set in sockets; and the *Archaeopteryx,* meaning ancient-
wings, having well-developed ones and teeth also and a lizardlike
tail. Continental drift is the old hypothesis that the present continents were once assembled something like 200 million years
ago into two great land masses in the northern and southern
hemisphere which, due to a slow convection process that carried
material upward from the mantle below the earth's crust, drifted
apart. Africa may be fitted into South America and the North
Atlantic regions may be matched. The evidence of glacial rubble,
the correlations in present plant genera and in mineral belts, the
studies of marine fossils in, for example, the Himalayas, and flora
fossils in central Antarctica, all are part of the supporting evidence
for the concept of two original large land masses.

This is the theory which best explains the fact that eels from
both North America and Europe swim from their rivers across
the ocean to spawn in the same Sargasso Sea near Bermuda, presumed to have been accessible to both continents before the drift
took place. If primitive birds traveled over the land easily as
they went south in winter and north in summer, and if over the
eons they adapted with the gradual drift to crossing greater and
greater water areas, it can be understood why certain species go
phenomenal distances. The Arctic Terns, whose route for long was
a mystery, breed far to the north; when the young are a few
months old they fly to the Antarctic, 11,000 miles away; they do
not go directly south but, supporting the Theory of Continental
Drift, if they have nested in Greenland or in Hudson Bay, gather
and fly across the Atlantic to join those coming from Norway
and all proceed together down the European shores and the African coast to Antarctica. If they have originated in the West—
Siberia or Alaska—they will head down the eastern Pacific Coast
to the waters farthest south. It is estimated that the indirect route
of the Arctic Tern covers 25,000 miles. When we visited the
Queensland Barrier reef off Australia once, we listened to the
Slender-billed Shearwaters, called Mutton Birds, moaning in their

burrows like lost souls; the local residents told us how the species would migrate in a clockwise pattern—to New Zealand, then northward skirting the Pacific basin following the wind pattern up the continent of Asia and finally down the North American continent, their route bearing out also the Continental Drift hypothesis.

One can only marvel at the fact of the Ruby-throated Hummingbird, three inches long, migrating from northeast United States three thousand miles as far south as Panama, making the five-hundred mile trip across the Gulf of Mexico without stopping, often barely skimming the waves. In contrast, I thought of the great blue herons on Graveyard Island on Lake Erie, spreading their black-tipped wings deliberately and taking their unhurried leave. The secret will most likely remain locked, but the patterns of migration are being continually studied and while the spectacle may not be understood, one can observe it with naturalistic awe.

Migration may take place nocturnally or diurnally and as a rule the smaller birds travel by night in order to escape their enemies and to feed during the days. Wading and swimming birds migrate either by day or night, as they feed at all hours. When diving birds migrate, they travel over water by day and land by night. Observers with telescopes focused on the full moon have estimated the passage of ten thousand birds an hour at the height of a migration season. The rates of speed and the heights at which the birds travel vary greatly among species.

In 1907, when the Dry Tortugas came under the protection of the Department of Agriculture, Dr. John B. Watson, later professor of experimental and comparative psychology at Johns Hopkins University, began to study the phenomenon of the homing instinct of the Tortugas terns. He painted sooties and noddies in bright colors, put them on board ship confined in cages below deck and let them go north a thousand miles. When released, they returned within a few days accurately to their nests.

Some think that migratory birds react to the magnetic field of the earth, and others recently have developed the theory that they are responding to what may be termed the scent or flavor in the air currents, much as the green turtle and the salmon are thought to react to the same in the currents of the sea. In the case of the latter, it is thought that a sun-compass mechanism aids them in the initial part of their migration, but when the coastline is neared they depend upon the sense of smell to identify their home river. Their identification is so accurate that they will return not only to a large stream, but to an artificial pool where they were reared connected to the river by a slim tributary. Scientists took sexually ripe silver salmon coming home to spawn out of two different branches of a northwestern river, plugged the noses of half of the group with cotton, and placed them back in the river below the fork to make the run again. The scent-blinded fish returned in a random way, picking the wrong as often as the right branch, whereas the others returned to the stream they had selected the first time. We have observed this accuracy of migratory return in wood ducks which return season after season to our pool not twenty feet across, in the back yard of our town house in a typical residential area.

During migration, birds seem to follow topographic lines—mountain chains, coastlines, and especially river valleys. They fly at great heights unless there is storm or fog and then they are in trouble. On Lake Michigan after a storm once, I saw thousands of washed-up migrants that had been traveling on the open water —juncos, sparrows, wrens, golden-crowned kinglets, brown creepers, thrushes, warblers, vireos, and more, mingled with drowned small fish and insects. Doubtless many had survived and continued on their way. It seems that migratory flocks are attracted especially in moisture-laden air to a fixed white light, which seems to dazzle them. We had heard that the lighthouse at Loggerhead Key was a hazard and we knew of ones on Lake Michigan that were and along the Florida Keys. The Washington Monument, the Statue of Liberty, the Empire State building and more, are famous for the phenomenal numbers of tiny passerine birds and larger migrants too, that are gathered by the bushel after freak-ish weather involving storm, fog, or freeze. At St. Catherine's Light on the Isle of Wight, the Royal Society has installed a grillwork of rests for birds above and below the light. It seems that the creatures do not kill themselves by dashing against the lighthouse as was once supposed, but by fluttering about until they fall and die from exhaustion. It has been proved too that if light-houses will employ a flashing or red light, it is less dangerous.

Barney had told me that frequently he had observed dozens of finches and warblers in season perching all over the riggings of boats he traveled on; they would accept crumbs and fresh water for a day before going on their way. He had made a pet of a Brown Booby that had lit on the *Sea Diver* and remained, eating from his hand; it stayed a week, skimming the sea and diving spectacularly the way White Pelicans do from the air. The Blue-faced and Brown Booby are seen in the Dry Tortugas all year around, large birds, somewhat like gulls with longer necks and larger bills and shorter legs. They are preyed upon by Man-o'-wars, who force them to drop their fish or even half-digested con-tents of their crops as they wing their way to their nests, which are hollows on the sand like the sooties make. In Audubon's time there was a tiny key, eight miles northeast of Fort Jefferson, which he said was called Booby Island, adding, "We found the sand bar not more than a few feet above the surface of the water, but covered with boobies, which lay basking in the sunshine and pluming themselves." The booby, accustomed from time past to come to earth only on deserted keys, has no innate fear of man who, not comprehending a creature that does not flee him, called it a booby.

The others were returning now from their investigation of Bush Key, perspiring in the heat. We waded out to climb in the little boat where John DeWeese was waiting. As we puttered away, I thought I might make another photograph of the key and got out the camera on which the telescopic lens was mounted, which I had used to record the perched Man-o'-war birds on our approach. I discovered that I had left the cover on the lens and announced my news to the rest of the party.

"Don't worry," Paula said, "I got plenty of shots." And she patted her camera.

"That's why we brought you along, Paula," Barney grinned.

John took us around Long Key and said that sometimes one could find nurse sharks here, who used the shallows for a spawning ground, but we saw none. It was nearing noon and Lauri kept saying she was hungry and didn't anyone want to eat? Barney went overboard to search for a place where we might want to explore the bottom. John said that next day we would visit the wreck of a French brigantine and dive off it. Paula and I were slightly seasick and said we would stay in the boat for the time being and wait until we returned to the walls of the Fort to go down. Barney and I split a cold beer from the freezer box. The underwater camera hung around his neck as he perched energetically on the stern, while I attempted to master my uneasy feeling as the boat gently rolled.

"It's due to overstimulation of the balance mechanism of the inner ear," he said.

"I know," I told him. "Don't talk about it."

"Sandwiches," Lauri said. "Try food. It sometimes works."

"Okay," Paula said.

"Why don't we circle out to the old coral forest?" Barney asked John. "I want them to see it. And then we'll head home from there."

Everyone agreed, and John took us toward the waters on the other side of the harbor of Garden City. "It's a tragedy," he said.

"This used to be a magnificent coral garden," Lauri told us. "That was some years ago. When was it, John?"

"Now it's a graveyard," John said.

"It's ironic, John," Barney said, "that you spent years trying to protect the Tortugas corals from the passing coral collectors and in a fortnight almost all the forest was lost in a natural disaster."

"It's coming back a little," Lauri sighed.

"It'll take a century to look like it did," John said. "Under favorable conditions, coral grows an inch or two a year."

Barney began to talk about when he had been here more than twenty years ago and had dived in these still waters. In the Red Room he had run off the film he had taken for Paula and myself. The Brain Coral heads had loomed six feet high, saffron yellow, brown, gold with tiny reef fish clustering about their rounded tops; and acres of staghorn coral standing up to eight feet, the finger-thick branches forming thickets, each darkened section seeming to have its own fish; and Elkhorn formations, reddish-mahogany, towering up to ten feet from the bottom with fronds and plates six feet wide.

It was in the winter of 1957–1958 that there had been a week of unprecedented weather for the area, the temperature falling to forty degrees and the coral, which thrives at sixty-eight degrees and can stand extremely high but not low temperatures, had frozen and died, the only mar upon the underwater ecology of the Dry Tortugas.

As our boat moved, we gazed through its glass bottom at the dead broken coral strewn upon the sea floor like whitened skeletons. Here and there a bit of new growth had started, particularly of Stubby Finger Coral, also called the Ground Pine of the Sea, and in one small section there still remained a grove of staghorn apparently spared. But what was once a coral forest, filled with countless varieties of fish, was now a bleak expanse. The De-Weeses said that it was only this particular area that had been destroyed; the rest of the sea floor in the National Monument was unchanged. Here, where it was ideal for snorkeling and was surrounded by high shoals, the warm currents from the deep sea could not protect it from an unusual cold.

The cool breeze and the speed of the boat as we returned drove away any of our sensations of seasickness. Paula and I applied the suntan lotion to our shoulders and backs as John skirted the Fort and approached it from the west, the side opposite the dock, so that we could drop into the water and make our way to the seaward wall of the moat where the underwater trail was contemplated. Lauri and he would meanwhile return the boat to its mooring and our gear to our room. We would come back through the breach in the outer moat wall when we were ready and return to the Fort through an opening that had been made in the wall to our quarters.

Barney reviewed us again on how to use the faceplates as we prepared to go in. "Wet them. Spit on them and rub it. Keeps them from fogging. If the water's rough along the wall, duck under. You can ride out anything, if your head's under. It's only when you put your head into a wave and get a mouthful of the salt sea that you're apt to panic."

"Now or never," Paula said, and plunged over and began to swim toward the Fort.

I followed Barney closely, hanging on to his trunks occasionally, as we headed for the wall. We found that along its southerly part, the water was more shallow and the underwater life more varied, while to the north because of the current and the deeper water the fish were larger and the waves strong. Sometimes I wandered far from Barney and he had no concern for me, for at any time I could grasp the wall for support and there was none of the insecurity that open water can give. In the clear water of the south wall were many solitary fish that Barney identified— a black-and-yellow Angelfish, a Demoiselle, Neon Gobies, a Blue-headed Wrasse, each seemingly with its own little cave in the wall. They were fearless and allowed us to examine them in their retreats, gleaming in the sunlight.

I heard Barney's shout and saw him wave: "Look here. A Toad-fish!"

We came to see the sluggish creature, nearly indistinguishable from the sea bottom, mottled grey-brown, scaleless, almost all head with fleshy soft appendages hanging from his lower lip. Not far from him walked an enormous hermit crab with a conch shell on its back. There were crabs of every size, many tiny ones and sea roaches, one of the isopods which are everywhere on land and sea. Unable to remain long under water and adapting to land, the roaches scuttled along the moat wall just above the waterline where the boards of the original coffer-dam still held. Purple and yellow gorgonians were attached to the wall—sea fans and sea whips and sea plumes, the horny material which makes up their resilient skeleton called gorgonin from the Latin *gorgo* or *gorgonis,* terrible or fierce. They waved in the surge like the serpents which made up the hair of the three sisters in Greek mythology. The gorgonians are of the coral family; being uncalcified and pliant, they thrive in areas where stony corals would break from the waves' force. There were clusters of knobby stinging or fire coral, not a true coral but a hydrozoan of the same class as jellyfish and the Portuguese man-of-war, bearing structures called nematocysts, made of contractile fiber and having a trigger that if touched released a piercing barbed thread which injected poison into the flesh of the intruder or prey and held it to the tentacle; it could cause a painful sting to man. We avoided them after Barney pointed them out, and we agreed with his statement that it was the pastel gorgonians waving in the surge which gave the utmost color and life and beauty to this old sea wall!

After an hour or more out there we found our way to the breach in the southwest outer moat wall. Barney hoisted himself up the rough side and gave us a hand to the top of the wall. We walked along it until we came to the sandy area that the DeWeeses had named Garden Beach, where quantities of sand had washed in over the years through a great broken section of wall. The craftsmanship of the masons had to be admired there also, for the piece that lay in the water was solid still, the weakness due only to the presence originally of a gate. We stepped down onto the beach and crossed to the Fort wall, entering the ragged opening that Lauri had said was made during WPA days to bring sand in for reconstruction work.

As we walked through the open archways toward home, I reported to Barney and Paula that I was delighted with the prescription faceplate, for the first time in my life unhampered by my near-sightedness under water. We rinsed off our sea-wet equipment, including the underwater camera, in the sink and laid them to dry in the three-foot-deep stone window shelf. We hung our suits on the clothesline strung outside our door along the arches. We looked forward to the excursion the next day, Paula and I feeling our new confidence in the underwater kingdom.

The next morning the little white boat was unavailable and so when we met the DeWeeses, we climbed into a shadeless outboard-powered skiff. The sun beat down upon the unrippled sea as we headed for Loggerhead Key near which the wreck of the French brigantine lay. John dragged a fishline behind us and the Fort, as we looked back, seemed gloomy and implicative across the expanse of water, growing smaller and smaller. The wrecked ship had gone down at the turn of the century and was no treasure vessel, but a place where fish had congregated over the years in the coral- and barnacle-encrusted metal remains. It was easy to find, for a jagged rusted piece of the ship's frame protruded from the clear aquamarine sea and two birds were perched on it, the bare blue skin behind their bills giving them their name, Blue-faced Booby. Barney cast the anchor and John pulled in his line; there had been no bids for the lure. Once we had seen a small Hawksbill turtle, not over two feet across, pumping along and then diving and disappearing, and again there had been a sting ray off to one side, a round dark shadow. Not far away on Loggerhead Key, the 150-foot black-and-white Dry Tortugas Light spired up. Another day John was to bring us over there and we hoped to see the tracks of the Green Turtles, who were laying now, and perhaps even one of the creatures.

The water about the wreck was near twenty feet deep and since it flowed in with the tide from the open sea, the visibility was a hundred feet, the water clearer than that around the Fort, where sand and plankton washed continually off the shallow banks around Garden Key. The skeleton of the ship rose from the bottom, its protruding spars and sections giving one something to hold onto in the strong tide. Barney said that the school of blue-grey fish circling through and about the wreck were jacks and that the ones below in the shadowy recesses of the iron mass were groupers, fanning in the current, their gills opening and closing and their pale eyes staring up as we floated above them. Clouds of Sergeant Majors or Zebra Fish, with vertical black stripes on a greenish ground, brilliant in the surface sunlight, contrasted sharply with the somber fish in the water-filtered light below. As I descended I saw a vague huge shadow. Coming closer, it wasn't there.

I surfaced with a splash and swallowed a wave and shouted, "There's the largest fish down there I ever saw in my life!"

The others came at once and Barney and John went down; they returned to the surface to listen again patiently to my description. Then John went back to his exploration and Barney to photograph a lobster he'd located. I continued to descend in the same place and it came out again, mottled grey, rolling its eyes at me, opening a mouth as big as a furnace door and turning with a movement of its blanket-big tail and vanishing. Later, all of the others saw it—the magnificent jewfish moving slowly from its hiding and returning.

No one could know the jewfish's age; fish never stop growing, some live one hundred years or more, and since ageing is not said to start until growth stops, it is not known when a fish can truly be said to grow old. It is possible that certain aquatic animals, free of the constraints of gravity and buoyed up by water, grow indefinitely until they are either caught by a predator or die of disease. On the other hand, it seems that the life span of multicellular animals on land is finite. Not even the tissues of an animal are immortal; if the skin of an old mouse is transplanted to a young one of the same inbred strain, it will wither and die before the young animal dies of old age. Cells of every tissue can divide only a limited number of times, even when grown in a tissue culture; after that they die. As Barney has pointed out, even if disease were abolished it seems that our human lives cannot be prolonged; as sleep occurs in a certain cycle, death does and may as well be accepted similarly. At the University of Edinburgh, I knew that there were several anemones that were now a hundred years of age. Their donator had had them for thirty years and fed them fresh liver weekly; they are in fine condition and every year produce the expected clouds of eggs and sperm. They are still at the university and perhaps will live indefinitely.

Jewfish are the largest species of the sea bass family, which includes the groupers. Carnivorous and powerful at maturity, weighing up to eight hundred pounds, the jewfish begins life as a tiny egg and then a hatchling of a fraction of an inch. Constantly pursued, alert and cautious, as it grows it becomes confident and bold; its problems of survival change from that of escape to that of the feeding of its large system. It is said that if a man enters the feeding pattern of a giant jewfish, the latter might be dangerous, as could be the sawfish, tarpon, barracuda, shark, wahoo, and a few others predatory in habit. One grouper of the Great Barrier Reef of Australia, nearly as big as a jewfish, is known to have bitten off a spearfisherman's arm; this is said to have occurred not so much because of the aggressiveness of the grouper but because it lunged for the bleeding fish or speared lobster at the man's belt and took his arm instead. If one enters the environment of these creatures slowly and without sudden movement, they are likely to see one as a part of it; and if one moves toward them, there is less danger than if one swims away. If a jewfish has been attacked with spears, not permitted in these waters any longer, it quickly learns to avoid man and is clever in escape. Ours was polite, we felt, and we took care to make no interference with its life.

On the outskirts of the wreck, barracudas went by now and then—slim and swift, pikelike, some two and three feet long. We had seen them up to five feet in the Bahamas, called the Tiger of the Sea, able to kill prey many times their size, their bite clean and straight. They will usually make a single strike, whereas a shark will attack again and again and rag its prey, tearing at it. Barney and John had advised me to remove my wedding ring and gold bracelet before going off the wreck. Barney said that a friend of his was trailing an aluminum spear from his wrist while underwater, and a barracuda struck and left toothmarks in it. Fast-moving fish, depending for their food on sudden strikes, seem to have a reflex action, such as our cat Snoopy has when a finch escapes the cage; although he knows the finches are taboo, Snoopy catches them almost simultaneously with their leaving the open door. He allows us to retrieve them unharmed from his jaws, but no amount of scolding can stop that first motion. A wounded fish will often show its light underside; this, coupled with its thrashing movement, can be confused with a bright flashing object worn by a swimmer. I watched Barney glide toward a barracuda, its eyes large and silvery; it gaped, showing its heavy compact teeth and retreated.

I was tired from the excitement and the long time in the water, the skin on my fingers shriveling; Paula was already in the skiff; the DeWeeses and Barney, sometimes swimming far off from the wreck, seemed inexhaustible. I was drowsy and settled back; we had no hats and the afternoon sun seemed to be a bucket of molten heat tipping slowly upon us; there was no breeze; the boat's movement was gentle and irregular. I had swallowed a good bit of salt water. When my mask fogged up, for I had not yet got experienced in managing the spit business, I had to remove it and in the process of putting it back on would often meet a wave unexpectedly. I also got a good deal of sea in me in the natural course of swimming in the strong tide. The voices of the three in the water sounded distant and I wondered if they were near or far; I opened my eyes. Paula's head was on her knees and she was very still and unresistant to the motion of the boat.

"I wouldn't mind being on the solid bricks of good old Fort Jeff," I sighed.

"It's not so bad," she lifted her head, her eyes half-closed, "if you can't complain and you just relax and prepare to perish. I'd rather not talk, if you don't mind." And she resumed her position.

Seasickness is caused by the overstimulation of the balance mechanism in the inner ear which informs one of changes in the body's acceleration or in its orientation to gravitational pull. It is composed of crystals of carbonate of lime, *otoconia,* that are attached to hair-like sensory organs, which they stimulate as they move in response to gravity or acceleration. In certain people, excessive stimulation of this system results in nausea or vomiting. Remedies lower the sensitivity of the sensory nerves and are often effective; they cause drowsiness as a rule, if taken in adequate doses. As Barney had explained to me, most people in the course of time adapt to motion and recover spontaneously from seasickness. As a child in small boats on Lake Michigan, I had often been ill when the water was rough; when it was calm never. I had taken the *Queen Mary* to Europe and smaller ships across the Adriatic and Mediterranean not feeling anything but exhilaration when there was a high sea. When I told Barney of it, he suggested that perhaps it was because I was so fascinated by the conversations with ship's passengers and officers and engineers that I adapted speedily; I was sure he was right. I remembered crossing the English Channel one time and over tea meeting an engaging tourist, who progressively became paler. I tried to help, "Can't you think of it as your mother rocking your cradle?" But he rose unsteadily and made his way up and out to the railing.

Now, not being pledged to endurance like Paula, I waited until Barney neared the little skiff and called out, "How would all of you like to dive closer to the Fort?"

"Right," he said, recognizing the message and relaying it to the DeWeeses.

Trailing my hand with its bracelet and ring in the cooling water, ignoring outright any cautionary remarks about predators, I looked with anticipation toward the docks of Fort Jefferson. When we landed, we retired to our quarters to rest and read.

Then late in the day, as the sun slanted upon the western wall of the Fort, we decided to take our faceplates and flippers and go again into the sand-filled moat of Garden Beach where the little boys of the Fort Assistant, of five and two years, had been playing and now were returning to their home. The shallow water was fed by the tides and waves of the sea so that it was never stagnant.

There was a variety of fish—grey snappers, slim silvery needle fish with long beaks, and large parrot fish, all of them fed from above by the Gallaghers, for that part of the moat was just below the sea side of the casemate outside their door, and by others who brought bread and scraps of meat to toss down. Barney remembered the same giant parrot fish and feeding them long ago. They were so conditioned over the years that the moment a human figure appeared in the casemates twenty-five feet above, they would rush in a pack from wherever they were in the moat and mill about in the water, leaping to catch the food as it fell.

As we snorkeled there, Mrs. Gallagher appeared above, waving to us and hurling shrimp hulls and fat trimmings and pastry crumbs into the moat. The parrot fish responded, passing us at full speed, the rainbow kind stunning under water, pink and blue-green with dark beaks, two feet long and more. Later, full-bellied from the man-dropped food, they moved sluggishly, not deigning to clean the coral from the inner side of the moat wall the way the ones on the sea side would do. There was a red of sunset while we stayed, getting slowly chilled. The twilight descended and we swam toward the beach, coming on the parrot fish, colorless now in the fading light, disembodied ghosts floating through the ruined moat.

We made our way home to put on warm clothes and sweaters and climb up to the second tier casemates; we leaned in the arches, the bricks still warm from the day's heat, becoming giddy on looking over the edge at the drop into the moat. Soon a thin moon appeared in the darkening sky, and Barney said it was the new moon that was the cause of the strong spring tides which had swept over the old brigantine and made the swells so that our boat had rocked. Despite all, Paula and I wanted to return to the mystery of the wreck and view again the quiet monster that made its home there.

CHAPTER SEVEN

The Affair

*When Pooh awoke in the morning, the first thing he
saw was Tigger, sitting in front of the glass and looking at
himself.*

"Hallo!" said Pooh.

*"Hallo!" said Tigger. "I've found somebody just like
me. I thought I was the only one of them."*

—A. A. Milne: *The House at Pooh Corner*

IN the night I was restless, sighing and turning, my shoulders
and knees and forehead slightly hotter than other parts of my
skin, but all burned from the sun, despite the aid of the Royal
Lyme Suntan Lotion. The air was still and hot and there was no
sound from the sea. While we were breakfasting, John came down
and reported that the little white Park Service boat that we had
found so comfortable the first day was still not available but would
be the next morning and so we decided to wait over a day to go to
Loggerhead Key. I spent the morning cleaning our quarters and
then, propped by bed pillows on the old wicker couch, writing a
little in our journal about the experiences of the preceding day
and reading Colette's reminiscences. Barney and Paula meanwhile
roamed about the Fort; the former who had kept on a cap and a
long-sleeved yellow jersey all the time in the skiff yesterday, removing only the cap when underwater, was but lightly burned;
Paula was red-tan but vigorous. At noon they returned with a

King's Crown conch, which Barney wanted to use for bait. He put it on the floor and with a hammer knocked off one of the knobs near the apex of the shell and inserted a knife to cut the ligament attaching the creature to its covering. He turned the conch upside down in the sink and the body slithered out; he examined it intently and then triumphantly pulled forth a six-inch thin transparent rod which rather looked like plastic.

"Remember the pisser?" he said happily. "And you can split it with me. I'll give the next one to Paula."

"Thanks," Paula said. "What is it?"

I accepted the gift from Barney, who had given me pissers before in Andros Island when he and Captain Joe brought up conchs from the bottom. I knew to eat it as if it were spaghetti, sucking it in and chewing; it was slightly salty with a not unpleasant cartilaginous consistency. Since my first try, I have always enjoyed eating the pisser, which is the name the Bahamian natives call it, considering it a delicacy. Barney has not yet been able to find out from his scientific or lay friends, or in any of our books, what the organ's purpose is.

He cut up the rest of the conch and put it with our fishing gear. Then after lunch, we got into swim suits and took casting rods and faceplates and flippers and went down to one of the coaling docks. The superstructure of the wrecked station had rusted away long ago, leaving only twisted iron pilings and their crisscrossed supports standing in the milky-blue water. On the shoreward side of the ruin was a board at water level which some fishermen had put there. We waded out from the beach, wearing our gear and carrying the rods and heading for the board and stationing ourselves on it. First we tried spinners, casting them into the open water; a few tiny Sergeant Majors followed them but there were no strikes from bigger fish. Then Barney took a line only and baited it with conch, and put on his faceplate and let himself down between the coral-crusted iron pilings; we could see below him the white conch flesh gleaming palely. The water was dark blue and shadowy and seemed filled with silvery minnows. After a while Barney surfaced.

"As I got accustomed to the darkness," he told us, "there was a pattern to the distribution of the fishlets; each in company with thousands of others is slowly circling the pilings in perfect rings, each spaced the same from the next. I tried to disturb them, swimming into them and they moved away in unison acting coordinately, as though parts of a superorganism which responded to my presence."

We had talked of this before, as to whether a hive of bees is a society of individuals or a superorganism with its parts dispersed according to the function of the various classes. We knew of Maurice Maeterlinck's work with bees and white ants, as well as that of J. Henri Fabre. We had heard of the South African naturalist, Eugène Marais, and his theory that a nest of the termites, taken as a whole, is like an individual animal—the workers and soldiers similar to the red and white blood corpuscles, the fungus gardens being the digestive organs, the queen the female reproductive organ.

Barney went down again to resurface with a splash. The water about him was alive with huge fish and he shouted, "Tarpon!"

The silvery shapes, ghostly through the unclear water, were four feet long and there were dozens, getting used to him and circling in and out slowly around the dock ruins. Sometimes they brushed by him but showed no interest in the conch; after ten minutes all at once they vanished. Parrot fish hung about, as large as the giant man-fed ones in the moat; they were disinterested in the conch too, as were a few roaming snappers. Our only bidders were two Queen Angelfish, over a foot long, and since they were too beautiful to capture, Barney kept moving the bait away from them. The Fort Management Assistant, coming along the beach with some workmen, shouted that the snorkel fishing would have been more successful if it were not high noon, and Barney agreed.

Although fishing was allowed in the Park, we knew that no species of coral, shells, shellfish, gorgonian, sponges, or sea anemones might be disturbed or taken at this national site. Crawfish, at least twelve inches long, and Florida lobster might be caught only in the legal season and then limited to two a day per person, the same applying to the Queen or Pink Conch. The sea turtle's nests and eggs were also not be to molested according to the regulations and it was forbidden to land vessels on Bush Key or any area used by the summer nesting birds without official permission.

We wandered over to the sally port to watch the Assistant direct his men in hauling up an old anchor that had been located off the key, which he wanted to place as a tourist attraction by the Fort Jefferson sign. As we went back home through the parade grounds, we stopped in to say hello to the Assistant's wife, a blonde Swedish woman, happy with the ways of the Fort and the freedom she could give her small boys, who roamed at will always clad in swim trunks, tow-haired and tan. About her house, on the shelves and in cabinets was a large collection of drift bottles which she had combed along the beach—many of them rare, coming on the strong currents of the oceans which circle the world, some from Japan, handblown, like those that Barney had picked up on the Pacific coast when he was stationed there in World War II.

We left for Loggerhead Key the next day, unharmed by the fierce sun because of the boat's canvas top and carrying straw hats to use when we left the boat. John trolled a line behind us and halfway over caught a grouper and then another, which we stowed in our cold box with the selection of beer cans and soft drinks and which we would share for supper. In the white sandy shallows off Loggerhead, over two miles from Fort Jefferson, there were sponges, eel grass, gorgonians, and the water was a light clear green. This key was the largest of the seven in the Dry Tortugas, long and low—the lighthouse white halfway up and black the rest of the way, the only functioning light on the keys. The flora seemed to be the familiar mangrove and buttonwood, cactus and much bay cedar; there was a grove of coconut palms, some date palms and Australian pine, a few of the taller ones leaning or down from the late hurricane. John said that in the great storm of 1919, almost all the palms had been destroyed, the island was laid low, and that there had been a vast fatality among the migrating birds who were attracted by the lighthouse.

The sun beat upon the scorching sand as we dropped anchor at the little dock and followed the path inland. We came upon the ruins of the Marine Biological Laboratory of the Carnegie Institution of Washington, hibiscus bushes blooming around them under the shaggy palms and pines. In 1904, the Carnegie Institution established the Tortugas Laboratory on a site leased from the government, where extensive research on all marine activity was successfully conducted; the station was unique in its day, world-famous. It was here the first underwater color pictures of marine life were made, creating a sensation. The problem with early color film was that it was too slow to use the natural light of the reefs; in order to illuminate them satisfactorily, a special raft was built from which quantities of magnesium powder were exploded underwater. In 1940 the laboratory was discontinued and the buildings abandoned, subjected to hurricanes and falling into a state of disrepair, until a fire completely destroyed them in 1965.

After looking about a little, we came on two men of the Coast Guard which had jurisdiction over the lighthouse, who were sawing a fallen palm in the brush. We asked them about turtles and they pointed to the southwest.

"They've been crawling every night. You'll see their tracks on the tip of the island if you go that way," one said.

"They like the full of the moon," the other said. "They're scattered now. Your chance of seeing them is slim, but you might."

We thanked them and went through the vegetation where there seemed to be no path but the DeWeeses knew the way. After a third of a mile we came to the end of the key and began searching for tracks; I hoped even to glimpse one of the gigantic turtles, although John said they crawled up only at night and at dawn returned to the water. Despite John and Barney's descriptions, I was not prepared for the massive tracks when we came upon them —two lines where the flippers had dug in the sand and three feet apart. The creature had left a wavering path, not directly from the sea into the brush, but following the shoreline for a hundred yards before turning toward the center of the key. There was such a disturbance in the sand over a large area that the site where the eggs were buried was completely disguised.

The Hawksbill, Loggerhead, and Green Turtle are all still found in the Dry Tortugas waters at nesting time. The Hawksbill, weighing under a hundred pounds, is sought after for its commercially esteemed tortoiseshell and its eggs as well; an omnivorous feeder, it will bite if disturbed. The Loggerhead, sometimes reaching six hundred pounds, can be vicious if interfered with; it is of no commercial value and feeds on jellyfish, molluscs and any fish it can catch. Its flesh, because of its diet, is said by some to be rank, but Barney has always liked it, and when we first visited Andros Island, we brought along a small loggerhead we had purchased at the Nassau docks, weighing about a hundred pounds. Our friend, Captain Johnson, cleaned it for us and Mrs. Johnson served it in varied ways—in thick soup made of the under part of the carapace and the flippers, which we found as glutinous and tasty as the best Green Turtle; the steaks and livers were braised and eaten rare; they had no fishy taste. It is the Green Turtle, however, vegetarian, gentle-natured, reaching up to four feet long and weighing up to five hundred pounds, once reported twice that heavy, which feeds in the shoal waters where there is plenty of eelgrass, that is a gourmet's delight; its meat is more delicate than the carnivorous loggerhead's and certain parts are fine-grained, white and rather like chicken. The Green Turtle, protected here, was we knew nearing extinction. When we were in the Everglades, John had talked about the Green Turtle Program under way at Cape Sable and how thousands of babies were released yearly. It was hoped that many would come to these government-protected keys as they grew.

The female Green Turtle makes her nest as deep as her back legs can reach, usually two to three feet; the eggs must receive proper moisture and stay warm and not be flooded out by high tides. When she decides on the nest site, she first makes a shallow broad pit in which to rest; in the bottom of this she digs a hole, flask-shaped, slightly lopsided, arranged so that the surface can be reached by the young through a narrow neck. The eggs are spherical and white. When Mr. Gallagher had been here last week, he found a turtle nest, uncovered it, photographed it and covered it back up; he had counted a hundred and one eggs. When we talked with Mrs. Gallagher last evening she said she didn't use the eggs because it was against the law.

"But I've talked with shrimp people," she told us, "and their wives say the only thing turtle eggs is good for is pastry—like cakes and such."

As we continued down the beach, we came on the giant tracks of two more turtles before we reached our little boat. There were flipper-marks over a large area, thought to be made on purpose by the mother turtle to baffle predators. John said that before the present day of protection, professional egg hunters probed for the nests with iron rods and dug when they saw yolk clinging to them. When the turtle is making her nest, and for a day or two after, it is said that there is danger from hunting predators; but for some mysterious reason, during the following sixty days no animals seem to be able to locate their hiding.

Baby turtles hatch into a world that wants to eat them, from pelicans to vultures, from raccoons to coyotes—all in the space of time it takes them to scuttle over the sand beach to the sea. The nest of turtles hatches all together; the first hatchlings do not dig until more come out. Every new baby turtle in the nest adds to the working space, the crumpled rubbery shells underfoot. When all are free of the eggs, the whole lot begin to migrate upward— wriggling and digging, the top ones freeing the ceiling, the lower ones packing the sand that comes down, their flailing movements spasmodic and instinctive. They remain a team at all times, as they make their way through the flask-like chamber, which it is thought is constructed to prevent cave-ins and to aid in their speedy simultaneous emergence. As the young reach the thin crust below the surface, they pause to rest. Then usually that night, but often waiting days for the right mysterious moment known only to the baby turtles, they all break through and start the hazardous trip to the sea, which is often hidden from their view and which they have never known. The cooperation of the group continues until they reach the beach, the constant movement of nestmates bumping and scuttling seeming to urge the group along and discourage resting stops along the way. It also seems to guide the hatchlings more directly to the water, by the same principle that migrating flocks of birds guide themselves more accurately and swiftly than a single migrant, the deviants correcting themselves to comply with the mainstream of traffic.

The baby turtle, on reaching the wet sand, has a new spasmodic surge of speed and as the first wave breaks, seems at once to know how to swim. His problem of getting through the powerful shore breakers is solved by diving for the bottom and avoiding the surge. His predators are now manifold; he may remain in the shoals and shallow water or may find protection in water vegetation like the sargasso weed, but no one is sure. The habitat of the young turtles has never been revealed. There were plentiful schools of small fish near shore as we walked, and we thought that the baby turtles might have their same or a similar problem. Systematically preyed upon by the water birds from the air and the predatory fish of the sea, they wavered between the two. Occasionally, a harried minnow leapt above the surface to escape his pursuer, and was at once snatched by a booby patrolling along the water edge. After a heavy storm the beach would be littered with tiny washed-up schools and the ghost crabs and wading birds would feast upon them.

The temperature was near ninety and augmented by the glare of sand as we reached the dock; our hatbands were wet, and we were happy to get in our boat again and set out into the sea. We were thirsty and slightly hungry and ate our lunch as the craft puttered along slowly. We were heading for the harbor of Fort Jefferson and planned to go through it and on to Long Key where John said the nurse sharks might be. We passed over coral gardens, seeing them through the boat's glass bottom, catching glimpses of parrot fish, snappers and grunts. After half an hour we were rounding the northern point of Long Key and because John knew this was a spring tide which was at the flood, we were able to cross the sandbar which divides the key from Bush Key on the northwest where the terns' fluctuating made a noisy cloud.

"There," John said.

And we saw two dorsal fins, a dark double horn above the water. He moved the boat toward it and there was the shadow of the great body and then we were nearly upon it—a nurse shark, ten feet long from nose to tail, gliding on the bottom. The boat drew close, and the shark began to move off, sprinting for a moment and leaving a wake. We waited, cruising, our cameras ready, and two more long shadows appeared far ahead, one trailing the other. Then it seemed the shallows about us came alive with sharks. We shut the motor off so as not to disturb them and drifted among the flock, a dozen, all mature, eight to twelve feet long, almost like elongated weed patches on the bottom until we came over them. Then slowly they swam away, one following another. Like the terns, the sharks were having their annual party. The spot, John said, was their rendezvous. Here they congregated from the trackless expanse of ocean every June, requiring shallow water to copulate.

"Look," Paula cried. "Do you think we could get a closeup?"

And we saw the splash in the distance and the brown long tail of the shark whipping five feet above water. We started the motor and made our way over. The shark was thrashing vigorously now— throwing water ten feet into the air. There was a second one; drawing near to within a few yards of the pair, we saw that one was lying on the shallow bottom, white belly up, and the other was attempting to grasp one of her front pectoral fins in his teeth, undulating over her and flailing his tail.

We knew that at the end of a number of mating seasons, the mature females were recognized by their ragged pectoral fins. The nurse sharks are sluggish with flat large heads and small eyes, weighing up to eight hundred pounds. Barney said he had never known one to be aggressive in any way and had swum with them many times, even riding them briefly, holding to the pectoral fins though their brown back hide was like sandpaper and not inviting. Before modern times, sharkskin had been valued by cabinet makers and carpenters as an abrasive to smooth their wood and was marketed as shagreen. Sharks and rays do not have true scales like the bony fishes, but placoid ones, which have enamel and a pulp cavity and are like tiny teeth and are scattered all over their bodies, giving them their typical roughness. If annoyed, a nurse shark may bite severely; its large jaws are equipped with rows of teeth which are modified placoid scales and are used to grasp and crush the shellfish, lobsters, conchs, clams and small fish on which it feeds. When the tiny teeth wear down or break they are replaced by others waiting inside the jaw and ready to work forward into place. Two short barbels are in front of the mouth, used in locating food. Slow-moving and bottom-cruising, the undeveloped lower tail lobes of the nurse shark distinguish it from its swift voracious brothers.

The sharks and rays, along with sawfish and skates, have a gristly and cartilaginous skeleton. In contrast to the fish of the class *Osteichthyes,* meaning bony, they compose the class *Chondrichthyes,* meaning cartilaginous, and have been around over three hundred million years according to fossil records. Their success over the eons is illustrated by the little variation within the class, which cannot be said of the varied bony fishes. They differ from the latter too in that whereas most bony fishes lay eggs, the cartilaginous ones fertilize internally and in most species the eggs hatch inside the female and the young are born alive. We knew that one of the predatory sharks hatched its young within the womb and that they proceeded cannibalistically to eat each other until at the moment of birth but one vigorous youngster, its carnivorous pattern established, emerged. The cartilaginous fish have no swim bladders to give them buoyancy and must swim constantly throughout their lives. If, for experimental reasons, a shark must be kept in a rigid position, water has to be artificially circulated through its gills or it will suffocate. Explosions in water which will kill bony fish since it injures their swim bladders, seem only to attract alert sharks.

It would seem that sharks are almost the only species of fish whose population is increasing of late. Some years ago, before chemists learned to synthesize vitamin D, the creatures were hunted for their huge livers from which vitamin-rich oil was extracted, and for their hides and for their fins which were dried and exported to China where they served as the chief ingredient of shark fin soup. We had ordered the latter in Bangkok one time, liking the rich glutinous turtle-like consistency of the dish. Nowadays, since trade with China has halted and since there is no longer a demand for the liver or hide, sharks are allowed to grow to adult size, and one hears increasingly these days of their boldness and of their attacks on people.

Now Barney was hanging the underwater camera around his neck and releasing the safety catch on the meter. "Would you hand me my fins?"

"Be careful," I told him.

"Well at any rate, you girls get a record of what happens," he said, alert.

But the pair of sharks were separating and slipping away, while over in the shallows a hundred yards away another commotion was beginning. We eased over, John cutting the motor as we got close and gliding up to them in the four-foot-deep water. The pair paid no heed to the boat or to Barney slipping through the shoals with his aimed camera. Clinging to the white belly of the overturned female we could see a twelve-inch Remora, a fish with a suckerlike disc on the top of its head with which it attaches itself to the flanks and bellies and under jaws of passing sharks and whales, waiting to feed on leftovers. In spite of the violence of the courting of the huge sea creatures, the little Remora had not been displaced.

Then the activity ceased abruptly. We could no longer see the white belly from the boat, and the female, brown on top and camouflaged in a cloud of sand, swam off. Her partner did not follow and we saw him as our boat drifted—seven hundred pounds of shark moving directly for Barney and over him. We felt that he mistook Barney's non-tanned skin for the female and watched Barney putting his hands on the huge snout and bracing himself and shoving vigorously.

I was alarmed. "Could you start the motor, John?"

He did and at that moment the shark, with a heavy stroke of his tail, swam slowly away. When we reached Barney, he was pleased though. He handed the camera up to me and bent to unfasten the little Remora which had left the female shark for his leg; there was a red patch of skin where it had clung. Barney seemed to want to repeat the adventure and asked me to reload his camera, which I began to do. We could see breeding sharks in the distant waters and Paula too wanted to get more shots of them. In my hurry, I forgot to rewind the film cartridge and opened the back of the camera; I realized my mistake and closed it again, rewinding the film, reloading it and handing it to Barney in time for him to try to approach another amorous pair. We had no such luck as the first couple though and decided to return to Fort Jefferson and perhaps come out another day.

As Barney climbed dripping into the boat, I asked, "Could I put a rhetorical question to you? What happens if someone opens a camera for only a second before rewinding the film?"

"Probably the film would be ruined. Why?"

"Well, it just happened," I sighed.

"Never mind," he said, "I don't."

And as we cruised toward the dock, I asked him, "Why are you smiling to yourself, Barney?"

He said, "Although I've had more pleasant love affairs, I've gained from this experience a reassuring thought. Now I know that no matter how old and repulsive I become by human standards, no matter if all who love me now desert me, as long as I keep my belly white, I can come to the Tortugas in June and be loved as I was in the days of my prime!"

CHAPTER EIGHT

The Discovery

This Sea that bares her bosom to the moon;
The winds that will be howling at all hours,
And are up-gathered now like sleeping flowers;
For this, for every thing, we are out of tune;
It moves us not.—Great God! I'd rather be
A Pagan suckled in a creed outworn;
So might I, standing on this pleasant lea,
Have glimpses that would make me less forlorn;
Have sight of Proteus rising from the sea;
Or hear old Triton blow his wreathèd horn.

—Wordsworth: "The World Is Too Much with Us"

WE were restless. This was our sixth day at Fort Jefferson. We had to stay for six more. The cots were uncomfortable, the food was plain, with the help of the DeWeeses we had covered the keys and their surrounding water so that we felt we could describe them and their history sufficiently. I spoke up at breakfast.

"Why don't we clear out? We've plenty of material and photographs. It's uncivilized; let's go somewhere else. What do you say?"

"It's up to you two," Paula said.

"All right with me," Barney said. "We'll go back to Pennekamp, if you like."

"But how can we do it? The *Bush Key* doesn't leave for six more days."

"Let's go down and talk to the shrimp boat men," Barney said. "I saw one come in with a load of Florida tourists yesterday."

"Listen," Paula said, "isn't that a helicopter?"

We went outside where the humming of the plane was clear off to the east, and saw the Management Assistant hurrying across the parade ground. We followed him, heading for the sally port. We felt sure that we could persuade whoever was the owner of the helicopter to take us to the mainland with him or wherever he was going. We crossed the drawbridge and went to the long spit to our right, where Bermuda grass grew shaggily and at the end of which were the old coaling docks. There was a large flat area between them and the Fort where there was ample landing room. The helicopter was changing its course, veering about so that it avoided Bush Key where the terns were, and was coming in from the west. Other personnel from the Fort were assembling to watch the landing. The Assistant's wife and her two tiny sons were there; she told us that it was a Navy helicopter and was delivering materials for the installation of a wind sock to be mounted on the south coaling dock for their convenience in making future trips. John had already said there was an excellent cooperative relationship between the Navy and the Park Service. She added that once when one of her sons broke his arm falling off a staircase, that plane had come over and taken them to Key West where there was a hospital. She thought they might accept us aboard, but doubted they'd handle all our luggage.

"We don't need our luggage," Barney said. "We'll take our cameras and we can rent underwater gear. Right?"

"Anything to get back to civilization," I sighed.

But the pilot shook his head. "Against regulations. Sorry."

"Think it over," I suggested. "Don't hurry."

"Nope, folks," he said, turning to the Superintendent briskly.

We stayed there a while, caught by the novelty of the event, as the other Fort people were. A few of the fishermen from the dock came to hang around and some of the tourists from the shrimp trawler. The latter were clad in casual dress—the men in old khaki pants and T-shirts, the women in bright shorts and blouses, barefoot or wearing sandals, two of them with their hair in curlers. The children wore crumpled assorted clothes. The men told Barney that a group of them had gotten together and rented the shrimp boat for a week to make the excursion. There were thirteen, including the children. They slept on the boat, fished, shelled in the moat and rowed about in an old dinghy. They had seen the coupling sharks too. These tourists from the lower income groups —mailmen, filling station attendants, clerks—somehow seem to have the same carefree attitude toward pleasure as the wealthy jet set. They are seen rumbling through Yellowstone National Park in trailers they have constructed themselves or in trucks with a room built on the bed, usually with an assortment of children at their sides. It often seems that the middle class, nervous, ambitious, anxious for prestige, misses certain delights that these two extremities experience.

We went down to the wharf to talk to their captain. He was ruddy-faced, a heavy wrench in one hand with which he was repairing some piece of machinery. "Sorry," he said, "this boat belongs to them folks for five more days and we're going up to Fort Myers anyways, day after tomorrow. Ain't going back to Key West."

"We'd pay you a hundred dollars flat," Barney said.

"You could leave them here while you run us back to Key West," I said. "If we left before dawn you might be back at dark."

"It's their boat," he said. "But tell you what I'll do. There's about twenty-five shrimp boats around here and I'll try to make contact with my radio for you. I know some of those boys could use that hundred."

"Wonderful," I said, as he disappeared into the cabin, swinging his wrench energetically.

We stood looking out to sea, and John DeWeese joined us. He had learned from the pilot of the helicopter of our problem. "You're not leaving! You're crazy. You just got here."

"Helga says it's not her idea of a vacation," Barney said. "And our work's done."

"I thought the beds would be softer, John," I told him.

John pointed out over the water. "See that boat? Yesterday the couple that own it told me they were going back to Key West in a day or two. Maybe you can persuade them to take you along."

"Great," I said.

"Let's get the outboard."

We climbed into the skiff and puttered out to where the forty-eight-foot cruiser was moored. We had noticed the owners during the past day or two, fishing from their dory on an outer reef. John said that they had found a big one out there and it had broken up all their tackle. He said they left a jug for a buoy to mark the spot, which was unlawful here as everybody knew. As we approached, a little old man came to the rail. John shut off our motor and Barney tossed him our line.

"Any luck with that fish?" Barney asked.

It was a mistake to have raised the subject; for the next fifteen minutes in unbroken narrative the old man, who we were beginning to think of as Captain Ahab, told us the story of his personal Moby Dick. Four days ago his wife had hooked the creature. After a short struggle, it broke the line and left with the hook. They thought it was a giant grouper or jewfish; I remembered the one under the wreck and how it had stirred me and how I wanted it to live forever.

Ahab was candid. "We threw out our water jug to buoy the place and went to get us a heavier line off the boat."

Then the beast had taken the hook and again ran off with it and most of the line. The pattern had continued for the following three days, the fish breaking heavier and heavier lines. Finally, they managed to hook it on a rope. Ahab said he and his wife had pulled and pulled until they had got the great brown leviathan halfway up.

"Big as a horse, ain't it?" he shouted into the cabin behind him.

His wife came out, a tiny woman in blue jeans, slim as a thirteen-year-old, so that we would have thought her his daughter. "He's right," she declared.

They said the creature weighed seven hundred pounds if it

weighed seven. When it saw the dory it stirred the water with its tail, straightened the hook in its mouth and swam away. Ahab hit the rail with his fist.

"He's still down there. And I'm going back to Key West in the morning to get whatever it takes to catch him."

"Could we ride back with you?" Barney asked. "We'll pay."

"I'll agree to take you, if you can be ready at seven sharp in the morning," Ahab said.

"How lucky can you get?" I beamed.

And so, at the appointed hour, we assembled our duffle bags and tossed them to Captain Ahab and prepared to board. We thanked the DeWeeses and told Lauri that we'd folded our sheets and left them on the cots and she was welcome to all the unused supplies in our rooms. We settled with the Management Assistant, paying the minor bill and thanking him for the use of the accommodations. We shook hands with all the people of the Fort, who came to witness our leaving. On board, Paula and I took our last camera shots of everyone, clicking as we moved away, calling back to the waving figures of John and Lauri.

"Goodbye, old Fort Jeff!"

The now-familiar shape of the red structure and the sound of the twittering terns dwindled to nothing as we cruised slowly into the channel. The motor was incredibly noisy; the fumes were inescapable; the boat seemed smaller than we had thought as Paula and I settled on the tiny top deck.

"I'm going to be seasick," I told her.

She nodded. "Let's get comfortable. It's a long way."

"Slow too," I said, for we barely moved through the water.

Barney went to see what the trouble was. "Port motor won't go into gear," Ahab told him.

Mrs. Ahab picked up the anchor and pitched it into the sea. "He's going to see what the matter is."

Ahab paused and gazed at his wife. "She is the best hand I ever had on this boat or other," he declared to Barney.

We began to roll heavily in the channel's swells. Ahab was on his knees in the cabin, starting to tear up the floor boards to get at the engines. I was becoming nauseous and settling myself for a long day. Even if the repair went quickly, I knew the boat could never travel as fast as the big *Bush Key* and we'd do well to arrive in Key West before night.

Barney in his firmest voice was saying, "Is there anything I can do to help? Tell me if there is."

"They aren't nothing." Ahab's voice was muffled.

When Barney looked up at the little top deck, I beckoned. "Make him take us back home," I whispered. "We'll never get there."

"Wait and see," he said. And tried again. "Is there something I can do?"

"If they are," Captain Ahab said firmly, "I'll tell you."

I was thinking of the swelling stretch of deep open sea between us and Key West. "Make him take us back," I called softly to Barney.

Ahab got to his feet. "We can make the Marquesas by nightfall even on one motor."

"Isn't that the Graveyard of Ships?" Paula asked me.

And then after an hour or two, Ahab gave up. His wife pulled in the anchor, refusing Barney's offer of help, and we limped back to Fort Jefferson on one motor. The dock was clear of our friends, though the shrimp boat people recognized us and waved. Barney told Paula and me to take only what gear we needed for a night and leave the remaining bags and the cameras where they were stowed. We arranged with the Ahabs to meet the following morning at seven. We stepped upon the hot dock and its stability was a delight.

Meanwhile something was happening—we were realizing that we had nothing specific that we had to do. I remembered my Uncle Steichen telling me once about having planned a visit to my family when I was little, and how my mother had phoned at the last moment to say that we had all come down with the flu and he should postpone his visit; everything had been arranged and he was just closing the door. He told me that one of the finest days of his life had followed, because while he stood there in disappoint- ment, he suddenly saw that he was being given a day to enjoy completely without plan. The Fort mechanic was sent for and Barney stayed to see how the trouble would be diagnosed. Paula and I walked back through the parade ground and home again. Lauri had put our sheets and pillowcases in the washing machine and was busy raiding the refrigerators and the cupboards, stack- ing the supplies in one of the A & P cartons. She put her hands on her hips and sighed.

"I wondered if this would happen," she said, "that port engine didn't sound right to me as you left. It kept missing."

"Can you and John come down for supper tonight?" I asked her.

"All right, thanks," she said. "And we're going shelling this afternoon. Do any of you want to come along?"

"As soon as we get the sheets on the line and this room tidied up," I said happily, "I'm going to sit here and read all day long."

"Me too," Paula announced.

Barney came in an hour later. The propeller shaft had come loose and was not turning with the motor, he reported. By night- fall, with the help of a Fort workman, Ahab would have it re- paired. "And then we'll be on our way," he said briskly. "You don't mind the delay, do you?"

"Not at all," I said. "And, what's more, I don't like Captain Ahab's boat. It's too small and the sea's too deep."

"Nonsense," he said. "A small boat's as safe as a big one. You couldn't sink that vessel."

"That's been said before," I told him, "and do you realize that there's nothing we have to do and nowhere to go today?"

"I tell you what," he said. "Let's take the mattresses and pillows up into the casemates and a book and you can read to me."

And that was what we did. We hauled the bedding up the stair- case and halfway down the alleyway past the DeWeeses' door and put the mattresses side by side in the western shaded edge of the wall above the moat. We packed a basket with crackers and cheese and coffee and orange juice and beer and a Du Maurier novel for Barney and me and *You and Your Congressman* still for ambitious Paula. When the sheets were dry in the sun, Paula went to get them and we spread them on the mattresses and fresh pillowslips on the pillows. The cool breeze blew in from the sea and over us and through the arches to the paradeground side. Past that, high in the air, we could see the continual movement of the terns above Bush Key and hear them, sounding from where we were like the peeping of a thousand baby chicks. We watched the scores of Man-o'-war birds and the thousands of terns circling in the updraft, around and about, a chimney of birds extending as high as we could see. Occasionally an ungainly pelican would soar up with them, not in search of food apparently, but as if he did it for sheer pleasure.

We spent the day there in the casemates, reading aloud, occasionally walking over to an archway to look through at the Bush Key activity. As the afternoon waned, the dropping sun entered the archway and we pulled the mattresses back from its heat. Then the sunset happened and Barney spoke.

"Tomorrow we'll be in Key West."

"And we haven't finished reading the book yet," I said.

"I'm glad you've decided to stay," Paula told us.

Before supper we walked through the parade ground where the bird-like Salt Marsh Mosquitoes were assembling and at the boat we explained to Captain and Mrs. Ahab that we would not be going in the morning and wanted to retrieve our luggage. Ahab tossed the duffle bags and gear over the rail to Barney and we returned to our quarters, content.

When it was dark, by a flashlight, Barney and I took two blankets and returned to our mattresses to spend the night there, Paula staying below. The moon rose, a red misshapen ball, later floating high and white and round and flooding its vague light over the ghost Fort. Just below our heads was the twenty-five-foot drop to the moat, unprotected by any rail. I awoke once with a start, dreaming of stepping off and falling and of the uncertain monsters lurking in the water below. Phantoms wafted by—perished seamen, murdered prisoners, thirsty explorers. It grew cool and we needed the blankets and there were no mosquitoes. After that, we spent every night in the open casemates, and most of our six days too. Sometimes we ventured down to Garden Beach or the outer moat wall to snorkel. One day we went out with the DeWeeses in the old skiff, floating about in the water where nurse sharks still were pairing; desultory, we watched them. Returning, we trolled for our supper, boating a couple of yellowtails in time. As we neared Garden Key, we cut loose the plastic jug Captain Ahab had left over Moby Dick's lair. We went back, lackadaisical, to our mattress in the casemates and took up Steinbeck in paperback this time, *The Pearl*. Kino was discovering it and Juana was telling him to open it: "Kino deftly slipped his knife into the edge of the shell. Through the knife he could feel the muscle tighten hard. He worked the blade lever-wise and the closing muscle parted and the shell fell apart. The lip-like flesh writhed up and then subsided. Kino lifted the flesh, and there it lay, the great pearl, perfect as the moon. It captured the light and refined it and gave it back in silver incandescence. It was as large as a sea-gull's egg. It was the greatest pearl in the world."

Sometimes we got out the journal and recorded incidents we recalled or information we had gotten from the DeWeeses about the Tortugas keys. Workmen would pass, nodding to our group. Mr. Gallagher came through, vigorous, pausing. "You folks still here? I thought you went off with some fisherman."

"We changed our minds," I sighed.

And all the time at Fort Jefferson, no matter whether we were reading, writing, drowsing, talking, swimming, climbing about the casemates, there was the continual background of the bird sound. We were told that when the terns left in September, they went in huge flocks and at night, the entire exodus taking place in two or three days; the only birds staying behind were cripples unable to fly. Bush Key would be silent until the following March or April.

Then one night the noddies would be heard, reconnoitering. And during the next they would have all arrived. A week later and the crowds of sooties would have come suddenly and the noise swelled to the crescendo which it would maintain for the coming months.

The DeWeeses continually shelled, usually in the late afternoons, along the outer moat wall, but also on the reefs and keys about. They brought their treasures by sometimes, carrying them in their faceplates for us to see. We had looked over their collection at their home in the Everglades—seventy-one species.

"No doubt," Lauri said happily, "there are more that we haven't found around here. This is just a representative assortment. We never take a shell we already have a good specimen of."

The rarest they showed us, found by John on Bush Key, was the Royal Florida Miter, *Mitra florida,* two inches long with six whorls, white and speckled with orange-brown. Of their two specimens of Cyphoma shells, one was rare too and we photographed it—the tiny Fingerprint Cyphoma, *Cyphoma signatum,* an inch long, creamy, its mantle pale yellow with many black transverse lines. The other of the genus was the common Flamingo Tongue, *Cyphoma gibbosum,* stunning, apricot with orange uneven squared spots ringed with black placed all over the mantle, like the Reticulated Giraffe of eastern Africa. Lauri had got it off a sea-whip and said they were fond of grazing on gorgonians where they made handsome living patterns. I thought that perhaps in the great wealth of the sea in the years before man now, one could substitute the bizarre beauty of these shells for the brilliant butterflies once common to our land. I wondered if man would protect the shells or whether they would go the way of the Lepidoptera, as poisons were placed into the oceans of the world.

In the opinion of the DeWeeses, the most beautiful of all the shells were the tellins, of which there are over twenty species that range from the West Indies to Alaska to Japan. We gazed at the three-inch Sunrise Tellin, *Tellina radiata,* like a flat oval dish, the pale red and yellow rays extending out, its beak tipped in carmine; and the Great Tellin, *Tellina magna,* soft-hued, pinkish, which is also uncommon and that they had found in the sands of Garden Beach at low tide.

"We wanted to show you the Great Tellin," Lauri said. "We have one and we're going to put it back now."

"Come with us tomorrow," John urged.

"Thank you," we said, feeling our isolation from all excitements.

The next day, they came with Lauri's sweater folded over a collection. "Look," she said.

"We're putting this one back too," John said, handing it to me.

It was spectacular and looked like its name: Lion's Paw, *Lyropecten nodosus,* over five inches across, heavy and strong, blazoned orange-red, with eight or nine coarse ribs. We stared. The others were the Jewel Box, the Turkey Wing, the Gold-mouthed Triton, whorled, with orange mouth and white teeth, the Purple Sea-snail, two-toned, lighter above and dark purple-violet below. We were reminded of a favorite book of ours, *The Voyages of Doctor Doolittle,* in which one of the characters, the Great Glass Sea-Snail, had an enormous pale-pink dome-shaped shell that towered like a rainbow, in which the doctor and his friends traveled across the ocean from Africa to Puddleby-on-the-Marsh in England, during which time the doctor, by learning the difficult shellfish language, obtained considerable information about the ancient history of the Animal Kingdom.

Snails inhabit the ocean from the highest coastal cliffs to the deepest canyons, eighty thousand species of them, from the minuscule two-millimeter *Helix Vitrinella* to the elegant two-foot Horse Conch. They may have a covering that is remarkable and they may have no shell at all, like the nudibranches, of the suborder *Nudibranchiata,* meaning without-gills. Sea-snails have been used by man for trade, tools, decoration and food. Early American Indians and pre-Columbian peoples of southwestern United States used them for ornaments and as a kind of wampum. In certain coral islands they were made into axes and knives; the Romans farmed edible snails and oysters; and in the Mediterranean a commercial empire was built upon the Royal Tyrian purple, the dye for it obtained principally from three species of marine snails: the Spiny Dye Murex, *Murex brandaris;* the Banded Dye Murex, *Murex trunculus;* and a Rock-shell, *Thais haemastoma.* I had recited Flecker's poem as a child.

> *I have seen old ships sail like swans asleep*
> *Beyond the village which men still call Tyre,*
> *With leaden age o'ercargoed, dipping deep*
> *For Famagusta and the hidden sun*
> *That rings black Cyprus with a lake of fire.*

The Phoenicians, superlative traders, navigators and colonizers since 2000 B.C., manufactured the purple dye chiefly in their cities of Tyre and Sidon, now in Lebanon, where Barney had heard of ancient piles of cast-off shells as huge as the hill called The Knob at our country place. The lengthy and arduous process involved in manufacturing the purple dye accounted for the rarity of the product. The colorless fluid from which the dye was made exudes from the elongate gland on the inner wall of the mantle of the spiny, spiraled, two- to four-inch long snail. When exposed to direct sunlight the fluid turns bright yellow, then goes into shades of green and blue and at last a strong red-purple. The snails were ground up or cracked and placed in huge bowl-shaped holes in the rocky shore of Tyre. Salt was added to prevent decay and the sun was allowed to act upon the mass for a few days. Then the fluid was put into cooking vessels, diluted with water and boiled for nearly two weeks. Our present concept of purple is a blending of red and blue, but in those ancient days when it rivaled gold and precious gems in value, the color covered the spectrum from crimson and magenta to purple-violet.

The Tyrian purple is often referred to in the Bible; Babylonians dressed their idols in it; Egyptians are said to have used it for mummy wrappings; in Rome, the dye was employed for lipstick and rouge and their senators wore it as a broad stripe on their

tunics. Then Nero proclaimed that no one but Emperors themselves might be permitted its use; when Mark Antony and Cleo-
patra voyaged to their unfortunate battle at Actium, their sails
were the only ones in the fleet of Tyrian purple; in time the Christian church, endowed by the wealthy, took over the crimson-hued
cloth used even today for the cloaks of its cardinals, and for particular celebrations. The art of producing dye and ink was known
not only to the Phoenicians; as early as 1000 B.C. the Celts and Lake
Dwellers of the British Isles were gathering the common Rock-
shell, *Thais lapillus,* to get the purple color. In prehistoric days
in South America, Central America and Mexico, the snails of the
genus *Purpura* were used to produce a violet dye. And they still
are today in Mexico, where the Tehuantepec Indians employ a
technique that we thought as worthy as our Stone Crabber friend's
in Key West; they milk the fluid from the snail and then return it
to its habitat to be milked again later.

Barney said, "I wonder whether shells like the Lion's Paw and
the Flamingo Tongue could be introduced and cultivated in protected areas in underwater parks like the moat below us?"

"There's an hour left of sunlight," Lauri said. And the two of
them went off to return to the outer moat wall.

We stayed in the arches and watched the night come down and
the stillness of the water, captivated, not wanting Fort Jefferson
to become a memory. The next afternoon thunderheads gathered
and winds began to blow. We pulled our mattresses back and prepared to watch the affair. The noise from the rookery became
higher pitched and louder and as their excitement mounted, the
birds came down to hover just above the key like a blanket. John
DeWeese told us the terns didn't like the rain because they
couldn't fly when they got wet, their feathers not being water-
repellent, and they had to wait for them to dry before they could
take to the air again. When terns fished, they scooped the prey up
with their beaks and did not submerge like a water bird; if they
were caught in the water by some accident or high wave, they
drowned easily.

We noted, as we looked down to the parade ground, that the little boys of the Fort's Assistant were running about as they caught the exhilaration that humans feel too before a storm. The children's voices became pitched higher also, and they shouted, jumping and rolling in the grass. It was the state of change. We were no longer lethargic either and paced up and down, leaning out over the sheer drop and peering at the skyscape of the sea.

At the first spot of rain, over eighty thousand terns, all that were able to be airbound, began to edge away from the storm, circling to our side of the Fort, where we could look out at them, darting and shrieking between us and Loggerhead Key, swooping over the sea, flying about the Fort, almost deafening our conversation with their cries. During hurricanes, they would move out of range, circling the storm, and not returning until it had passed, the DeWeeses said. They talked of hurricanes they had known at the Tortugas, when palms lay flat, everything moving changed its place, and the residents would go into the inner parts of the bastions, like the hideout we had seen, where ammunition once had been stored and the noise was muffled. The rain fell, thunder rumbled and the little boys below moved slowly to their house; we too, felt stilled again.

That night it was cold in the casemates and we brought up extra blankets. In the early hours of morning, with a drowsy recollection of the past storm still in our minds, suddenly the whole key was shaken violently. The great building trembled and bits of mortar and bricks fell about us; noise reverberated.

Barney assayed an answer: "We've been struck by lightning."

But we knew there was another reason, for the stars were shining and the storm long past. We speculated a while before falling back to sleep; in the morning John explained, "That was a sonic boom from a jet coming out of Key West Naval Base. Some day one of those is going to shake down old Fort Jeff. It's built on nothing but coral debris and every time a boom comes, we find more cracks in the walls. The nesting terns don't like it either."

We had seen, on our tours about the Fort, cracks in certain arches, sometimes an inch wide, marring their beauty and down which the limestone and mortar seeped, forming series of icicle-like white stalactites. Below were hardened pools where stalagmites were building up as the moisture fell drop by drop. Barney had said he did not remember them from former days.

And then it was time again to leave the Dry Tortugas; we went to the Management Assistant's office once more and paid the few more dollars for the extra days and shook hands with him and everybody. We were happy to be traveling on the familiar old hulk, *Bush Key*, stable and firm upon the water, with the DeWeeses for company. We talked about the future of the Dry Tortugas National Monument.

Barney said, "I've been watching Fort Jefferson for more than thirty years, and it's one of the few places in America that over so long a time has shown no important change. Except for the devastation of the coral gardens by the freeze, the sea and bird life and even the pattern of human life in the Dry Tortugas is much the same as it always was."

"It's planned to be a basically holding operation," John said, "with little change."

We knew that and Barney complained, "They shouldn't have torn down the officers' quarters."

"It was dangerous," Lauri said. "The walls were shaky and they were afraid of an accident."

"It puts too heavy a load on the manpower here," Barney said. "The Fort becomes filled with earth-moving equipment, old boards, bricks and stones, and loses the charm of an unspoiled monument. They should have fenced it off if they couldn't repair it."

"What about taking care of tourists?" I asked.

Lauri said that a commercial twin-engined amphibian plane was to begin transporting people daily for twenty-five dollars a person. The flight took half an hour each way and sightseers could spend three hours looking over the Fort. Now and then an excursion boat started a ferrying service between Key West and the monument, charging fifteen dollars per fare, but they usually discontinued service during the summer.

"Both plane and boats," Lauri told us, "are bound to be governed to a degree by the weather, and they have to have enough passengers to make the trip worth their efforts, too."

"Suppose someone brought in a retired liner and anchored it in the harbor?" Barney said. "It could be used as a floating hotel. They're doing that with the *Queens* in America. Passengers could stay over a day or more and return by the same boat."

We knew that it was next to impossible at the Tortugas to take care of more visitors than came on chartered boats or private yachts or in the company of the Park Service or the Navy or the Coast Guard. Because we were with the DeWeeses and this book was to discuss the monument, we had been allowed to stay at a nominal fee in the barren quarters that we had become so attached to.

"We're going to have a storm," Paula said, pointing toward Rebecca Light.

Far off the port bow, where the triangular base and pillar of the distant lighthouse's superstructure rose from the sea, cumulus clouds were gathering. By the time the *Bush Key* was abreast of the light, the clouds were blackening and rain squalls were following us, here and there a water spout twisting down in a dark funnel from the flat horizontal base of the sky formations. Although it was raining sporadically around us and the wind was blowing twenty knots, the sun shone brightly on the sparkling sea. The *Bush Key* began pitching in the eight-foot waves wrought by the squalls, that soon developed into ten- and twelve-foot ones. The spray flying over the foredeck made rainbows in the sun. We felt no indication of motion sickness, delighted by the movement and the scene. Flying fish, taking advantage of the updraft that the wind made as it hit the waves, soared for seemingly impossible distances, each making a miniature rainbow of its own as it plunged into the sea again.

Ahead we saw a flock of fifty sooties, noddies and gulls that had come out miles from shore, wheeling and dipping over the water to grasp in their beaks the tiny bait fish now being driven to the surface by the hungry ones behind and under them. As we neared them, we saw that the silvery throngs flashing along were not minnows, but sizeable fish, six inches long. John said the terns could handle that length and even larger ones and often snatched flying fish. Occasionally from the depths, one of the pursuing predators would arch himself out of the water, leaping what seemed twenty feet and making an arc and falling back almost splashless. When this happened, we would not see it directly, but off to the side and by the time we perceived the motion and focused on the fish, it had passed the summit of its arc and seemed descending from the heavens.

The sporadic rain was becoming a drenching flood now, and we sat on the hatch or stood in the door of the cabin, watching it. I thought of the origins of the sea, how over the unreckonable years as the heated planet Earth cooled, the vapors turned into raindrops and the chasms began to fill. And how in time, through some chemistry, life awoke. I was familiar, as every schoolchild is, with Michelangelo's "Creation of Man" in the ceiling of the Sistine Chapel and God's extended arm and pointed finger touching that of Adam. I thought of a photomicrograph Barney had shown me recently in which the transfer of genetic material from a bacterium resistant to antibiotics to one that was not, was accomplished through a finger-like extension of protoplasm called the pilus. The transfer endowed the recipient and its descendants with the ability to survive in the presence of the formerly lethal antibiotic; in its implication of the gift of life, the photomicrograph recalled the forceful Renaissance painting.

I knew that fossil records demonstrated that some seven hundred million or more years ago there were jellyfish, flatworms and soft corals; and that after three hundred million years more, animals with backbones began to evolve and primitive relatives of fish appeared. In another one hundred million years, fish life became dominant and several species came upon the shore and learned to live there, one of them being the far-distant ancestor of man. In time the land areas would be reigned by the monsters which developed—dinosaurs and their kin. Some of these would return to the sea and others adapt to freshwater lakes and streams. Among them were various types of reptiles, one the Ichthyosaur, with a powerful fin where the lizard tail had been and paddles instead of legs. Then, ninety million years ago, while dinosaurs, soon to be doomed, kept thundering across the land, dragons of reptiles were lashing through the waters—the crocodile-like Tylosaurus, over twenty-five feet long; the sixty-foot-long Cetiosaurus, called the Whale reptile; and the Pteranodons, which are thought to have launched their heavy bodies from high places to glide on eighteen-foot parchment-like wings over the water where they swooped to catch their marine prey, coming on land only to lay their eggs. Of these giants, the crocodiles, marine lizards and sea snakes survive. The latter have nostrils which close by a valve, they are fish-eaters, and most of them have lost the belly scales common to land serpents. Marine snakes have been observed behaving in a communal manner that brings to mind the single writhing sea dragons that once lived on earth—for great numbers of them will congregate in a slithering mass which covers ten miles wide by fifty long; it is thought they may be copulating.

Gazing at the seemingly endless expanse of sea and the cold rain ragging it, I thought of the earliest recorded explorers; the Phoenicians circumnavigating Africa in 590 B.C., the Greek philosopher Posidonius setting out by sea for Spain in 100 B.C. to find out if the sun hissed when it set in the western waters, the Greek astronomer-geographer Pytheas sailing in 325 to Iceland for the purpose of marine exploration, the Viking Leif Ericson crossing to North America near 1000. Thousands were drowned or destroyed or frustrated or betrayed in their attempts, and then there were the famous ones: Marco Polo in 1292, Bartholomew Diaz in 1488, Christopher Columbus in 1492, Amerigo Vespucci in 1499, Vasco Nuñez de Balboa in 1513, Ferdinand Magellan in

1519, Martin Frobisher in 1576, William Barents in 1594, Henry Hudson in 1609, William Baffin in 1616, Abel Tasman in 1642, Captain James Cook between 1768 and 1776 on his ship *Endeavour* scientifically recording all and the first to cross the Antarctic Circle.

"After having been twice driven back by heavy southwestern gales, Her Majesty's ship *Beagle,* a ten-gun brig, under the command of Captain Fitz Roy, R.N., sailed from Devonport on the 27th of December 1831," Charles Darwin's journal begins. The Royal Navy's surveying expedition was due to voyage around the world, and Darwin was the naturalist who had been nominated and appointed. During the five-year trip, he was plagued with my problems of seasickness and on land suffered from various intestinal ills. However, he managed to work while nauseous and weak, remaining, stubborn, at the rail while observing and collecting marine life. He experienced storm at sea, unearthed fossil giant sloths, observed an earthquake, explored jungles and wild shorelines, scaled the Andes, rode Galapagos tortoises, gazed at the duck-billed platypus, and returned to England on the second of October 1836, his trunks and boxes filled with specimens, his notebooks with records, eager to unpack the multitudinous crates that had been sent home ahead of him and with certain ideas and implications he wished meticulously to set before the world.

I went into the cabin to sit on the bench in back, feeling the motor's vibrations, taking out my journal to report on the storm and my feelings. Soon we were chugging into the harbor of Key West and pulling up to the old wooden dock where rubber tires were hung to keep boats from bumping against the jutting pier posts. Barney threw the *Bush Key* lines up to be made fast to the dock. We stayed on board a while, reluctant to leave, claiming that we wanted to wait until the rain grew more gentle. Then we picked up our gear and headed for the DeWeeses' station wagon; they would drive us to the Key West airport, where a little plane would take us to Miami and we would board a larger one for Cleveland. We waved back to the *Bush Key*'s crew of two.

"I wonder how soon I'll get to go back?" Paula said. "I miss Fort Jeff already."

"How about you?" Barney asked me.

"I feel just the way you thought I would. I miss it too." And he laughed.

CHAPTER NINE

Under Seven Flags

Sweet and low, sweet and low,
Wind of the western sea,
Low, low, breathe and blow,
Wind of the western sea!
Over the rolling waters go,
Come from the dying moon, and blow!
—Alfred, Lord Tennyson: "The Princess"

WE had planned our trip to the Virgin Islands for the twenty-second of January. The Park Service people wrote us that the underwater park was at Buck Island Reef National Monument just off St. Croix, but that we should also visit St. John because there was an underwater trail there and certain marine features of interest. We were informed of the rangers, historians and other officials we should get in touch with. Then on a visit to Washington, D.C., on the twelfth of January at a little after midnight, the taxi we were riding in was struck by a car careening toward us in the wrong lane and ten of Barney's ribs were broken, his spleen was ruptured, and my right wrist underwent a multiple fracture because I saw the collision coming and put my hand on the seat before me to break the impact.

After a few days, we knew that Barney would live and then before long we were back in Cleveland. We spent much of our days in the Red Room, Barney propped in his white leather chair, pillows at his back, reading a little but mostly writing—completing a medical book that had been waiting on just such an opportunity. As soon as he had been out of the Constant Care area of Washington Hospital Center and we could discuss it, we had set our vacation date ahead to the twenty-sixth of March. We planned to stay in the Islands for eight days and looked ahead to it. I worried a little about my wrist's response, for the arm was still in a cast, the upper half of which was removed daily to bathe and massage the frail weakened white limb.

"I'll bump it on a staghorn branch and break it again," I told Barney, "or trip coming down the airplane ramp and that'll be that."

"I'll be all right snorkeling," he said, "but I wonder what it'll be like going down twenty feet. I expect I'll be as good as ever."

Paula, in her junior year of college, would not be coming along. We would miss our Chief Photographer, and I reviewed with her the instructions for the underwater camera and meter before they were packed into the red duffle bag. There was a special plug on the bottom of the camera housing which she cautioned me about, that must be in place with the greased "o" ring about it when one went down. In order to take flash shots above water, the plug had to be unscrewed and an adapter put in its place from which the flash attachment worked. It was also important that the camera be rinsed off with fresh cold water after every use and the camera be allowed to dry if possible before opening. As for the problem that had come up when Barney was photographing the amorous sharks in the Dry Tortugas shallows and I forgot to rewind the film cartridge before opening the camera to reload it, the film apparently was protected and not exposed and the shots were a successs.

Early the next afternoon Paula drove us to the Cleveland Hopkins Airport, where we would take a Pan American tourist flight by way of New York to Puerto Rico, arriving in the evening and staying overnight. We would make the hop to St. Croix early the next afternoon. The sun was low as we arrived at San Juan International Airport. We put ourselves into the charge of a taxi driver, who advised us to stay over a few days.

"Is most beautiful place in world—this Puerto Rico," he said firmly.

He told us that of all the forests under the jurisdiction of the United States Forest Service, El Yunque, twenty-five miles out of San Juan, was the only tropical forest. There were about 30,000 acres, containing a rain forest, a palm forest and dwarf trees on the peaks, where the vegetation was not over six feet high.

"You stay over and I take care of you," he urged. "I do that with you American tourists all the time."

"You're American too," I protested.

"How about it?" he smiled. "Or you like to see a cockfight? I can tell you wheer the *galeras* are if you stay over."

"Tell us where to eat tonight," Barney said, "where there aren't any of your American tourists. Where would you go?"

"I take you to a place my friend manages," he said. "Very Spanish. I wait for you."

We protested, but he assured us that he would have supper himself and then come back and return us to our motel. We liked the café. The food was good—peppered marinated fowl, chickpeas, and *pasteles* wrapped in plantain leaves, with a local beer. A flamenco dancer came on the tiny stage and then an elderly guitarist with a tin bowl in which people now and then dropped a coin. In the morning we had time to see a little of Old San Juan before our flight, and our persuasive friend was waiting outside our motel as we emerged and led us to his taxi on a side-street. The air was hot but dry.

He drove us along the Avenida Ponce de León to the walled city that was a peninsula jutting into the waters of the Atlantic and San Juan Bay. We viewed the two ancient forts, El Morro and San Cristobal, and walked up one of the worn step streets near the Cathedral. Our driver waited while we got out to go past the busy shops on the narrow ways where there was an Old World

feeling like Capri or some continental town. We knew that Columbus on his second voyage, traveling with three large ships,
fourteen smaller craft and crews that totaled fifteen hundred
men, including high-born Spaniards and Columbus' brother,
James, and carrying lemon and orange seeds, horses, sheep, pigs,
goats and cattle, had touched in on Puerto Rico in November
of 1493. Ponce de León, who had already visited the Dry Tortugas, came in 1508 to settle on this island with his family, as
its first governor. Reluctantly, we drove back out of the Old City
and to the airport.

The flight to St. Croix on the Virgin Islands Airways was a
short one, costing something like twelve dollars a one-way fare,
and covering a hundred miles to the southeast. We would land
at the Alexander Hamilton Airport, named for the illegitimate
son of Rachel Levine who was born on the island of Nevis in the
British West Indies in January of 1757. Hamilton's mother had
been unable to obtain the divorce she sought from her elderly
husband and it being a time of relaxed morals and customs in
the islands, had lived illegally for seven years with James Hamilton of Scotland. While Alexander was an infant, the couple
moved to St. Croix, where three years later his mother was sued
for divorce by her legal husband who declared that she had
"absented herself and went whoring in the Barbados." When
the boy was six and his younger brother a baby, the father of
the children took a boat and left for another of the West Indies
islands, never to return. Five years later Rachel Levine, who
had been in declining health and struggling to support her small
sons by running a store, died at the age of thirty-two and was
buried in the family's cemetery at Tuite's plantation on St.
Croix, according to the Registers of St. John's Church of the
island.

Alexander Hamilton was reared by his maternal relatives; he
left plantation life early for Christiansted and tutoring in Latin
and mathematics. After his mother's death when he was eleven,
an opening was sought to provide for his future; at the age of

twelve, a delicate child with a quick intellect, he was appointed apprentice clerk and general factotum in the trading house of Nicholas Cruger, a wealthy merchant of Christiansted. Hamilton disliked the work and wrote a young cousin, "I contemn the grovelling condition of a clerk . . . to which my fortune condemns me . . . I shall conclude saying, I wish there was a war." He was advanced shortly to bookkeeper and sent to Frederiksted on the other side of St. Croix where his diligence and quickness were so remarked that when Nicholas Cruger suddenly was taken ill and had to leave for medical treatment in New York, to everyone's astonishment he appointed the boy-clerk in complete control of his business. By the time the merchant returned a few months later, he found the fifteen-year-old doing a flourishing business. Delighted, he sent Hamilton out to tour neighboring islands and to buy and sell and report on business conditions. On the boy's return, a tremendous hurricane occurred, which almost wrecked Christiansted; having lately been reading much of Plutarch, Pope and the classics, the young West Indian wrote a sensational report which he sent to *The Royal Danish-American Gazette,* the island's chief newspaper. It was accepted and so impressed Hamilton's family and friends that, although they were in financial straits themselves, they pooled their resources, placed letters of introduction in his pocket, and put him on board ship bound for Boston and the future. That was October of 1772 and Alexander Hamilton, who was destined to be a leading statesman, President George Washington's Secretary of the Treasury and the youngest of the Founding Fathers of the American nation, was not yet sixteen years of age.

We gazed below at the white sand beaches and smooth green hills of St. Croix. We had been told that the western end of the island was a rain forest and the other dry and almost a desert and that the name St. Croix was not pronounced as it would be in France, but the long way: *Sānt Croy.* We picked up a Volkswagen we had ordered at the airport and were given a map to guide us to Christiansted, near ten miles away on the other side of the island, which is twenty-eight miles long and about six and a half miles across at its widest. We were cautioned to remember to drive on the left-hand side of the road. That rule had been established in the days of the Danes, the Volkswagen people said, and in all but a few backward countries traffic still proceeded that way. They related the legend that once it was believed that the heart was on the left side of the body and men would carry their shields on their left arms to protect themselves. Since the sword was necessarily wielded by the right hand, travelers felt safer if they met approaching riders and carriages from the left side of the road.

We found it not too difficult. About us, as we drove, was a jungle of small trees in the sparsely settled landscape. When we reached Centerline Road, the main paved one that went down the middle of St. Croix, we saw abandoned windmill towers occasionally about the ruins of old buildings. We knew that once St. Croix had been called one of the Fabulous Sugar Islands and that over half of the land had been planted in cane and more than forty-six million pounds of sugar had been produced in the top year of 1812. Six-ox teams with mules occasionally replacing some of the oxen had hauled high-wheeled wagons along this way, bound for King's Wharf with kegs of the dark raw sugar called *muscovado,* which is what remains after molasses is extracted from sugar cane juice.

We drove through the narrow streets of Christiansted to our hotel in the center of the town, not far from King's Wharf and overlooking the harbor. It was the Club Comanche, advertised as "completely renovated," and having air conditioning and a smart blue salt-water swimming pool with no one in it. We looked over our room, where the air was cold and stifled, the machine humming steadily under the window. We left our duffle bags in a pile and went down to the open-aired room below where the bar was for a draft beer. We listened to sports fishermen, who had been up to Lang Bank near Buck Island during the last few days, where there was a 100-fathom edge, and they had been catching kingfish and tuna and wahoo, one of the latter weighing 110 pounds, the record for that week. They said the wahoo was considered by many the prime game fish hereabouts and that it was a scrappy fighter. They directed us to follow King Street down to the water, which was Gallows Bay, and we would be at the Christiansted National Historic Site. We had been told by the parks people that their Management Assistant had an office in Fort Christiansvaern and would see about setting up our Ranger-guided trip to Buck Island.

There was little breeze; the air was hot and few people were about. We went down to the dock, where a decorative stone windmill stood, and watched the hotel fishermen, some of them natives, who were cleaning their catch on a wooden table for the evening menu. We had been told that the native-born people were called Crucians or Cruzans, and one pronounced it *cru-zán,* and that the local dialect was a little hard to understand. But these men spoke rather like the Andros Island people we had visited, using a heavy British intonation, their syllables clipped and their speech attractive. They were descendants of freed Cruzan slaves, whose overseers, employed by the Danes, had been largely Scotch, Irish, and English. Spanish is the second language of the Virgin Islands, since Puerto Rico is so close; some of the churches of the town say masses in both Spanish and English.

The fishermen showed us a dolphin which they called *dorado.* Barney gave them our name and tipped them and said we would like some saved for our supper as I had never eaten the once rainbow-hued fish. They promised and we asked about the Buck Island Ferry and the glass-bottom boat. They said both were out now and that the latter was called *Reef Rover* and made five excursions daily; the ferry left once a day all year round from the Club Comanche Dock. It departed every morning at half past ten for the five-mile ride to Buck Island, and returned at four. The fare, which included gear and instruction, was five dollars a person. Barney asked them to tell the captain we would like reservations for two the next morning.

"Sure mon, we will," they said.

To our east along the shore were sailboats and yachts and cruisers moored to the docks. Directly to the west, next to the little windmill, was the landing ramp where the Antilles Air boats went in and out that linked the midtown harbors of St. Croix, St. Thomas and St. John. We planned to take one of the amphibian planes in a few days to St. Thomas. The fishermen pointed out our way to King Street. The sidewalks were of brick or cut stone and there were long arched European-type arcades, with many bright flags flying outside and having balconies above with their white shutters opened to what trade breezes they could catch. It was dusty and still and pleasant, as if everyone were asleep.

Big red Fort Christiansvaern was built in 1744 by the Danes, with bastions and dungeons that reminded us of Fort Jefferson. We were told by a guard that behind one of the great wooden doors, with the small peep hole for observing prisoners, Alexander Hamilton's mother had been confined in 1750 by order of her lawful husband when she first ran away and refused to live with him. The guard said that the fort now housed the offices of government officials. He pointed to the cupola of the nearby Steeple Building and said it originally was the Lutheran Church of the Lord of Sabaoth from the century between 1753 and 1834, and that it now was the St. Croix Museum. He directed us to the office of Management Assistant Richard Ward of the National Park Service, which administered the Christiansted National Historic Site in cooperation with the Government of the Virgin Islands. We talked awhile of our project with Mr. Ward, telling him that we would be taking the Club Comanche Ferry in the morning. He explained that there were no accommodations on Buck Island and there was no intention to have them and that the Park Service hoped to keep the island in a natural state. Buck Island had only been established as a monument since December of 1961, and the Ranger who had been in charge there had been assigned somewhere else and just departed. There was to be a four-man staff in the office of the Site, consisting of Clerk, Ranger, Historian and Management Assistant. The recent Historian, who knew a great deal about Buck Island, had also been transferred by the Department of the Interior to another area in line with their policy of not keeping their people very long in one place. The positions open for Historian and Clerk had not been filled yet, but a Ranger had been appointed and had arrived. Mr. Ward said that he would be breaking him in, and the Ranger would be in charge of Buck Island as soon as he knew the ropes, and that if we weren't bored by their conversations about routines and demonstrations of techniques of boat launching and the rest, he would try to answer any questions we had. We were delighted to be accommodated and agreed to meet them in the same office the day after tomorrow at nine in the morning.

Mr. Ward gave us some brochures and told us that the intention of the Christiansted National Historic Site was to preserve examples of the Danish management of the islands, and that the site had been established in March of 1952 by order of the Secretary of the Interior. The Government House across the way had been the residence of the incumbent Danish Governors and housed the colonial government's offices. It was a stunning eighteenth-century structure with an elaborate ballroom and accurately reconstructed kitchen. We went to visit the Steeple Building where there were Indian relics from times before Columbus and a record of the seven flags that had been exchanged back and forth on the little island over near five centuries: Spanish, French, English, Dutch, Danish and Norwegian, and finally the United States. It is not known if the various Indians, who claimed the island before the restless continentals arrived, had flags, but likely they had national symbols, which are not recognized by civilized man. St. Croix has also been inhabited by pirates and owned by private companies and even once by one of its governors.

Columbus on his second voyage over, leading his fleet with its load of animals, plants, seeds, sailors and distinguished men of Spain, had anchored off Salt River, five miles up the west coast on the fourteenth of November 1493 to fill his water kegs. The Genoese had claimed the island for Queen Isabella of Spain and named it *Santa Cruz,* Holy Cross, the same name it now bore in French. St. Croix was the first territory now under the United States flag to be discovered by Columbus, who also gave the Virgin Islands their name: *Las Virgenes.* He had seen the multitude of peaks, some one hundred in all, the westernmost part of the Lesser Antilles, and he thought of St. Ursula and her 11,000 virgins. It is said that in about the third century, eleven ships had transported the British Princess Ursula of the Christian faith and her companions on a long voyage prior to her unwilling marriage to a pagan king. After three years they came to Cologne on the Rhine, as it was being sacked by the savage Huns; all of the virgins were slain and thereafter Princess Ursula was made a saint.

Once peaceful Arawak Indians had populated St. Croix, and then a hundred years before Columbus arrived, the Carib Indians had come up from the south to attack and enslave the Arawaks. Columbus gave the Caribs their name; hearing them called Calinago or Calino, he altered it to Caribales. This corruption of their name, since these Indians practiced cannibalism, was the origin of the name *cannibal.* And since they inhabited all of the Lesser Antilles, the Caribbean Sea was named for them. It was thought at the time that all the people of the New World were as fierce and it was inscribed under one artist's woodcut that they "eat each other . . . become a hundred and fifty years of age, and have no government." After Columbus' battle with the Carib Indians, during which he captured a few, he continued on his way. Although Spain claimed the island, she took little interest in it, spending her time on the rich Aztec empires, the looting of which took all her attention. Occasionally Spaniards arrived at St. Croix as well as others of the Virgins in order to capture Indians, whom they needed for slaves to work the gold mines on nearby Puerto Rico and Hispaniola. In time it was not surprising that all Indians disappeared from the island; it remained uninhabited except for French buccaneers who used it for a base much as the Dry Tortugas had been.

In 1587, John White of England stopped in for a few days at Santa Cruz and claimed her for the British Empire. Some English colonists, who had already settled on St. Kitts, still owned by Great Britain, followed him around 1625, and Dutch settlers too. Twenty years later, ships from England and Holland arrived at the island and a battle ensued and the English were driven off. A few years after, they returned with a formidable force, and this time it was the Dutchmen who were ousted along with any French who were there. Spain then began to evince new interest and in 1650 an expedition arrived from Puerto Rico with over a thousand men to throw out the British. Later the same year the French sailed from St. Kitts, 125 miles off, to seize Santa Cruz from the Spanish. The victorious French declared that Santa Cruz was now St. Croix.

The commander of the French fleet was Monsieur de Poinci, after whom the brilliant-flowered poinciana tree has been named, and who became the governor of the French West Indies. Because the French crown was in financial difficulty, de Poinci bought the island from his government, later in 1653 selling it to the Knights of Malta, an ambitious wealthy religious military order. They began to clear plantations for sugar cane, indigo and coffee. They had little luck with the project, though, and were glad to sell it in ten years to the French West India Company. Before long that company went bankrupt due to poor management, and St. Croix was returned to the crown. But for twenty years the economy remained so poor that Louis XIV of France finally decided to transport all of the more than seven hundred colonists to what is now known as Haiti.

St. Croix, although still a French colony, was not being occupied officially. Certain Dutchmen, English, free Negroes, as well as a scattering of Frenchmen, remained on the land. The English still were interested in claiming St. Croix for themselves and three times tried to take over and were driven off as often by fleets sent by the French king. In 1733 trouble erupted on St. John; the slaves on the plantations revolted and although the rebellion was squashed, the captives remained restless. At the same time France was warring with Poland and needed money. She was looking about for offers. A charter had been granted to a group of Danish merchants years before in 1671, by the King of the United Crown of Denmark and Norway, to colonize St. Thomas. The merchants called themselves the Danish West India Company and were responsible for introducing sugar, cotton and tobacco on that island. Three years later they decided to merge with the Guinea Company, a Danish slave-trading group, and became the Danish West India and Guinea Company. They had their eye on St. Croix, larger and more adapted to agriculture, and when they approached the French crown in 1733 a treaty was concluded and St. Croix was sold for 750,000 *livres*. The vigorous company proceeded to survey the island, divide it into nine quarters, and subdivide the quarters into plantations of 150 acres each, which they offered at reasonable rates to attract the immigration of new settlers.

One of the buildings in the wharf area of the National Historic Site was the Danish West India and Guinea Company Warehouse, now the Christiansted Post Office. There were also the Danish Customs House, now the Library Building, and the old Scale House where rum barrels were weighed, presently used by Virgin Islands officials. Everywhere were exhibits demonstrating the instable history of the island. Under the control of the Danish West India and Guinea Company, slaves, sugar and rum were traded at the expense of the colonists themselves, and while the company did well, the planters complained about the monopolistic practices and petitioned King Frederik V to take over St. Croix for a crown colony. In 1755 this was done; St. Thomas and St.

John were included in the sale and the three composed the Danish West Indies, with Christiansted protected by Fort Christiansvaern, its capital, and a Governor General appointed by the king. For the first time St. Croix began to prosper. King Sugar and the byproducts rum and molasses ruled, and the plantation owners lived like aristocratic lords. Wooden structures were torn down and replaced by decorative handsome masonry buildings. By 1796, nearly a hundred and fifty ox or mule mills and almost as many stone windmills—the little one that we had seen at our hotel an imitation of them—ground the sugar cane on which the prosperity was built. By 1804 there were over twenty-seven thousand slaves. The opulent economy, although built largely on debt, was not shaky as long as sugar prices remained stable. For fifty years this state continued before a decline set in, due to fluctuations in the price of sugar, the abolition of slave trade, sugar tariffs which the United States levied to protect its Louisiana sugar growers, mortgage foreclosures on planters, a shortage of capital, slave rebellions on St. Croix and subsequent emancipation of slaves, the introduction of labor-saving tools and machines making the windmill suddenly extinct, the centralization of factories, the Christiansted fire of 1866, the earthquake and tidal wave and severe epidemic of 1867, the hurricane of 1872, another violent one in 1876, a riot of freed Negroes in October of 1878 called the "Fire Burn" when forty estates were destroyed and never rebuilt and much of the town of Frederiksted was damaged; bankruptcy became common and the island was at low ebb.

The United States in 1867 offered to buy St. Thomas and St. John from Denmark because of their strategic harbors for seven and a half million; in 1902 she offered five million for the three West Indies islands with no success; then during the first world war, to keep Germany from establishing a submarine base, the United States raised the offer to twenty-five million; it was accepted. It was the highest sum she ever paid for the smallest territory she ever acquired, and three times what she had paid for Alaska in 1867. One of the stipulations of sale was that the three islands should continue their established free-port status. On the thirty-first of March 1917 the Danish flag was lowered and the Stars and Stripes run up. The first move was the stopping of the manufacture of rum, for prohibition was in full sway. It was a serious blow to the island, dependent on this prime sugar cane product. Congress, benevolent, voted great sums for rehabilitation and St. Croix struggled to survive. After repeal, the rum trade was restored; two large industrial plants—oil and aluminum—have been established; and with the advent of air travel the island has flourished as a vacation spot, its tip being the most easterly point of United States territory.

We walked slowly about Christiansted's streets as the afternoon waned. I needed a hat against the sun and got a huge-brimmed floppy one that would fold into my bag for another trip. The shops were becoming active and we noted the many advertisements about St. Croix being a free port. Japanese pearls, famous Thai silks and French perfumes, bone china from England, liquor from Scotland, leather from Italy, binoculars from Germany, Swedish crystal, Danish teak and a multitude of Swiss watches seemed to be offered in duplicate in many of the shops. Barney's old watch had been in trouble lately and so he bought one of the latter for twenty-five dollars; we were assured that it was worth four times the sum. We stopped in at a West Indian straw market and got a basket to keep our cameras in and I felt that its price was the same as for a similar one at home.

We returned along King Street to our hotel; it was after five and we stopped at our bar in the large open room that was used for dining also and opened to the sea at one end where there was an iron-grill railing. At either side were steps leading down to the rectangular salt-water swimming pool, and past that was the long walk to the tiny windmill and the dock. The bartender, hearing that we wanted to try the renowned native rum, mixed the house's special for us using the juices of some island fruits, slightly sweet, and finishing it off with a sprig of mint.

"Local Cruzan rum, mon," he sighed. "Best there is."

"May we take them over by the railing?" I said.

"Anywhere you like, modom. I make that with the dark. Next one I make you different with the light rum. See which you prefer."

We thanked him and settled at a far table in the nearly unoccupied room. I was grateful to rest; I disliked thinking of going to the cold stifled room above and wanted to stay awhile before changing for supper. Beyond us in the blue-green harbor, where the sun was slowly nearing the horizon, were a multitude of sailing vessels of every size, anchored and tied, which seemed from their names to come from everywhere in the world to Christiansted. We had noted one at the Club Comanche dock earlier in the day which bore the name *Alaska*.

A blonde attractive woman was hurrying up the stairs to our right, a clipped toy poodle at her heels. She paused at our table. "Everything all right? I'm the proprietress here and we want you satisfied."

We talked with her awhile, ordering a drink for her too, and found that she was the owner of the *Alaska*. She had come down here three years ago on a cruise, for the boat was her home, and liked it so much she settled here and was still living on board with her poodle Klondike Jake. She advised us to catch the show that night—a new Haitian dance group that she said we would enjoy; they did the familiar Limbo act that we had seen in Nassau, where a man worked his body under a rope or bar made lower and lower by his assistants, while the band's beat grew louder, until the acrobatic torso was nearly to the stage floor. We said we would like a table held for us and that we had been promised fresh-caught dolphin for supper. And then Barney asked what the windmill was for.

"The chambermaids call that the Honeymoon Windmill," she said. "The couple that were there just checked out."

"Is someone coming in?" I glanced at Barney.

"Not until next week."

"Could we look at it?" Barney said.

"Is it air conditioned?" I asked.

"We're practically honeymooners," Barney said.

"How romantic."

And we all walked down together, Klondike Jake in the proprietress' arm, carrying our fresh drinks made with light rum by the helpful bartender, to inspect our new home. It was four-storied and on the first bare floor was a long-used unmatched metal set of table and chairs. Our friend sat there with her poodle while we went up. The stairs wound about to the next floor which was divided into two bathrooms, one in pink tile and one in blue, each with the proper facilities including showers and cupboards; although mystified, I felt this was a distinct continental touch. We continued up to the curtained third story, which except for two tiny end tables held nothing but an enormous bed. There was a little balcony outside this floor and a metal spiral ladder led to the railed open top, where the windmill turned round with a plaintive noise and the pivot went up and down to no purpose. And there was no air conditioning anywhere.

Barney went down to make the arrangements with the proprietress, who said that our bags would be sent over straightway. We stayed on the windmill's lookout, while the sunset came about us golden. Broad-winged pelicans dove with resounding splashes; murmurs came from the boats on the bay; a Man-o'-war bird soared overhead. Dusk came and on a promontory down the curving shoreline, where the hills were silhouetted to the west, a native woman stood casting a line into the water still reddened by the sunset sky, where a few ancient crafts belonging to the Cruzans were floating. Presently we stirred ourselves and went below, where we found our bags piled in the narrow way outside the double bathrooms.

After a while, we returned to the dining area, now crowded with guests, the silver, china, glass and small talk making a steady sound. All seemed to know Klondike Jake, who wandered from table to table selecting the best morsels from those proffered. We settled at our same table which bore our name and nodded to our busy hostess. The dolphin was served, baked and succulent in its crisp brown paper. We watched the bright-garbed enthusiastic dance troop awhile before returning to our windmill. Tomorrow we would dive off Buck Island and I was a little unsettled about my wrist, not yet healed, which still ached now and then and to whose inefficiency I was gradually becoming accustomed. The trade breeze blew steadily from the northeast through our windows and we went to sleep to the rusty soft-sounding "Oh, oh, oh," of the machine overhead.

CHAPTER TEN

The Barrier Reef

Yea, slimy things did crawl with legs
Upon the slimy sea.
About, about, in reel and rout
The death-fires danced at night;
The water, like a witch's oils,
Burnt green, and blue and white.

—Samuel Taylor Coleridge: "The
Rime of the Ancient Mariner"

WE were up early, walking down to the wharf and about the town streets. At breakfast, we had asked the waitress about box lunches and she said the hotel was accustomed to supply them and would bring us two. I carried them and Barney had our red duffle bag of gear and the basket of camera equipment when we boarded the ferry at a little before ten-thirty. The boat was bright, its upper part red and white, across the dark blue lower expanse were the yellow letters BUCK ISLAND: COMANCHE DOCK. The American flag fluttered under the white clouds in the blue sky; a talkative score of people in swim clothes, slacks, and straw hats were assembled. A little dory was tied behind us as we chugged off. A box at one end of the vessel contained flippers, snorkels and underwater masks of all sizes and colors. A cold chest of soft drinks was stashed in the cabin, available to passengers for a small fee. Our crew was composed of three native Cruzans, the captain in spanking white with the ferry's name in red script on his shirt back, the others in trunks.

We looked back at the gentle hills and the quiet town, passing the ruins of Fort Louise Augusta as we left the bay and tiny Protestant Cay, privately leased and in the old days a hangout for pirates and later the home of the Danish Harbor Master. Further along we went by Green Cay. The word cay is pronounced *kēy* here, the Spanish *cayo* meaning a reef or low island. Other boats were leaving Christiansted for the underwater park too; the swifter ones passed us, the skindivers on board waving. There were trim native sloops with white sails, a catamaran with two hulls and the sail mounted on the crosspiece high above the water, a trimaran with the hull in the middle and two small balancing ones at the sides for stability. Our destination was five miles away, to the east.

We knew that Buck Island had been under United States ownership since the treaty with Denmark in 1917 and that in the twenties it had been leased to a private individual, Cornelius Pentheny, who had raised goats there, the flock increasing to over a hundred, prey to passing vessels whose crews shot them for sport and food. In 1936 the Virgin Islands government took over the island, and in 1948 Buck Island Park was created by ordinance. Then spurred by the new interest in skindiving, snorkeling and spear fishing, Buck Island Reef National Monument was established by President John Kennedy in December of 1961 to be run in conjunction with the National Historic Site at Christiansted. The island itself is a mile long and a third of a mile wide; the park area, including the island and surrounding reefs, contains 850 acres. Its distinctive feature which makes it so desirable as a national monument is the barrier reef which hems the eastern half of the island. The waves spend themselves upon it, which protects the placid shallow lagoon within, where marine life flourishes and can be viewed even by novice divers without danger or disturbance.

I sat in the open sun on the bench with others, not wanting to go under the shade of the cabin where Barney stood talking to the skipper, his camera about his neck. It was the end of March and it had been a long winter; Swedes are sun-worshipers by nature and half-Swede, I basked in the hot light. The water was calm. My right wrist ached a little, and rubbing it, I said nothing to Barney about my concern for its performance. He was listening to the skipper who said that there was a Buck Island for all three of the Virgin Islands and that the one in Coral Bay off St. John was called *Le Duck* on marine charts, but local people paid no attention to that. He said we would be putting in at the sandy beach on the western end that was shielded from heavy sea swells by St. Croix on the south and the patch of reefs off the northern coast of Buck Island in that direction. The purpose for landing there rather than going straight to the reef was to enable those unaccustomed to skindiving to receive instructions on the use of fins and faceplates and snorkels and practice with them during the morning, before setting out for the reef itself, where the trail was, in the afternoon. He said that many people took the ferry just to picnic on Buck Island and they would not come along for the visit to the reef, but wait to be picked up on the return to St. Croix.

"My wife's worried about her wrist," Barney said. "She broke it. Is the reef rough?"

"No, mon," the skipper said. "And Andrew there will tow her in one of those tires. Sometimes we string a dozen of them on a rope if they're new tourists."

"Good."

"Your wife's going to get a burn," the skipper told Barney. "It's the water; the sun reflects off it."

"I know," Barney sighed.

The boat moved steadily; passengers leaned on the rail somnolent, their chins in their palms or pointing to the varied boats in full white sail. No one spoke with vivacity; all seemed to be waiting for something. And then the white sand beach was stretching ahead and before long the anchor was overboard. Everyone began fitting on their gear, the experienced ones plunging into the water and heading for land to walk awhile or snorkel off the beach,

others listening to the crewmen who were outfitting them and explaining techniques. Barney had his fins on and handed mine over;
the water was emerald-clear as I lowered myself on the ladder and
into it. We swam to the beach, my right hand holding onto
Barney's swim trunks, and paddling with the other. We wore our
masks, not bothering with snorkels which I was not accustomed to
yet and leaving our camera which we would use later. Sometimes
we slowed and treaded water and looked under, where schools of
neutral-hued fish went by now and then. The fins gave one such
speed and stability in quiet water that of course there was no hazard. We went up on land and walked along the hot sand a hundred yards apart from the others, and entered the water, bathtub-
warm close to shore. We lay down in it, moving slowly along looking through our faceplates. One can submerge at a two-foot depth
and view a world that, because of surface refraction, is seldom observed from above.

We knew of the Beaked Chaetodon Fish of the Polynesian seas
with its elongated muzzle and how it could shoot a drop of water
in the fashion of a blowgun at insects resting on underbrush beside
the water; it is a habit the fish will continue in captivity and they
are commonly kept as household pets by the Japanese. We knew
of the Archer Fish similar in its hunting habits, but more powerful and adept and able to strike a fly four feet away; and of the
four-eyed fish of Central American lakes and rivers, *Anableps
dowei,* its bulbous eyes bifocal, so that it lies like a tiny submarine
on the surface, the upper half of the lenses adapted to the air and
searching the surface for food, the under half watching for attack
from below. Although evolution has developed various ways for
creatures to focus effectively both above and below the water, varying from the bifocal lens of the four-eyed fish to the angular one of
the flying fish, man in the principle of the faceplate has worked
out the most efficient of all. By interposing a layer of air between
the curved cornea and the water, it is possible for the eye to focus
as well under water as above, the principle which is employed in a
glass-bottomed boat.

As we observed some flickering blue minnows schooling near

the surface, we decided it didn't take coral reefs or quantities of marine life to make underwater viewing interesting. "I've always said that all you need," Barney declared, "is clear water. If you can see ten feet away, there's apt to be something going on."

We found a sea cucumber and now and then a solitary sea star. We saw no sea urchins on the white sand bottom and had been told that this was another of the assets of this beach as a practice spot for snorkeling novices. The sea cucumber, star and urchin belong to the *Echinoderma* phylum, from the Greek *echinos* or hedgehog and *derma* or skin, their skeleton having calcareous plates with projecting spines. In the sea cucumber these plates are scattered so that their skin is leathery and flexible, the sea stars' plates are close together forming many movable joints, and in the sea urchin they are locked tightly, making an immovable shell. All of the echinoderms move by means of hundreds of little tube feet, operated by internal bulbs, each pumping water into a foot making it expand and sucking it out making it contract. We knew to let alone any sea urchins we came across, round and black or purplish with thin tapering spines and usually three or four inches across. The length of the spine varies with the variety, but they are used for locomotion and to keep off enemies, to capture food and to transfer it toward the mouth, and in certain kinds they may contain poison glands at their base. The spines are able to pierce flesh easily, even working into leather gloves or shoes; they usually snap off at the surface; their tips are tender and barbed. I had come across sea urchins long ago at the Greek seashore, called *impiastro,* sea-thorns. I had tried to dig a spine out, getting most of the stem; the spot had been stained with the purplish fluid peculiar to the urchin. I told Barney about the adventure.

"How big a hole did you make," he asked, "and how long did it take to heal?"

"I feel the same way about splinters," I told him.

"There's no point in trying to dig out the urchin spines," he said, "and if one will just be patient, they have the quality of dissolving and absorbing."

"I never can wait to get splinters out either," I sighed.

In the village of Con-con, Chile, on the Pacific, Barney and I had ordered sea urchins once, five to a plate, with a tiny bowl of chopped onions, red peppers and chives on the side and cruets of vinegar and oil to season them. We liked the sectors of greyish eggs tasting like mild but salty caviar.

We came on a sea cucumber and when Barney picked it up and brought it into the air, it spurted a jet of water; he said they are famous, if violently disturbed, for contracting their body and ejecting most of their internal organs which have the power of regeneration. They are found from tidewater to the deep seas and range from an inch in length to several feet. In certain countries they are relished for food and are called *bêche-de-mer*. We had had them in Singapore, served in a thick sauce, glutinous and a little like flippers of Green Turtle. The sea cucumbers are host to a tiny fish called a Pearlfish with a large head and a tapering body, which enters the cloaca tail first. Pearlfish, in parts of the world, live in clams and starfish also, and oysters where they have been found trapped and covered with mother-of-pearl. They use the sea cucumber's body for a protective home and venture out to search for their food of tiny crustaceans, returning at will. Occasionally a species will live within its host and feed on its tissues, but the sea cucumber has regenerative power and seems not permanently harmed. We thought of Prometheus, whom Zeus had chained to a rock where a vulture came and fed on his liver each day, the organ renewing itself each night.

We handled some sea stars and let them go—five-pointed, red, brown or yellow. We knew they were carnivorous on bivalve molluscs. One would settle on a clam or oyster and begin to pry the shell open; whether it uses chemicals to weaken the creature or does it simply by pressure is not known, but when the shell at last opens, the sea star protrudes its stomach into the bivalve and digests it within its own shell. I saw one, reddish with an almost ten-inch spread of rays, magnified by the water, so that on first glance it seemed of startling size compared with ones I knew in northern waters. Starfish are a problem to the oystermen up there because of their depredations upon the beds; the men used to catch them and break them up and throw them overboard; then it was noted that each piece was regenerating into a new sea star and the population was being multiplied.

We had been told, on a visit to Heron Island on the Queensland reef off Australia, part of the Great Barrier Reef, that erosion was taking place on miles of the northern part of the reef due to a plague of a sea star called Crown-of-thorns, *Acanthaster planci,* a foot in diameter, black and prickly, which crawls over the coral on its fifteen to seventeen arms, throws its stomach over a colony and consumes it *in situ.* Within a few hours, the crown star moves on, leaving a coral ruin behind. Bounties were set on the star, but the efforts of man against the hordes were puny. Finally it was discovered that the Triton, a large carnivorous snail similar to our Horse Conch and reaching near eighteen inches, was the natural enemy of the Crown-of-thorns; however, so decorative and popular is the Triton shell and so avidly was it collected by tourists visiting the reef that this was thought to be a factor in the plague's onset. Thirty thousand dollars worth of Tritons were then imported from Fiji, and it was made illegal to possess a Triton shell. Already results are apparent, for a Triton may devour as many as fourteen Crown-of-thorn stars a day.

When our travels took us further, to Fiji, we saw the reverse of the picture. There all the souvenir shops carry Triton shells collected from the depredated waters where the thousands had been exported. We were told by the natives that the Crown-of-thorns was appearing in numbers for the first time on the reefs and we saw many. They said also that the only successful method of killing the Crown star was to spear it, carry it ashore and bury it in the sand. Shelling of molluscs of all types has become such a big industry, and so many live ones are taken, that it is not possible to say whether it is solely the removal of the Tritons which has caused the glut of Crown-of-thorn stars or whether it is due also to the removal of all small molluscs which prey on immature or smaller forms of the predatory star.

It was noon and we looked back and saw that people had picnic hampers along the shore where they spread towels, put up umbrellas or sat by their dories pulled on land. Others were lunching in the sloops about and the ferry passengers were standing along the rail eating sandwiches. We swam out to join them; the Comanche people had put in fried chicken, pickles, a ham sandwich and we bought a soft drink to go with it and sat in the cabin's shade. After half an hour, we were on our way to the underwater trail.

We moved southeast around the island and approached it. Most of the West Indian reefs are Fringing Reefs, the coral lying in patches or close to shore. Their life is precarious, for the water can be rough in unsettled weather, the heavy surge disastrous to marine life. The *Barrier Reef* is more stable; it is continuous, lies somewhat offshore and is separated from the ocean by a placid lagoon. Charles Darwin explained the likely formation of a barrier reef due to subsidence with care in his book on the subject, published in 1842: as a rocky-based island slowly sinks a few feet at a time, or even quite insensibly, the living masses of coral bathed by surf on the margin of the reef continue to regain the surface. The water encroaches upon the shore little by little, he wrote, the island becomes lower and smaller, and the space between the edge of the reef and the beach becomes proportionally broader. The width of the reef and its slope on both the outer and the inner side is determined by the growing power of the coral and the force of the breakers and currents to which it is exposed. A number of factors helped the reef formation off Buck Island. There was no contamination from fresh water, for there were no streams on the island; the spillover from the sea was sufficient so that it never became stagnant; and there was a high enough reef to amply protect the marine life within the lagoon.

The ferry crew told us that there had never been an accident to any of their passengers. They attributed this to the care with which they instructed their charges and their system of first visiting the western sandy beach. Andrew the Cruzan, tall and sleek, with powerful legs and great energy, was prepared to pull a string of any number of divers wearing innertubes through the channel. No one asked for the service but myself and a round red-faced businessman who was here on something to do with aluminum and claimed that he had not been underwater since he visited Coney Island as a child. As we drifted after Andrew, the latter sometimes submerged, bored with his work, and could be seen on the bottom like a long dark sea creature, perfectly in his element. There were markers below and I read one alongside a picture of a gorgonian: SEA FAN / A FORM OF CORAL LIFE / PLEASE LEAVE FOR OTHERS TO ENJOY. Behind it stood clumps of top-heavy massive brain coral, its surface smooth and convoluted and attended by tiny fish; there were thick branches of elkhorn probing up through the water, which was of such clarity that one could see a hundred feet ahead. There were flocks of reef fish too, but I paid little heed knowing we would be coming out the next day with the park men to identify them. I could see over on the rough terrain of the edge of Buck Island a group of Man-o'-war birds perched there or taking to flight and circling in the prevailing winds.

I was a little tired from the excitement of the first day out on the water and my pleasure with my wrist's reasonable response and when the businessman seconded it, Andrew towed us back to the ferry. I had a Coke with him while waiting. When Barney arrived, he was delighted, climbing aboard dripping, his mask pushed up on his hair, his flippers in his hand. He had photographed a sting ray, a vague mound of sand on the bottom far below, the two eyes and the spiracle showing; the latter is a part of the breathing pattern of bottom-loving forms, water coming into the spiracle and going to the throat and gill cavity. Man has a vestigial spiracle in the eustachian tube, which is between the middle ear and the pharynx and serves to equalize the air pressures on both sides of the eardrum. Barney had approached and touched the ray on the middle of its back lightly; the creature had exploded out of the sand and gone flapping off into the blue. Like the shark and the skates and the sawfish of the same order, the ray has a cartilaginous skeleton and is covered with placoid scales; when these scales are greatly modified they may become the barbed teeth of the carnivorous Tiger Shark, the spiny pectoral patches of the skate *Raja,* the extended snout bearing teeth of the twenty-foot Sawfish, or the Sting Ray's tail spine which can be dangerous.

One of the returning girl passengers was coming aboard with a purple sea fan and I asked the captain whether that was permitted. He said it was one of the problems of an unusual park like this— everyone wanted to take a piece of seaplant or a shell home for a souvenir. It was bad for his business if he complained and the officials censured him if he didn't. Another passenger clambered up with a Queen conch, almost a foot long, its flaring outer lip a sensuous pink, and set his prize beside him in the sun. The captain told us, and we knew it was true, that each visitor was permitted to collect two conchs if he desired. We felt that that was why we had seen no living conchs about the reef, and Barney said that even in the weedy pastures of the flat bottom where they liked to graze, and which he had explored, he had noted none. We saw the skipper walk past the owner of the conch to where the girl sat; he talked quietly with her and she nodded and laughed, pleased nonetheless with her souvenir. As in other underwater parks, the taking of corals, gorgonians, and certain marine life is prohibited, but the enforcement of the rule is another matter. Since most of the spectacular sea life grows very slowly, its quick replacement is impossible.

The ferry was heading for the sandy beach to pick up the passengers who had remained there, and then we were making our way back to Christiansted, feeling at home seeing the speck that gradually became our windmill. I had a sunburn, and it was pleasant to climb all the stairs to the top, where the breeze blew and the wheel turned with its soft squeak. We were told that there were three pairs of Brown Pelicans who lived in this harbor all year round. This was their hunting hour and they flapped along the sunset-colored sky, diving with a noisy splash, surfacing and swimming along while gulping their catch. The cloud formations were spectacular for a while and then the blue and grey of dusk came down and highlighted the masts of the boats and their dark hulks rocking in the still-shining water. We talked about the day and looked ahead to the morning.

Promptly at nine, we were at Fort Christiansvaern, going into the office of Management Assistant Richard Ward, who was wearing the park uniform of dark green, a badge on his shirt, the bison insignia on his sleeve, his cap on the deck before him with the initials USNPS. Talking with him was the new Ranger, vigorous, in Bermuda shorts and T-shirt. We had our Volkswagen outside and followed their car down to the wharf where the *Park Ranger*, a white thirty-three-foot National Park Service boat, was tied. We waited, impressed, while Mr. Ward went through the complex system of ropes and trusses whereby at any time, single-handed, one man could launch the boat. The ferry had made the trip to Buck Island in a leisurely fashion; now we sped over the dark blue-green water, the two men talking constantly of their various problems, not the least of which was the attrition occurring on the reefs about the Virgin Islands since they had become so popular. Spearfishing, once practiced here, was of course forbidden. But it was almost impossible to control heavy trap fishing and hook-and-line fishing; and many boats anchored carelessly into the reefs, breaking the formations, which would take years to replace. There was a problem too, with the local people, including the Cruzans, who searched the islands regularly as their forebears had done, for booby and tern and turtle eggs as well as the adults to eat. And they set tangle nets for the Hawksbill and Green Turtles too.

The waters off the sandy western beach ahead where we would land were aquamarine in contrast to the open sea and there were no sloops filled with tourists, for we were ahead of the daily influx. Off to the east we saw the crowd of circling Man-o'-war birds that we had seen yesterday, and we asked if they had a rookery here on Buck Island. Mr. Ward said that the flora abounded in prickly plants including cacti, but that nevertheless the island had been well searched and no Man-o'-war nests had been spotted. There were plenty of breeding pelicans, especially on the north side of the island. There was a predator problem, he said, with the mongoose, which had been brought to many of the West Indian islands in the old days when sugar cane was the prime product in an attempt to control the abundant rats. The latter, it seems, adjusted to the presence of the new creature, which increased as the ecology was upset. The Small Indian Mongoose, *Herpestes auropunctatus*, his body a foot long and his tail of the same length, bright-eyed and voracious, small-muzzled, robbed pelican nests, each containing two or three of the white thick-shelled eggs, and ate the young nestlings too, dark-fleshed and with loud voices at that age which would diminish to muteness in time. They were fond too of turtle eggs and newly hatched turtles and also of iguanas and the ground lizard *Ameiva polops* and had reduced the latter's population almost to the point of extinction. We have a number of chameleons in our country house which live in the plants that are in the windows and keep the fly population down; we felt it was a pity that the gentle lizards were nearly gone. It was known that in Tobago, the British Windward Island near Trinidad, the Man-o'-wars commonly nested; it was thought that they had abandoned Buck Island because they were wary of the little predator. Mr. Ward said that attempts were being made to control the mongoose, and we said we hoped it wouldn't be done through the introduction of yet another predator.

It is known that through the eons, evolution brings about a balance between parasite and host and between predator and prey. Because of this the latter are not exterminated, for if they were the predator would consequently perish. Barney told of a situation in Australia where a grazing animal, the rabbit, was introduced into grassy areas ideal for its culture, but in which no natural predator existed. When the rabbits eventually reached the proportion of a plague, myxomatosis was introduced by releasing rabbits infected with it. The virus spread quickly and nearly all of the infected rabbits died; it appeared that the species was about to be extinguished. Then two things happened: a few rabbits had genes which made them resistant to myxomatosis and survived as did their descendants; at the same time the virus itself underwent a mutation, becoming less toxic. This latter strain survived better than the original because creatures infected with it lived longer and transmitted the virus more widely throughout the rabbit population. Thus, in the course of a decade, evolution brought both the rabbit population and the virus into balance.

Mr. Ward said that it was unlikely that another prey species would be introduced and more probably that poison would be used for a control. We disagreed with this too. Poisoning with non-specific chemicals destroys indiscriminately and a chain is set up which can harm or kill desirable fauna. This was the case with the Golden Eagle of our west, which fed on coyotes that died when poison bait was put out by sheep herders. It is the case with the sick squirrels which our neighborhood children bring me every now and then in spring, during that season when midwest man is stirring himself after the long winter and begins distributing insecticides as he grooms his lawns, bushes, and gardens. It is why we never hear a whippoorwill in the long summer twilights when once one could tell the time of night accurately by the moment they began their haunting calling. It is why the familar robin has become a rarity.

Now it is beginning to be evident, and Mr. Ward was familiar with some of the literature, that the safest control is the biological one. Recently tests were performed by the Czechoslovak Academy of Sciences with the linden bug, the male of which may mate twice daily. The Czech scientists used a synthetic juvenile hormone prepared from the balsam fir and known to be effective in almost all insects, but particularly in a group of true bugs, the *Pyrrhocoridae*, which include some of the most destructive pests of commercial crop plants. Natural juvenile hormones, which are secreted by insect larvae, must be absent when metamorphosis from larva to adult insect takes place; if present, metamorphosis is disrupted. The scientists applied one milligram of the synthetic hormone to each male linden bug. When they mated, the females were contaminated and made sterile by the hormone; it was also found that the contamination of the females was sufficient to damage normal males with which they mated later. The process continued until almost the entire laboratory population of linden bugs was rendered infertile. We knew of the X-ray sterilization of the male screwworm fly, one of our western cattle pests, and how the species had been successfully controlled without damage to the multitude of beneficial or harmless insect species about.

The Ranger was dropping anchor, and we took our cameras as we went ashore on the white sand, which stopped abruptly where the vegetation began twenty yards inland. A handsome Department of the Interior sign stated that this was BUCK ISLAND REEF NATIONAL MONUMENT and further along before a grey-barked spreading tree was another of the park markers: THIS IS A MANCHINEEL TREE, telling how the tropical tree was poisonous and had a blistering milky juice and how its fruit, the manchineel apples, had been eaten by early settlers who became ill and advising the tourist not to try them. There were other signs explaining the purpose of the preserve, and beyond was a small frame shelter in which were dressing rooms and first aid and emergency equipment for the use of the park people.

There was a stony path up the side of the rocky island and we started up. The air was fragrant and Barney was reminded of the maquis in Corsica, a dense prickly flowering barrier that for centuries gave shelter to wild goats and cuckoo birds and Corsican *banditti*. A Zenaida Dove flew up before us, whimpering the way our mourning dove will when startled and fleeing, the same soft grey but larger than our dove and its tail square.

We were surrounded with alien plants—the frangipani and the Turks Head cactus, some of the latter enormous, their green grotesque prickly shapes topped with bulbous brown fruit. We plucked out the misshapen red beans which lay within the fruit and could be taken with no danger of being stung. Barney insisted upon tasting one and said it had a flavor rather like the scent of orchids, so faint that one is never sure it is there. The path was narrow and tortuous and the thorny-branched trees were continually in the way. Sage was fragrant and everywhere were pipe organ cacti, so abundant in our southwest, orchids and air plants hanging upon them and flourishing. Halfway up, hot, I said I would wait while the men climbed to the top where there was a forty- to fifty-foot tower which had a ladder on the outside and Barney wanted to ascend to photograph the reef from there. The elevation of the highest point of Buck Island is 329 feet.

I sat on a rock beside a Gumbo Limbo tree, its branches huge and snake-like; I knew it yielded a certain aromatic resin called çachibou, that name coming from the Arawak Indians who once lived here. As the men's voices dwindled away the life about me began to be evident. A small lizard crawled up a branch of the Gumbo Limbo tree. I saw the Ground Dove, smaller than the other, and emerald-throated hummingbirds, unmistakable, appearing black in the distance but green with throats iridescent emerald, their tails forked. And Black-faced Grassquits, little finches, smaller than a goldfinch, short-tailed and black. And Bananaquits too, like our wood warblers, to which the species is related, black and white above with yellow breast and rump and a distinctive curved beak. I had been told that they like fruit nectar and small insects, their tongues adapted to this method of eating; they called, wheezy and sibilant, "Zeeee-sweee-te!"

The men were returning, their steady voices hushing the buzzing insects and birds so the forest sounds almost ceased. Barney had photographed the reef from the tower's top, the lagoon almost aqua above the white sand, the coral in patches and beyond the dark blue water. He was anxious to return to the underwater trail which Mr. Ward said was 250 yards long and only a tiny section of the extensive winding reef. By now as we descended, we could see the Buck Island Ferry and the many boats congregated from Christiansted and elsewhere. We boarded and went on to the reef, passing the flock of Man-o'-war birds, all of the roosting ones facing in the same direction, looking to the sea and the light wind, ready for take-off. A few would land and others take off and then the whole crowd would wheel up and soar.

We anchored at the beginning of the trail and put on faceplates and flippers, Barney with the camera, and taking snorkels so that we could stay under for long observation. I felt at home in the mild temperature of the calm water. The trail was clearly marked with heavy triangular pieces of cement, their bases resting on coral rock and a plate of glass fixed to the side protecting the sign. The glass continually became covered with algae and Mr. Ward said it was a problem and he and the Ranger kept diving down to clean it off. Tiny fish were pecking the signs all the time, eating the algae. Before an enormous brain coral was the message: WHAT WOULD YOU NAME THIS CORAL? / YOU ARE RIGHT / BRAIN CORAL. On other markers were the names of fish and their pictures and warnings not to touch the fire or stinging coral. We were directed: TO THE CORAL FOREST and, following the narrow natural passage through the reef, came to the information: THIS IS A FOREST OF ANTLER CORAL. Below was a solid stand of it, fringed with Elkhorn coral; all of the branches pointed the same way as if a strong wind were blowing through. I asked Barney and he said that just as trees on windy hills are molded by the wind, coral is molded by currents; the trees, however, bend away from the wind while the coral bends into the current from which the individual growing polyps gather their food.

We came to a brain coral which made a pedestal ten feet tall with a huge globe atop; Mr. Ward stood on it while he spoke with us. He had pointed to a Peacock Flounder, *Platophyrs lunatus*, flapping out of a bed of gorgonia, its small blue spots and larger dark rings arranged in an uneven pattern and camouflaging it. We spoke of the confusion of names. reminding us of the dolphin-porpoise business when we had argued on the *Sea Diver*. The Peacock Flounder was one of the Flatfishes, the suborder *Hetero-somata* or differing-body including the flounders, halibuts, turbots and soles. In the northern waters a sole means a flounder; the Peacock Flounder that we had seen belonged to the turbot group. Barney argued that it wasn't the turbot he was familiar with and had often caught in these waters. But the Rangers said that species is the ocean triggerfish, *Canthidermis sabaco,* and belongs to the suborder *Plectognaths* or jaws-woven-together, referring to the odd arrangement of its spiny or dorsal fin.

The Peacock Flounder, in common with others of the suborder, began life like other fish, swimming as they did and feeding on microscopic plankton. But before long it began to exhibit the tendency to turn upon one side and then in a remarkably short time, a few days, the eye on its under side began to migrate, the optic nerves being so placed as to provide for the 120-degree travel of the organ. If the eyes migrated to the right side the fish was *dextral,* if to the left it was said to be *sinestral.* Barney told us that the migration of organs was not an unusual biological process and is common in the course of embryonic development. The cells in man which make up the spinal cord and brain migrate from the skin, and those forming the thyroid and parathyroid, as well as the thymus, descend from the area just below the mouth that in the embryo are gill slits. These slits later disappear, but are examples of the fact that in the course of its development the embryo goes through the various stages that its species did in evolving from an amoeba through the fish and finally into man. This is the principle of Haeckel's Law—ontogeny recapitulates philogeny— the embryologic development of the individual recapitulates the evolutionary development of the species. As the flatfish spends time on its side, the upper eyed side becomes pigmented and camouflaged and the under blind one pale. The flatfish is one of the most adept at simulation of its background. The halibuts have large symmetrical mouths and are either sinestral or dextral; the flounders have asymmetrical mouths and are largely dextral; the turbots have asymmetrical mouths and are mostly sinestral. They may be found in limestone reefs, but are particularly fond of the ocean floor, sometimes burying themselves in the sand so they resemble a tiny ray, the two eyes visible, and flapping off when disturbed. Since water must pass out of the gill on the blind side, the flatfish does not rest upon the ocean floor like a ray does, but supports itself slightly off the bottom on its fins.

In the same gorgonian bed as the mottled flatfish were Yellow-tail Snappers, *Ocyurus chrysurus,* their fins and tails luminous and dandelion-yellow on a blue ground. Barney photographed a pair of Four-eyed Butterfly fish nearby; we knew there was a symbiotic relationship between them and the snappers, the butterfly fish having a pointed long snout suitable for exploring crevices of reefs, and also for plucking parasites from larger fish and even predators' bodies and on occasion from their open mouths and throats to the pleasure and benefit of both species. The butterfly fish is a well-known case of protective coloration, the ones we saw a pale yellow with many fine rows of spots and a prominent mock eye on the rear of each side of their bodies, the eye nearly identical to the ones I was familiar with on the rear wings of the giant moth I had known as a child, *Telea Polyphemus.* A predator snatching at them would find them darting away apparently backwards. There are at least two hundred species of butterfly fish in the world's tropical waters, their flitting about, their brilliant colors and their solitary habits giving them their common name. They are of the same family as the Angelfish, *Chaetodontidae,* which is a larger edition of a butterfly fish, reaching two feet and more in length. The angelfish are friendly, often travel in pairs and move their spectacular bodies with majestic calm.

We continued on our way, coming across parrot fish in the same areas as the butterfly and angelfish; a large blue one, two feet long, was attacking coral with its beak; we heard the crunch of the bite and knew it could cut a nail in half. Since the chief item of its diet was living coral, it ate at the same time great quantities of calcified skeletons of the polyps; we saw the great blue fish passing this indigestible material as it swam off leaving a white streak like the vapor trail of a jet in a blue sky. Barney said he had seen parrot fish standing nearly vertically while small wrasse pecked at them, cleaning off the coral bits about their heads and mouths. The wrasse are the most common of all reef fish, distinguished by their exaggerated buck teeth and thick lips, their elongate bodies, greenish, with variations of yellow, blue and red, the males of one variety blue-headed. They belong to the suborder *Pharyngognathi,* or throat-teeth, and eat shellfish and invertebrates which they crush in their heavy teeth situated in the region of the pharynx.

Moving seaward, we came to the edge of the barrier reef where the white sand bottom fell off sharply into the open deep. I felt dizzy and insecure, gazing into the hazy depths that stretched away and turned back into the reef. There were many channels and depressions, some twenty to thirty feet deep. Now and then a narrow chasm could be seen leading to the ocean and Barney would cross the reef's top to view it while I waited, resting on a smooth brain coral. He took care not to be scratched on the elkhorn or stung by the fire coral. I preferred the vast stretching meadows where a fresh sight met one at every moment.

Barney rejoined me and we moved slowly over the reef. We were leaving the underwater trail now and prowling on our own and sometimes catching something on the camera. The Ranger and Mr. Ward were resetting some of the markers and discussing the former's duties and we wanted to stay out of their way. Each species of reef fish has its specialized niche in the ecology of the reef. Some feed on other fish or plankton, some on vegetation, some crack the invertebrates' shells or crush the coral, some pluck the spines from the sea urchin and devour its succulent flesh, some eat the coral worms protruding from the coral, some become immune to poison and steal the prey held by the venomous living coral polyps or the tentacles of sea anemones. The competition for food is for the greater part not between the various species but intraspecies. It is thought by many ichthyologists that the dazzling display of color in certain reef fish may be the signal evolved to notify others of the same kind that the particular feeding ground is already occupied and those of another species that they are not competing. The coral reef is heavily populated and differs from the open sea where the feeding problem necessitates gradations of soft concealing colors, or iridescent blending rainbow hues or variations of countershading and top-lighting, rather than specific bright fantastic patterns of bands and stripes and spots and dots.

For long it was thought that fish made no sounds, but along with the discovery of the porpoises' squeaking and clicking, whistling and grunting have come bioacoustic studies of the noises fish produce for the purpose of signals and not connected with their eating or moving about. Mammals and songbirds produce their vocal sounds by the passage of air through their larynx or syrinx respectively. Fish, having no vocal organs and being in quite different conditions under the water, must use other parts of their bodies to produce the wanted crackling, beeping, groaning, grunting, blatting, buzzing or various other noises that have been observed to be going on continually. When listening devices were first employed during World War II, it was thought that the many constant queer sounds came from other ships. It is believed that the fishes' deliberate noises have to do with intra-species communication rather than being a threat or signal to other kinds of fish.

Water is a far better conductor than air, being about a thousand times more dense; more energy is required to start sound through water, but once on its way it is transmitted farther and faster than in air. The sound-producing marine animals come under three groups, the cetaceans, which we were familiar with; the invertebrates, which click or rasp or snap their claws and mandibles and other parts of their shells; and the vertebrate fish, which rub or rasp or gnash their teeth or placoid or true scales, or which vibrate their swim bladders, the latter highly efficient sonic mechanisms originally designed to control the fishes' buoyancy but now employed for signals regarding feeding or territory definition or spawning, sometimes being unique to one sex. Vibration of the swim bladders is characteristic of drum fish, sea basses, catfish, squirrel fish and the Toadfish, *Opsanus tau*, common in these waters, mottled yellow-brown, sluggish, uttering a croak like a faraway foghorn if disturbed or caught. Its relative, which lives in the Gulf of Mexico—the Midshipman, is commonly called the Singing Fish for the peculiar humming sound it makes when snared.

In the elkhorn branches and about the coral, we came upon

hosts of tiny fish, active and vigorous, like Christmas tree lights—
yellow, blue, scarlet. These were the Demoiselles of the suborder
Chromides; jewel-like, they are noted for their boldness and speed;
there are so many species and the color change is so dramatic between young and adult and between the sexes that there is constant confusion about their identification. There were Sergeant
Majors, greenish yellow with black bars; and Beau Gregories, who
are called Jewelfish in one of their color phases because of the
shimmering iridescent blue on which are many lighter blue spots;
and bright gold Garibaldis, their young differing and being green
with blue dots; and Yellowtail Demoiselles, with pale yellow un-
dersides and almost orange tails.

We saw a pair of two-foot-long Black Angelfish cruising up to a
clump of gorgonians. They slowed and stationed themselves outside
the waving coral, their fins idling. At once three or four blue neon
gobies appeared and began to groom them, plucking here and
there over their bodies; these latter were the cleaning fish, who set
up stations on a reef to which larger fish come for their services,
very like the African Rhino and its tickbirds, which serve the
pachyderm by eating the pests which they find in the folds of its
skin; and the bacteria that live in the digestive tract of termites and
break down the wood they eat into a substance the termites can
absorb; and the crocodile, noted in the fifth century B.C. by Herod-
otus for its manner of opening its jaws and allowing the Egyptian
plover to enter and pick the leeches inside its mouth. When scientists have removed all the cleaning fish from certain sections of a
reef without molesting other varieties, it has been noted that in
a few weeks the reef is deserted by most of the host fish and that
those who remain are sickly, their fins ragged and their skin eaten
by parasites and injured by fungus growths.

There are a number of cleaners, but the wrasses apparently are
the most common and specialize in it. They will even pluck offend-
ing parasites and fungi from predators, who wait with gaping jaws
and lifted fins to encourage the tiny fish that are observed to enter
their mouths too. When a great grouper moved up as the Black

Angelfish departed, we watched the neon gobies dart over and zig-zag about before him, which we knew was the invitation signal, and the client comprehended, opening his huge mouth. Since nature has a way of filling every possible niche with a creature adapted to it, it is not surprising that there is a species of tiny blue sharp-toothed predator fish which resembles the cleaner fish and mimics their invitational display and then proceeds to tear the flesh and fins of the host fish, who flee in alarm.

We had noted the grouper's color had adapted to the area in which it arrived. Barney said that in its skin were chromatophores, large cells with star-like branches containing granules of pigment ranging from yellowish white through orange, red, brown and black. When the granules of the chromatophore are concentrated in a tight ball in the middle of the cell, they have little effect on the color of the skin, but if the pigment is dispersed and covers a wide surface area the skin will take on the color. It has been determined that in the brain of the creature is a center responsible for interpreting the environment and deciding the body's color changes. In the octopus, the branches of the pigment-bearing cell shrink tightly and when the creature moves along the bottom, as the environment changes, the chromatophores contract or expand, making waves of color change over the body and tentacles. This process is not only a means of camouflage; if the octopus is irritated or disturbed it will become flushed and red. Certain fish employ dramatic color alterations when ready to mate or wanting to warn rivals of the same species or predators of another.

In the same coral bed, camouflaged by a different technique, was the Trumpet Fish of the family *Aulostomidae,* brownish-yellow, hovering vertically, head down so it resembled a branch of the gorgonian. It reminded me of the common bittern of our swamps which stands with extended neck among the reeds and is difficult to spot. Preferring no company, the long-snouted trumpet fish feeds on crustaceans and smaller fish; it has been observed swimming above the back of a parrot fish, presumably to conceal itself from predators below.

Beyond the bed of gorgonians was a brain coral and above it were two Yellow Grunts of the family *Haemulidae*, related to the Yellowtail Snappers we had seen but known to be less wary and smaller, under a foot long. They faced each other with scarlet-lined mouths wide open and occasionally approaching and touching. Barney said he had often noted this behavior among the grunts, which was still unexplained but thought to have to do with sexual, territorial or aggressive display. For a while we watched the two creatures, their bodies alternating longitudinal stripes of blue-grey and yellow, their fins yellow, their prominent eyes glassy, opening their red-lined mouths so widely in respect to their size that it seemed as if a swallowing contest were going on in which the first to close its mouth might be engulfed by the other.

Far below in the tall stem of the brain coral, apparently disinterested in the pair of grunts although they were its natural prey, was a Green Moray Eel, big around as a man's wrist, its head and neck protruding from the coral, the rest hidden in its lair. It opened and closed its long-fanged mouth, and Barney said it was not threatening us; that was the way it circulated water through its gills.

Barney motioned me to the surface. "Don't put your hand near one of those. It has teeth like needles and when it bites it sets its jaws and fixes its tail in the rocks so that if you try to pull away, you'll cut your hand to ribbons. If by chance one does get hold of you, grasp it around the neck and get it up to the air and wait for it to release its hold."

I respected the moray and knew that it stayed close to its hole from which it ambushed passing prey. I knew the legend that ancient Romans fed slaves to Mediterranean morays in their fish ponds, but knew too that it was not this creature, but an eel-like fish, *Muraena*. I had no intention of interfering with this moray's life. We knew that spearfishermen had often been in trouble when taunting an eel and that if an injured one were brought up into a boat, it might attack its captors and be dangerous. They are nocturnal creatures and the Green Moray Eel, commonly six feet long,

may reach ten. The morays about the West Indies are not poisonous; the other common variety here is the Spotted Moray which
seldom exceeds three feet. They belong to the order *Apodes,* with-
out-feet, which contains the common eels so famous for their migrations to the Sargasso Sea to breed.

The spawning habits of the eels had for centuries been unknown. Aristotle in his firm way stated: "There is no doubt that
they proceed neither from pairing nor from an egg. Eels are derived from the so-called 'earth's guts' that grow spontaneously in
mud and in humid ground; in fact, eels have at times been seen to
emerge out of such earthworms, and on other occasions have been
rendered visible when the earthworms were laid open by either
scraping or cutting. . . . So much for the generation of the eel." It
was determined before the present century that a certain small
transparent creature which resembled a fish and was called *leptocephalus,* narrow-head, was in reality the larvae of the eel and in
time transformed into an elver or baby eel. Then in 1913 a Dane,
Johannes Schmidt, brought up nets full of the *leptocephalus* from
the Sargasso Sea and the mystery was solved. The evolution of the
eel is unknown and stories of sea serpents have been always related to the creature. A few years ago, off the coast of South Africa,
what appeared to be a *leptocephalus* larva, six feet long, was hauled
up and there were speculations among marine biologists that this
could produce a sixty-foot adult eel; one such animal might accurately be called a sea serpent.

The eel is an isolated and highly adapted form of fish, living in
holes and either swimming like a snake or slithering along the
ocean bottom. The Common Eel is the most primitive and has
small scales embedded in the skin and pectoral fins. Snake Eels
are spotted and have two short barbels on their nostrils with which
they explore the sea floor. There are other groups of fishes which
closely resemble true eels and one is the renowned Electric Eel of
the Amazon.

Fifty-eight per cent of the weight of *Electrophorus electricus* is
contained in the modified muscle cells of the electric organ. Be-

cause of varied concentrations of potassium, sodium, chloride and organic ions, it is able to generate a total tension of 600 volts which can be released at will. It has been thought that the electric charge was for use in defense and immobilization of its prey; it is beginning lately to be proposed that the organ is also for communication with others of the same species in a territorial sense. The Electric Eel belongs to the order of rays which is *Hypotremata,* openings-beneath, and includes the sawfishes, skates, devilfishes, true rays and electric rays. Some of these can shock severely; certain of the skates have an organ on their tail which can administer half a volt; and the electric rays, depending on their size and variety, can deliver up to 220 volts, enough to temporarily disable a diver. Sting Rays, which include the Stingaree common in the Caribbean, employ another device for offense and defense—at the root of their whiplike tails is a protruding stinger, a serrated blade, along the edges of which are glands that secrete poison.

Barney has had a long acquaintance with the venomous creatures of the oceans over the world, and when we glided again over the underwater trail and then returned to the two men and climbed into the *Park Ranger* which would return us to St. Croix, he talked on the subject with Mr. Ward and the Ranger. He spoke of the Lion Fish, which he knew in the Red Sea and which I had viewed with him in the rocky crevices of the reef off Tautira, Tahiti, where the surf plunged over and they hung brilliant and grotesque, red and yellow and brown, with fleshy protuberances swaying about them, their stings often fatal to humans. The men mentioned the bits of protoplasm that at certain seasons crowd the surface of the Tongue of the Ocean in the Bahamas, looking like fragments of pine needles and when brushed against the skin, causing a rash rather like poison ivy. Barney has had sea urchin needles embedded in his skin, been hit by the sting ray's barb and lanced by the spines of countless species of fish whose dorsal fins, if not venomed, caused wounds that festered painfully. He has been knocked flat by the shock of the electric ray, been stung repeatedly by the trailing tentacles of the iridescent Portuguese Man-of-war, been wounded or poisoned by one or another of the various virulent sea creatures and felt that the only principle he had evolved if one didn't wish this to happen, was to wear gloves in the water and not to let the skin touch anything gaudy or monstrous or that wasn't clearly recognizable as harmless.

I felt, as in the case of the moray eel we had seen and similarly with all of the creatures of the water, that we were intruding curious, upon their territory, and that all we could do was to gain what knowledge we could about their ways and to behave accordingly. I had had friends made nauseous and breathless by the painful sting of the Portuguese Man-of-war and knew that on occasion there had been deaths from it; the tentacles are often thirty feet long and the triggered stinging nematocysts may engage the skin of swimmers who are not even aware that the creature is about. The Portuguese Man-of-war is one of the huge family of the phylum *Coelentera*, hollow-intestines, since they all possess a large central cavity.

The Coelenterata are the polyps and include the hydrozoans, jellyfish, anemones, gorgonians, and corals. A polyp is a tube, radially symmetrical, with a mouth at one end surrounded by a series of tentacles that are armed with batteries of stinging cells, the nematocysts. The polyps feed upon algae, small organisms and fish which are killed or stupefied by contact with the nematocysts and are drawn into the mouth by tentacles which serve that purpose. They reproduce asexually by budding, and certain of them do not resemble their parent polyp but form cup-shaped buds which eventually become free-swimming and are the *medusae*, the jellyfish, their mouths turned down and their tentacles dangling instead of flower-like and up-reaching. These *medusae* have male and female forms which produce polyps, and the process repeats itself.

The stinging nematocysts are a characteristic of the Coelenterata and occur in clusters; each is a cell with a cavity filled with a fluid that surrounds a coiled hollow thread-like tube. The top of the cell is pointed and triggered; in response to being brushed by a swimming creature, the cell will contract and shoot out the tube which turns inside out. Barbs in it are exposed and poison is simultaneously extruded. The thread holds the victim which, as it struggles, becomes entangled in more nematocysts and shortly, like prey in a spider web, is rendered helpless. We were familiar at home with the wild Jewel-weed, *Impatiens biflora,* during the summers bearing its profuse golden flowers that in fall become seed pods which when touched, curl and throw their ripe seeds for a distance.

There are nearly three thousand species of *Hydrozoa,* water-animals, over the world, of great variation from the minuscule and colonial to the gigantic and solitary. They include the stinging or fire coral, *Millepora,* mustard yellow and knobby, that Barney had pointed out along the sea wall of Fort Jefferson, which has small pores from which the polyps extend their tentacles. And the Portuguese Man-of-war, in reality a colony of polyps and one medusa, the latter forming the bell or float for the colony and the polyps performing the roles of digestion, reproduction, and defense and feeding; the first individual of the Portuguese man-of-war is an egg which produces the medusa; all the rest of the colony bud off from it. Many of the hydrozoans have more than one medusa and they become swimming bells that propel the assemblage, but the Portuguese Man-of-war depends upon the wind and tide for direction. It grows to a foot or more across, sometimes travels in a fleet of a dozen and in its tentacles, living in symbiotic relationship, often is found the little Man-of-war fish, *Nomeus gronovii,* which dodges the poisoned strands that are known to kill it occasionally when the pair are confined in captivity. In payment for the protection, the Man-of-war fish lures in other fish for its host's benefit; it has also been observed to feed on the nematocysts and has a pouch at the back of its mouth where the poisoned cells are stored and neutralized before going further.

The True Jellyfish, the *Scyphozoa,* cup-animals, are a small group of perhaps two hundred species characterized by a high squarish bell, the medusa, at each corner of which are stinging tentacles. The jellyfish propels itself, often speedily, where it wishes to go by moving water in and out of its mouth so that the bell is expanded and contracted; some varieties are plankton eaters and others devour fish, but all are carnivorous; some have no sting and one which has a dangerous one is the Lion's Mane, preferring arctic or boreal waters and seldom entering warm seas and reaching a diameter of three yards and having tentacles a hundred feet long. A jellyfish called the Sea Wasp, *Chironex fleckeri,* of Australia, is one of the most dangerous creatures of the sea and has exceeded sharks in known fatalities over a given period. As in all the coelenterates, fish often live within the protection of jellyfish's tentacles, sometimes in great numbers.

Barney said that these venomous creatures of the sea often have a singular beauty. Seen in the tropical sunshine, the iridescent float of a Portuguese Man-of-war is as bright as an opal and from beneath the knobby purple tentacles trailing in the tide and the swarm of minuscule creatures seeking protection in them, form colorful patterns of an infinite variety. A jellyfish, drab when found stranded on a beach, is an organism filled with light and diaphanous color when viewed through a faceplate as its heart-like beat pulses it rhythmically through the water.

The anemones, gorgonians and corals are the *Anthozoa,* floweranimals, having no medusa stage at all. The polyps may be small and congregate in colonies comprising an entire reef like the hard corals; or may be solitary and large like anemones; they are all carnivorous and many are nocturnal and are said to bloom at dusk. The anemone is fairly stationary though capable of slow movement. A passing fish touching its outspread flower becomes paralyzed and is drawn into the mouth, which closes and pulls in the tentacles holding the prey, so that the anemone is a smooth bulge. Delicate cleaner shrimp and various little fish may live within the tentacles of certain anemones, one being the Anemone Fish. It has been speculated that a protective slime covers the latter which neutralizes the poison, but at any rate, in payment for its role of bellwether that leads the sheep to the slaughter pens, the Anemone Fish maintains its sanctuary and is rarely eaten itself. Few species of anemones are dangerous, most causing a burning sensation when touched which disappears shortly. However, recently in Australia we were told of a red sea anemone not yet catalogued and roughly the size of a little fingernail, which ejected nematocysts from its mouth as well as its tentacles and produced a violent reaction in the marine biologist who discovered it ten fathoms under the water; the creature is one of the world's most venomous organisms in proportion to its size.

A coral reef is a congregation of polyps, in some ways resembling a hive of bees or wasps, a nest of ants, or perhaps a city of men, each creature complete within its own stony shell, but flourishing only in the colonial system. Coral needs a hard bottom to build upon, there must be moving water but not violent surge, there must be proper salinity without freshwater drainage, the temperature should be not much under 70 degrees or over 125; and the water must be not too deep, two hundred feet the maximum as a rule, so that the microscopic creatures which live symbiotically in the polyp congregation may thrive. The polyps feed on plankton, and many varieties are nocturnal, blooming at dusk. Corals vary greatly in form and size; they may be stony and brittle, flabby and spongy, or branching and resilient and having a skeleton of non-stony material like the gorgonians that withstand ocean turmoil which would destroy stationary hard corals. Most species of coral are brown, especially the stony varieties, but may be blue, green or a dark yellow. The color is due to pigment and also to the presence of symbiotic or parasitic plants and organisms which live in their tissues. The iridescent Purple Sea Fan has its name from its color; the rare Mediterranean *Corallium* has had its beds almost depleted, due to its red hue being so prized by mankind.

Most of the anthozoans are non-poisonous, although a scratch of non-stinging coral can produce a sore which heals slowly, due to the reaction of the tissues to the organic matter, and is liable to infection. Most coral stings will wear off in a few hours. In coral poisoning, there is always the factor of an allergic reaction in the same way that bee or hornet venom may cause violent illness and even death in certain persons and not in others.

Among the creatures of the sea, the list of mutual relationships seems endless. We knew of a coral which uses the shell of a hermit crab to transport and feed it: the *Hydractinia,* resembling a plant and growing branching upon the hermit's shell and protecting its host by its sting. There is a species of crab, *Melia tesselata,* that arms itself with two venomous tiny anemones in each front claw, which it uses for defense and also in the capture of food. There is even symbiosis that seems the reverse of the Portuguese Man-of-war and the Man-of-war Fish living in its poisoned tentacles, in the *Hydrichthys mirus,* a colonial polyp which attaches itself in a network under the scales on the side of a fish, *Seriola Zonata,* defending it with its nematocysts and thriving itself.

Mr. Ward said that two species of sponges are found in the West Indies which produce severe stings: the poison-bun sponge, *Fibulia,* and the fire sponge, *Tedania.* The latter is a brilliant reddish-orange and the former brownish, its texture bread-like. These animals are of the phylum *Porifera,* pore-bearers. They resemble plants, have skeletons, and are nearly always involved in symbiotic relationships with a variety of crustaceans and worms; they range from an inch or two high to the Basket Sponge, *Hircina,* which is large enough for a man to sit in. The venomous species are of the class *Demospongiae,* the Horny Sponges, and have many needle-like calcareous spines that break off easily in the flesh.

We were told that in these waters there were no dangerous snails, but Mr. Ward was familiar with the cone shells of the tropical Indo-Pacific, of the family *Conidae,* which had many varieties around here. The large *Conus* snails are shy creatures and withdraw if handled; within the proboscis of each are radular teeth, harpoon-like and containing venom, much like rattlesnake fangs. The snout is extended and jabbed into the skin, the poison flows from its sac back in the head; death sometimes takes place within a few hours; it is advised to treat the wound in the same way as a rattlesnake bite, and perhaps applying tourniquets intermittently every half hour followed by removing them for five minutes. Although the cone shells in the Caribbean are said to be non-poisonous, it is recommended that they not be handled indiscriminately;

they are recognizable by their cone shape, and over the centuries have been the most desired by shell collectors. The most valuable of the species, the Glory-of-the-seas cone, is priced at six hundred dollars today.

I asked about poisonous fish and they spoke of the Scorpion Fish, *Scorpaena grandicornis,* of the Rockfish family, which may grow up to a foot long and is marked in a bizarre way and has fleshy protuberances and spines about its head and conceals itself in rocks and reefs. Some of the sharp stout spines along its back are hollow and have glands at their base full of neurotoxic poison, causing pain and occasional fatalities. It is not to be confused with the Scorpion Fish or Nohu, *Scorpaenopsis Cacopsis,* found only in Hawaiian Island waters, which delivers its venom in the same fashion. All these predators employ the concealment device of disrupting the body and jaw lines with fleshy vari-colored appendages so they blend into the grassy bottom or a weedy coral patch. The Toadfish is another of these, a bottom-lover, scaleless, mottled dark brown, with fleshy tabs hanging from its lower jaw. I had seen one in the Dry Tortugas, reminding me of our pet toads in the amphibarium at The Unicorn's Lair, which have two parotoid glands upon their backs, irritating to mucous membranes if rubbed and causing the creatures to be ignored by our experienced dog. Mr. Ward said that some controversy existed as to whether the West Indian species of Toadfish was venomous.

"These poisonous creatures may be of use to man in time," Barney said. "The sea hasn't been tapped in this realm. Recently the common honeybee was experimented with for control of outbreaks of staphylococcus infections that are penicillin-resistant, and a substance was isolated from the bee venom that was effective against strains that were resistant to most other antibiotics. Cobra venom, too, has been used off and on for the treatment of a variety of diseases, though with indifferent success. And until recently most of our effective medicines, like digitalis, quinine or opium, came from poisons of plants. Antibiotics also are derived largely from the poisons of molds."

They talked about poisoning from eating the flesh of certain marine creatures. Upon occasion, barracuda and some jacks and groupers have caused illness and death. Barney said that although the toxicity of the flesh of carnivorous fish may be caused by their eating an intrinsically poisonous fish, it is more often the result of a food chain phenomenon such as exists in inland areas with DDT, which is transmitted from insects to the birds which eat them and to those who then eat the birds. In the ocean, one of the most important of the poisons in the food chain is introduced by a bloom of red protozoa, *Gymnodinium brevis,* which in hot weather will occasionally multiply to such a degree that the water becomes a muddy red and the vapor rising from it is irritating to mucous membranes. Some of the organisms in it contain saxitoxin, potent and responsible for typical shellfish poisoning, which involves partial paralysis. Barney was familiar with the "red tide" in the Caribbean during which millions of fish would perish; and he had been stationed on the West Coast in the early forties when a red tide occurred and rendered the mussels and lobsters that fed on it so poisonous that people who ate them sometimes died. He had seen dozens of sick lobsters stranded on Pacific rocks, tempting bait for unwary beachcombers.

"Sometimes fish are safe to eat on one side of an island and unsafe on another," he said, "and what is safe at one spot and one time may not be at another. When there's any question about the edibility of a fish, the best practice is to follow the advice of the natives."

The Chimaera or Ratfish is said to be deadly poison, not only the flesh, but the dorsal spine too, which when touched exudes venom. The fish to be most wary of, though, in the case of the laymen, are the triggerfish, filefish, trunkfish, and the puffers and porcupine fish, all of the suborder *Plectognaths.* While the former three are occasionally questionable and Barney says he has eaten them all without qualm or reaction, the latter two, the puffers and porcupine fish, ought to be avoided by the inexperienced.

It was Captain James Cook who first reported having tasted the

liver and roe of the *Maki-maki* or Deadly-death Fish, now identified as *Tetraodon hispidus,* off New Caledonia in the New Heb-
rides on the eighth of September 1774: " . . . we were siezed with an
extraordinary weakness in all our limbs attended with a numbness or Sensation like to that caused by exposeing ones hands or
feet to a fire after having been pinched by frost. I had almost lost
the sence of feeling nor could I distinguish between light and
heavy bodies, a quart pot full of Water and a feather was the same
in my hand . . . one of the Pigs which had eat the entrails was
found dead." The most recent account we knew of poisoning by
the same fish was when ninety fatal cases were reported in Japan
in 1957 out of 176 poisoned. The symptoms came in quick order—
within ten minutes numbness and tingling of the lips and tongue
and inner surfaces of the mouth, then weakness and paralysis, and
often within half an hour, death. The poison, which has been
recognized always in Japan, where chefs who were considered competent to prepare puffer fish were granted a license, has been of
interest to scientists as a painkiller and lately as a tool in nerve
physiology. The same powerful non-protein toxin, tetrodotoxin,
has been found to be present in an almost unrelated creature, the
true newt of the family *Salamandridae.* This discovery was made
inadvertently when a biologist was grafting parts of embryos of
the California newt, *Ambystoma tigrinum,* into salamanders and
noted that the latter became paralyzed.

The puffer fish, called *Maki-maki* in Hawaii, *Blaser* in Indo-
nesia, *Fugu* in Japan, and *Botete* in Spain, belongs to the family
Tetraodontidae, four-toothed, their teeth being fused into a
divided beak with which they crack the invertebrates on which
they feed. The porcupine fish is very like the puffer except his
fused teeth are not divided and his family name is *Diodontidae,*
two-toothed. Both species are active about reefs, amusing and
friendly, and I had met them in the Bahamas when Barney and I
were there—cruising about independently, hovering like tiny helicopters about the coral—known for their ability to inflate themselves speedily with air or water and erect their quills at the same

time so that predators cannot swallow them. The puffers are silvery and up to one or two feet long and smooth; the porcupine fish are much the same, although often much larger and with tough strong spines. The liver and roe and testes of both may be toxic and the flesh too, especially in the tropics.

As our boat sped out of the channel and into the open sea, I looked back at the greenish water where the underwater trail lay. I thought of the pioneers of the sea and those who first tasted and touched the unknown creatures under the surface, which often appears at a distance to be metallic or of some silken material, deceptively concealing the world beneath. I knew of the Great Alexander, King of Macedonia, over three hundred years before Christ, said to have been let down by his crewmen into the sea in an enormous glass ball with an air-pipe, and riding in it towed by them. And of Aristotle speaking of the diving-bell that the men took along, filled with air so that they might work upon the sea floor. I thought of Leonardo da Vinci writing coldly in his manuscript regarding his secret diving-dress, "How or why I do not describe my method of remaining under water, or how long I can stay without eating; and I do not publish or divulge these by reason of the evil nature of men, who would use them as means of murder at the bottom of the sea, by breaking the bottom of ships and sinking them together with the men in them. And although I will impart others, in those there is no danger, because the mouth of the breathing-tube is visible above the water, supported on bags or corks."

The small boat was cruising into Christiansted's harbor as evening came on. The sunburn I had gotten over the last two days prickled slightly and I looked forward to a shower of fresh water in my pink room of the windmill, and to our little lookout on the top of the small stone tower. The three pairs of pelicans were resting on the hulls of the vessels, awaiting sunset when they would start diving for their evening meal. Mr. Ward demonstrated to the Ranger the method of mooring the *Park Ranger* to the dock at the wharf without help, since he would usually need to do it that way.

Before we got into our Volkswagen, we invited them to come along to the Club Comanche for refreshments, but they declined, wanting to talk over their day. We were grateful for their help and for the knowledge we had got from them. We parked our car on the narrow street, crowded with tourists at this hour, and went up the steps to the large room where our friend, the bartender, was stationed with Klondike Jake, the proprietress' toy poodle at his feet.

I asked him if I might photograph him and he said to go ahead. While I got the bulbs and put the flash attachment piece into the socket, Barney asked advice.

"What do you recommend?"

He smiled into the camera lens while expertly cooling a glass with crushed ice. "Local Cruzan rum and the fruit, mon. Cools the lady's sunburn, too."

We thanked him and took our glasses home with us, to watch the pelicans flapping against the sky and hitting the water with a loud splash. Through the squeaking turning wheel of the windmill, I took pictures of the brilliant panorama of the harbor, the outlined cloud formations and the continual movement of boats, not wanting to forget. Below, the ship *Alaska* rocked at her dock near the ferry boat and far down the shore in the dusk was the same native woman we had seen before, tossing her line out into the sun-red water where the boats' shapes gradually became silhouettes that lost their clarity at last, merging insensibly into the night.

CHAPTER ELEVEN

Las Islas de las Virgenes

For my part, I travel not to go anywhere, but to go.... The great affair is to move ... to come down off this feather-bed of civilisation, and find the globe granite underfoot and strewn with cutting flints.

—Robert Louis Stevenson:
Travels with a Donkey

THE next morning we slept late in the great bed on the windmill's third story, the sunburn making me lackadaisical, the Trade Wind breeze steady through the windows. We went down to King Christian's Wharfside Restaurant around eleven to have a beer and talk about driving around the island of St. Croix before taking the Antilles Air Boat late in the afternoon for St. Thomas. We could see one of the white twin-engine amphibian planes, trimmed in red, approaching from St. Thomas now, the engine noise increasing. We had been reading in the local paper how after three years of no mishaps, there had been two accidents in the last couple of weeks, one a near-disaster. A Grumman Goose yesterday had come down in a rough sea in the Charlotte Amalie harbor and the strut connecting the left pontoon to the wing had snapped. None of the nine passengers had been injured and they were ferried by a nearby boat to the waterfront. The week before, in the same harbor, one of the busy air boats had flipped on take-off and turned over on its back. The pilot had gotten the passengers into

harbor boats and the damaged plane had been towed away for repair. The tourists at the table beside us were discussing it as the
little air boat touched down into the water and then puttered over
to its ramp by our windmill.

"Made it again!" one cried.

"And you owe me five dollars," another said.

"Right."

The day was warm as we climbed into our car and set out. We
wanted to see the spot where Columbus had anchored those near
five centuries ago. We drove west on King Street and out of Christiansted and a few miles from town took the North Shore Road toward Sugar Bay. We turned off on a gravel road to look at the
ruins of the estate called Judith's Fancy, once the largest sugar
plantation on St. Croix. We wandered over to see the bay to the
west, turquoise and still. It had been the Genoese's second visit to
the new country and with him were hundreds hot for the treasures
they planned to take. There were no tourists about, and we could
feel how it had been a wilderness and the Red Men had seen the
stranger band and the seventeen ships and, territorial, had driven
them off.

The landscape seemed abandoned; we saw no people, no cars.
The stone walls, some in the process of reconstruction, stood
crumbling, the tall mill rearing like a tiny deserted pyramid. Once
slaves had worked the fields, mules and oxen circled to turn the
wheels when the wind was still, and the air had been scented with
the heavy odors of molasses, rum, sugar and sweating bodies. In
the stillness now bees were audible, humming over a flaming hibiscus, four-petaled, near five inches across. We drove away on the
dusty road and found ourselves on a primitive unfinished way,
often rocky, with unfenced cliffs and paths that led only to the sea.

There were coconut palms and strange trees, almost leafless and
covered with long withered brown pods. We saw termites' nests in
trees, like enormous black balloons, and down the trunk would be
a wavering dark line that was the protective tunnel which led to
the ground, used by the insects. Sometimes there were cotton

plants, formerly domesticated and now wild, white-tufted. We passed through the mountain country where the heights reached a thousand feet and then the rain forests of St. Croix, verdant and damp, the flora mango and mahogany and turpentine and bread-fruit, the mosses and airplants and vines thick. We knew three species of orchids were native to the tropical area.

As the day wore on, we decided to return as I had not packed yet, and we stopped at a café on our way back for lunch, over-hung with seagrapes, their large rounded leaves shading the open tables. They brought us crab salad, seasoned with curry, fruit juice, a ripe papaya with a sliced Persian lime to put on it, both grown locally. We tasted the tamarind fruit, which they said the children liked and the natives used in making jelly and that the beans I had seen were of the tamarind tree. When we asked how close we were to Christiansted, we were startled to find that we were on the western end of St. Croix, twenty miles or more away, and on the out-skirts of Frederiksted. The roads were vaguely marked and the island so narrow at spots that one glimpsed the sea on what seemed the wrong side sometimes, which we found confusing.

We decided to drive on through the city and passed Fort Frederik where the Danish Governor General, Peter von Scholten, had ruled. He had had an unusual regard for the Negro race, perhaps influenced by the free mulatto who was his mistress, beautiful Anna Heegaard. Forbidden to marry her by Danish law, unofficially he regarded her as his wife and be became the first on the island to invite Negroes to his twice-weekly official receptions and to see that they were employed in government jobs. In July 1847, the Danish King Christian VIII had decreed that every slave would be made free in eleven years and that every baby born mean-while would be free. The restless slaves refused to accept the slow verdict and riots became common. Then on the third of July 1848 Governor von Scholten, without consulting his king or the local people, abruptly from the balcony of Fort Frederik ordered that all unfree slaves were to be emancipated at once. The shocked planters turned upon their governor, insisted that his powers be revoked and declared martial law to control the insurgent Negroes. Ten days after the act, Governor General Peter von Scholten was on board ship for his homeland. Although King Christian exonerated him, he was never to return to St. Croix and died six years later, followed to the grave in a few years by Anna Heegaard, who never saw him again.

Outside Frederiksted, we found ourselves confused again for the sea seemed on every side and came to a dead end at a wide white beach. We were told by a native that this was Sandy Point and we must go east, and he directed us back to the paved main Centerline Road that ran through the island. Two miles out of Frederiksted was another of the estates, all of which bore odd names: Lower Love, Mary's Fancy, Betty's Hope, Catherine's Rest, Hard Labor, Betsy's Jewel, Wheel of Fortune. This was Whim Greathouse and there we saw the tombstone of Anna Heegaard. Everywhere were coconut palms and bougainvillea in bloom. With the Caribbean waters as a backdrop, there were sugar cane fields, the black cutters wearing red or blue shirts and straw hats in the sea wind, slicing the stalks with their machetes while about the white egrets circled. The cane resembled bullrushes and was eight to ten feet above the men that chattered and shouted, the loaded wagons coming and going. In other fields were sleek cows—Holsteins and Brown Swiss —and many goats too, always accompanied by their egrets which flew up in white distrustful clouds as our Volkswagen buzzed by. A long brown mongoose like a rat-squirrel dashed across the dusty pavement.

We went by industrial plants, sprawling, one at least with its own port, and wondered whether the island would change in character as energetic manufacturers took over parts of its limited space. We felt the other age, seeing the small stone Children's Huts along the road now and then, where the young of slaves, not old enough to be in the field yet, had been tended. Barney spoke of Haiti that he had visited, where technological and social change had left a civilization stranded on its own customs and traditions, unable to adapt, its ruins overgrown with jungle. The freed slave,

Henri Christophe, had declared himself king and then entered upon a tyrannical reign, building a fantastic palace, *Sans Souci,* and a citadel, *La Ferrière,* on a mountaintop, living in almost ludicrous splendor until his prospering kingdom rebelled under his cruelty, his insurgent troops deserted, and his obsessional fear of Napoleon and the armies of France ended in paranoia and Christophe's suicide on the eighth of October 1820 by a silver bullet in the halls of *Sans Souci.* Barney said that there was a problem on St. Croix when descendants of slaves, with no tradition of working for a living, who found life with aid of the dole pleasant enough, might never be stirred to vigorous ambition. As a result most of the work at good wages was being done by Spanish-descent immigrants from Cuba or Puerto Rico in such large numbers that Spanish was the second language of the island. He was familiar with the Bahamas where, when little or no government support to descendants of slaves has been available, they have managed to do for themselves and maintain a standard of living that seems at least equal to those of their race in the Virgin Islands on relief.

By the time we reached Christiansted, there was less than an hour before the Antilles Air Boat would depart. While Barney turned the Volkswagen in and settled with the Comanche people, I hurried to pack the duffle bags. Then we were in line waiting to climb in, waving to the woman from Alaska with Klondike Jake in her arms. The fare over to St. Thomas was eight dollars a person, which we thought reasonable. Aloft, one felt the jewel-like quality of the islands set below in the tremendous sea. St. Thomas was forty miles north, geographically similar to St. John and not of the same island group as St. Croix, the ocean between sounding nearly 12,000 feet, over two miles. We would be met by Frank Givens, Superintendent of the Virgin Islands National Park, which included about two-thirds of the island of St. John and was administered from the National Park Service office in Charlotte Amalie.

Mr. Givens was the park official who had notified Ranger Richard Ward of our arrival in St. Croix and our interest in Buck Island. He had asked Mr. Ward to radio St. John if we were flying there directly, but Barney had called him yesterday and said that we had friends in St. Thomas and wanted to visit them and would need reservations for three nights before our return to Cleveland. Dr. Floyd Mowry had practiced obstetrics at the University Hospitals in Cleveland many years ago, and had decided to retire to the Virgin Islands when he was offered the position of training midwives and supervising their work. He had fallen in love with the tropical way of life on vacations there and refused to return to the seasonal climate of America. He had built his house in the hills above Charlotte Amalie before St. Thomas became a popular vacation spot. Barney wanted us to visit his hospital while we were here.

We had another friend that stayed on the island about four months of the year, Warren Corning, who had a home in Ohio near us in the country. He had bought land years ago on the western tip of St. Thomas—Botany Bay. He was interested in setting up a sanctuary there and had had a survey conducted regarding the exploitation of marine life along the shore. I had sat next to Warren at a dinner party a few weeks before and he had spoken darkly of what was going on.

"The tourists are stripping the sea fans. We swam in Trunk Bay and there isn't a blasted one left. I know where some are and I'm not going to say where for your book either!" He nodded vigorously. "It used to be that you'd anchor in one of the island bays and if another vessel came along and saw you, they'd go on to another spot for themselves. Now there are boats all over the place. No one expects to be alone any more." He told me that he wouldn't be there when we came, but that we were welcome to swim off the place and look it over. He had waved his hand. "You have to snare, not spear, lobster, but you can't tell that to spearfishermen. I used to spot a baby lobster and I'd go back next year and it would be bigger and the next year bigger yet. I knew their lairs. I'd take people to see one but I stopped doing that. I've learned never to tell anyone where one is or I find it's gone. There are one or two now that I'm watching."

Below us was the wide harbor of Charlotte Amalie, looking

rather like a resort of the Riviera banked upon the green hills. As we descended, tall swells became apparent and recalling the former mishaps, I braced myself. We scooted into one and it seemed that we were turning over, but then we straightened and skidded to an abrupt halt. The pilot came down the passageway and opened the door; a boat was arriving to ferry us to the dock. While the passengers clambered into it, the pilot told us that one of his problems was the wakes made by the big boats moving through the harbor, which often made landings interesting.

As we approached the stonefront of the harbor ahead, we could see two officials in the familiar green uniforms of the Parks Department. We stepped up from the rocking boat and they shook our hands and congratulated us on our safe arrival. When our bags from the air boat were handed up, we piled them into their car; we were driven through the winding narrow streets that sometimes became modern broad avenues. We proceeded slowly, often bumper to bumper. The contrast with Christiansted was pronounced; we had got used to the sleepy provincial feeling, so that these lively shops and continual traffic seemed sophisticated. Superintendent Givens and Ranger Carr, who was with him, said that there had been some trouble getting reservations for us and that there was a scarcity of rooms in town and that neither one was familiar with the hotel we were booked in but it was a new one. We said anything would do; I was tired and still felt the effects of the burn I had gotten over the past days. They inquired about our plans and we arranged to have them pick us up at eight-thirty the morning after next; we would remain on St. Thomas tomorrow and spend the last day at St. John.

We came to our lodgings, a white-fronted building in modern style with an outside grille staircase which led onto the various floors. Mr. Givens and the Ranger helped Barney take the bags to the office on the first floor and then they departed. We rang the bell at the desk, but no one came. We waited, ringing now and then for a quarter of an hour. Then a young native girl came in, yawning. Barney asked about our rooms.

She sighed, "I didn't have a pencil when they gave us your name and I can't tell if we have a room or not." Her voice was soft, disinterested.

Barney was firm. "We intend to stay."

"All right." Resigned to the ways of vigorous outsiders, she searched for a card.

While Barney checked us in, I took the key and went up ahead with the camera basket. There were no hangers in the closet and I shouted down to him about it as he slowly mounted the stairs, three duffle bags in each hand. "I'll tell her," he called.

Half an hour later, smiling and patient, the girl brought me a few while I finished unpacking. I wanted to shower and there was a drip, not a cascade; the commode cover struck back when I lifted it, paining my stiff wrist. Barney was stretched on the hard flat bed, grinning. "We'll get out of here tomorrow. I'll phone Floyd Mowry in the morning and he'll know the right place. Tonight I'm taking you to Bluebeard's Castle!"

"Wonderful."

We sat on the darkened terrace that night, having a Bluebeard specialty, a foaming rum drink that used the juice of the island's fruits, about us well-groomed tourists in the seventeenth-century decor. The *maître d'* declared that the story of the ogrish bluebearded Chevalier Raoul and his wives published in 1697 by Charles Perrault had its basis in local legend here. We ordered glazed duck and fried green bananas, and then before midnight we took a taxi down to the waterfront where we had landed, walking down the Promenade in the carnival air where people from all over the world and every walk of life seemed to mingle. We walked back into the city a block to the main thoroughfare, Dronningen's gade, where the shops were and back to the waterfront again. Sometimes we stopped in and drank a glass of Danish or Dutch beer. We knew that the town was the largest of the Virgins with close to 20,000 inhabitants in the three hills on which it was built, some of the streets so steep that they became flights of railinged brick stairways; a quaint one always pointed out to visitors was the Ninetynine Steps.

Fort Christian loomed darkly up above; we knew it had been

used as a church and residence for the Governor, as well as a fortress, and that pirates had been hanged there occasionally; we were aware that ancient cannon flanked its heavy walls. Sixty years before the United Kingdom of Denmark and Norway bought St. Croix, they determined to colonize St. Thomas in order to engage in the profitable trade of the Caribbean seas, being exploited by France, Holland, England and Spain. St. Thomas was then the stronghold of certain pirates, who included our Bluebeard and also Blackbeard, Captain Kidd and others celebrated in legend. Privateers used the port freely too, their distinction from pirates supposedly being their policy of not murdering the men whom they robbed of ship and cargo and personal effects.

King Christian V granted a charter to the Danish West India Company to establish a trading post on *Sante-Thomas,* and on the twenty-ninth of February 1672, the ship *Faerø* left Bergen on the west coast of Norway with a hundred and ninety passengers, chiefly convicts and social outcasts, many indentured. The remarkable Captain Jørgen Iversen, who was also appointed the leader of the new settlement, brought them in after three months at sea to *Sante-Thomas* with the loss of seventy-seven due partly to hardship but also to the captain's pious nature which inclined him to lash at the mast anyone who cursed, using the name of God, and to insist that if any eating were done by passengers it was to be accompanied morning and evening by fervent communal prayer. Before nightfall on the twenty-fifth of May the *Faerø* anchored about where our air boat had dropped into the swell. During the next seven months, the list of survivors would become twenty-nine, including the righteous Captain Iversen. And it was reported that during the following three years, of the 324 who would arrive from Europe, sixty-four would remain.

Cotton, sugar and tobacco were cultivated, and slaves were imported from Africa by order of the king after 1680, when it was proved that European labor was incapable of similar efforts under the Western Indian sun. There were well over three hundred in the town including the Negroes by 1681, and in that year it was christened *Charlotte Amalia* in honor of King Christian's queen by Governor Nicolas Esmit, the tyrannical successor to Iversen. Among the first planters and traders who came to St. Thomas, the greatest proportion was Dutch; in the census of 1688, there were 66 Dutch, 17 Scandinavians, 31 English, 17 French, and a scattering from other European countries. The population remained predominantly Dutch over the early years and that nation's language as well as its leaning toward bright colors in its clothes and architecture and its independent ways, is still stamped upon the island.

Observing the signs on the shop windows emphasizing the freeport tradition of the town, we remembered that back in 1716 under the rule of the Danish West India and Guinea Company, which had not yet acquired either St. John or St. Croix, it was first established that ships of any nation might buy and sell in St. Thomas on payment of a five per cent import and a six per cent export tax. Unlike St. Croix, the island never lent itself to agriculture and a sugar aristocracy was never to develop; instead, because of its strategic location in the Caribbean and the magnificent harbor, it became the center of West Indian trade, filled with warehouses and export-import lines. At one time the importation of slaves from Africa was so heavy that St. Thomas was noted as the greatest slave market of the world. When the sugar and rum empires folded and slavery was abolished, St. Thomas still flourished while her sister islands declined. But then the riots of free workers combined with new methods of refining sugar from beets in other parts of the world, followed by the disastrous year of 1867 with its rapid succession of epidemics, earthquakes, hurricanes and tidal waves, resulted in the Danish government being ready to call it quits. It was on the seventeenth of January 1917 that the *Dansk Vest-Indien* became part of the United States.

The moon was rising as we walked the blocks to our hotel and climbed the iron staircase up to the hard bed, in which I refused to sleep late the next morning. Barney persuaded the hotel concierge to let him use the telephone and he called Dr. Mowry. They decided that we would meet at the hospital later in the morning to look it over. Meanwhile Dr. Mowry advised us to go to Yacht Haven on the northeast side of the harbor for our last two nights.

"I'll phone and say you're coming, Barney. Expensive, but worth it."

And we agreed as we followed the boy up the Yacht Haven outside stairs with our bags. The room was enormous with a great bath area and a tub, double beds, a writing desk, and a spacious balcony outside framed by an arch and looking out to causeways and piers and well over a hundred vessels from tiny cruisers to elegant yachts. On the balcony were two brown friendly lizards of the same genus as our chameleons, *Anolis,* their brown color not varying to green the way our pets at home did. While Barney went down to arrange another Volkswagen so that we could go over to the hospital and then to Botany Bay, I settled in, content. And then we were off.

Dr. Floyd Mowry told us that all three Virgin Islands used the hospital in Charlotte Amalie on occasion. Prenatal care and uncomplicated deliveries were handled by the midwives we met under his charge and by those trained there who were sent to the other islands. They were of varied races and nationalities and recruited from here and everywhere. There were always obstetricians in attendance at the hospitals in the event of complications. In spite of the low socio-economic status of the majority of the mothers, Dr. Mowry said that the maternal and infant mortality rate was no higher than in the average American city. We were delighted with his enthusiasm with his program and his pleasure with his life on the island. We would have dinner that night with him at a small place on one of the high hills above the town. Dr. Mowry wrote down instructions so that we could find our way to his home first. And he looked at the map we showed him and pointed to the Harwood Highway that we should take now to drive to the island's west end where Botany Bay was. Tomorrow we would go to the easternmost part to Red Hook and take the Park's boat over the sound to St. John.

This island of St. John was not so large as St. Croix, being three miles wide and twelve long. The mountain range across it is primarily of uplifted granite and conglomerate and rises sometimes to 1600 feet. At the high spots we always saw the Caribbean. Eastward reared the rough hills of St. John and past them Tortola and Virgin Gorda of the British West Indies. In the other direction were the western islands. These were *las Islas de las Virgenes* which Columbus had named, being the tops of a spectacular underwater mountain chain separating the Caribbean Sea from the Atlantic Ocean. We drove up Constant Hill to a mountaintop, continuing on the road that was rocky and dusty and seemed to run through nearly deserted countryside. It was hot and dry and the road was bumpy, but all this lent to the pleasure of the unexplored day ahead. We were reminded of traveling through parts of southern France and Spain where the terrain is similar. Now and then a roadway led off so that we were uncertain whether we were holding to the main one, and the map did little to reassure us. We passed the ruins of one of the ancient sugar plantations and a straw-hatted native family leading two loaded burros and then we reached a padlocked gate with a mailbox nearby with Warren Corning's name. While we stood there deciding whether to make the trek through on foot or to return to Charlotte Amalie, a jeep drove up in which were a young couple and six children, the man proving to be Mr. Corning's caretaker. He had been expecting us and opened the gate, closing it after us and locking it again. He gave us the combination to use on our return and pointed to the road to the big house.

We left the car in the drive and walked down to the shoreline, carrying our masks and flippers in case we decided to go into the water. We knew that Warren Corning was attempting to preserve the ecology of the area, named for the famous inlet in New South Wales, Australia, whose variegated vegetation along the shores had prompted Captain James Cook to call it Botany Bay. In 1964–1965, Mr. Corning had supported a survey to determine the value of setting aside a littoral zone for a marine sanctuary and nature study center. It had covered the Greater Botany Bay area that belonged to him, including West Cay Bay, Little St. Thomas Channel, Mermaid's Chair Bay, Sandy Bay and Botany Bay where we were. The shore was so precipitous and rocky that I waited there while Barney left his clothes and took his gear and went out to take a look at the bottom. The diversity in Greater Botany Bay of tidal flow, depth of water, sandy and rock or coral rubble bottom, all combine to make it ideal for the study of a vast variety of grasses, sponges, corals, fish, invertebrates and all typical underwater life of these tropical islands.

Warren had explained to me that there is no legal way to prevent divers and fishermen from despoiling water areas off privately owned land and that there is no official protection for the marine life. When Barney finally came ashore and dressed and we were driving to the padlocked gate, he said that it would be a great advantage to resort hotels and private establishments if they were able to control the waters adjacent to their properties, not only keeping them from being fished out and made sterile, but encouraging the life there the way our friend Art McKee had tried to do with the artificial wreck he had created off Key Largo that attracted reef fish looking for new protected spots. Art had had no redress when the wreck was speared out and blown to bits; and Warren had none when his lobster friends were removed.

We started back eastward on the dusty way toward Charlotte Amalie. At a crossroads, we saw a parked car with a party of vivacious young men and women who hailed us. They were lost and explained that their trunk was full of spearguns and scuba gear and they were heading for a place someone had told them of where huge fish could be speared. They had an attitude of excitement and determination, and as we gave them our map, we understood their feeling that there was an endless supply of fish for their spears throughout the world.

A few miles outside Charlotte Amalie, we stopped by the wayside, wanting to swim before coming in. As soon as the road had bordered the harbor, we had seen casual groups in the water—natives or visitors or residents. We changed into our suits beside the car, as the others seemed to have done, and went in. There was a lot of eelgrass and few fish, the water was murky and cold, and then, sitting on our towels in our suits, we drove refreshed back to Yacht Haven. Before going up to dress, we stopped at the huge room where the bar was to have the drink of the house, The Palm Kiss, which was given gratis to new arrivals.

After a while we visited Floyd Mowry's house perched on a hillside and replete with brilliant tropical blooms inside and out and cooled by the breeze from the sea. As dark came on, we drove higher yet to a small place he knew, quiet and frequented rather by older residents than tourists, where thick steaks were grilled to order on an open fire by a chef with a high white cap, and we filled our plates with green salad from a wooden bowl the size of a washtub. The lights of Charlotte Amalie flickered and those from the boats moored or moving about the harbor or from far distant hills. There was no sound but the slow wind and the people's low satiated voices, and we felt we understood Dr. Mowry's attachment to St. Thomas.

One Man's Dream

Away with a corrupt world! Let us breathe the air of the Enchanted island.

—George Meredith:
The Ordeal of Richard Feverel

IT was our last day in the Virgin Islands. We were up in the dusky early light, walking about the deserted harborfront before our hotel. The sails were furled on the masts of the vessels on the quiet water, and they rocked back and forth. Sometimes an occupant of a boat, clad in torn shorts, was seen painting or scraping or repairing some part or again just stretched along the bow, nodding to us as we passed the somnolent scene.

At eight-thirty, we were in the Yacht Haven office, our camera basket and bag of underwater gear in hand, and I wore the floppy-brimmed hat I had bought in Christiansted. Wise now, I had packed our long-sleeved jerseys too. We recognized Ranger Carr, who said that Superintendent Givens was tied up and that he would drive us instead and answer any questions. We were going to Red Hook Landing, nine miles away on the bay at the easternmost end of St. Thomas, where the Park Department's launch would take us to the park entrance at Cruz Bay. There we would meet the naturalist assigned to us, Ranger Richard Zani. We inquired about tourist accommodations and Mr. Carr said that taxis from the port of Charlotte Amalie to Red Hook cost three dollars a person, with a fifty-cent charge for each additional passenger. A ferry went on a regular schedule between Red Hook and Cruz Bay, a four-mile thirty-minute passage, daily from 7:35 A.M. until 5:50 P.M., the fare a dollar for adults and fify cents for children. There were taxis on St. John for transportation to the beaches and campgrounds, and sailboats and various vessels could be rented or charter boats engaged at twenty to fifty dollars a day for deep sea fishing. Drive-it-yourself jeeps were available at about twelve dollars daily, and a jeep taxi service was prepared to take visitors on a tour of the entire nine-mile-long and five-mile-wide island, the smallest of the three Virgins.

We thanked Ranger Carr, who would meet us on return to the landing. The Park boat was waiting at the Red Hook National Park Dock; Captain Williams was large, jovial, black and competent. He asked Ranger Carr's permission for a group of his relatives to accompany us; they wanted to spend the day at a Cruz Bay beach. We admired their bright wear and continual gaiety on the way over. We sat under the shelter of the tiny cabin out of the path of the blazing seemingly innocent sun. Our skipper told us that the long running waves across Pillsbury Sound which made the trip over so quick could make the return eventful.

The southeast end of St. John as well as the area around Coral Bay, totaling about six square miles of the island, is privately owned and there are near fifteen hundred inhabitants. The remaining two-thirds of the land comprises the Virgin Islands National Park. Ranger Carr had told us that the park had an extensive offshore boundary where spearfishing or possession of a speargun was outlawed. There were a variety of boats in Cruz Bay; the nine o'clock ferry was getting ready to leave, sunburned vacation campers and overnight excursionists from St. Thomas on board.

We greeted Ranger Richard Zani, recognizing him by his uniform. He was young, darkly tanned, muscled, his hair crew-cut, his attitude serious. He had some business with Captain Williams and we looked over the Information Center while we waited for him to join us. Detailed maps of the island were provided, listing the jeep roads and the foot trails and the ranger stations, one at Cruz Bay and one at Lameshur, four miles away. There were schedules listing the nature walks, the historical talks, the snorkel trips and campfire programs; there were exhibits of features of interest in the park. And lists of regulations for keeping the campsites and the park intact, one declaring that the injury, defacement, removal or disturbance in any manner of any sign, ruin, relic, vegetation, rock, animal or bird was prohibited. No water-skiing might be practiced, no firearms or motorcycles might be used. No person might cut, carve, injure, mutilate, remove, displace or break off any underwater growth or formation. Nor might anyone dig in the bottom or attach to any coral or rock a rope or wire or other contrivance whether temporary or permanent. No wrecked or abandoned watercraft might be tampered with. All known means of taking fish, crustaceans, molluscs, turtles or other marine life was prohibited in Trunk Bay or any waters where there was a marked underwater trail. Certain fish, lobster, conchs and whelks might be caught, but in explicit quantities. We were impressed and asked Ranger Zani when he returned if there was much poaching. He said it was a continual problem, due to the small staff and size of their boats, but agreed with us that the answer lay in the education of the public rather than in a huge police force.

Ranger Zani, as the Park Naturalist, was due to lead a snorkel trip through Turtle Bay, a part of Caneel Bay Plantation, at ten o'clock, less than an hour away, and we would accompany him. We would visit the Trunk Bay Underwater Trail next which was self-guiding, and then return to Caneel Bay for the buffet luncheon; in the afternoon we would drive about St. John.

We climbed into the dusty sturdy jeep and jounced off. Barney asked Mr. Zani about his background and he said he had a bachelor's degree and was interested in too many things to specialize. We found him candid and knowledgeable about insects, birds, trees, plants, fish, and coral. He pointed, as we drove almost at once into the Virgin Islands National Park.

"That little dark bird there is a Grassquit."

Zenaida doves that we had seen on Buck Island flew up before us, their wings whistling. We saw the same Ground Dove and the commonest of the thrushes which Mr. Zani said we would see everywhere—the Pearly-eyed Thrasher.

Before going to Turtle Bay Beach, we went on to see the facilities for swimming, picnicking and camping at Hawks Nest Bay and Cinnamon Bay. We knew that camping was not permitted on Buck Island or on St. Croix or St. Thomas. We were impressed with the handy beach cottages under the coconut palms, furnished and screened, costing near ten dollars a day for two persons. Mr. Zani said that bedding and cooking utensils were included and that there were camp stores nearby where supplies were available and one could also shop at Cruz Bay's little stores. At Cinnamon Bay we saw the large beach, free to the public for camping and the handsome tables and fireplaces and spigots of cold water spaced here and there. There was a one-month camping limit, our guide said, and if tourists wished, they might rent completely equipped tents for twenty-five dollars a week per couple. At Hawks Nest, Cinnamon and Trunk Bay, there were lifeguards at posted times, as well as scheduled snorkel trips along the reefs like the one we were taking.

We parked in the Caneel Bay Plantation stone lot, changed into our swim suits and long-sleeved jerseys in the rest cabins provided, and carrying our masks, snorkels and fins, Barney with the underwater camera, followed Ranger Zani down the path. The water of Turtle Bay was aquamarine under the fierce sun. On the beach was a crowd of men, women and two or three children, as well as an authoritative native lifeguard with two small red-and-white safety rafts in his hand. It was just before ten. Mr. Zani told us that one could rent simple underwater gear at the camp concessions and that the ambitious who liked the more elaborate wet suits and scuba—self-contained underwater breathing apparatus—tanks could find them, as well as service, over on St. Thomas.

We watched Ranger Zani, as he counted off twelve snorkelers

for the first trip out, the limit that had been officially set. Then he reviewed everyone's equipment on land before each rinsed his fins and put them on and followed, awkward, into the shallows. The foot fins, he said, should be a part of the diver, the shoe-part fitting tightly but not so as to blister heel or toes. One can trim the rubber if there is a point of friction and many prefer to wear socks. Some fins are made with straps but these too are liable to cause discomfort. The fin itself should be pliable and long, not short and stiff, so that the skindiver can propel himself with a true fish-tail effect.

With the help of the amiable lifeguard and Ranger Zani, the masks and snorkels of all neophytes were tested for leaks and proper fitting. There are a variety of masks on the market, some enclosing the entire face and having a built-in snorkel, some with a piece for a rubber nose so that the diver can pinch his nostrils to clear the eustachian tubes. Barney's old one was of the latter type; mine was a simple wide glass plate, but both of ours enclosed only the eyes and nose. The test for leaking is to try on the mask and breathe gently through the nose; the mask must pull against the face. Of course the glass should be unbreakable.

The skindiver's mouth must be free so that he can always surface and gasp in air, even if the faceplate should leak during rough waves. One had to learn, too, not to breathe through the nose at all. Mr. Zani cautioned that before going beyond one's depth, one should practice removing both faceplate and snorkel while treading water, and replacing them. He also said that the novice should never swim in anything but calm waters and he should know how to float on his back if in trouble. If he could not float he should confine his snorkeling, as should very young children, to the shallows. He also advised the use of rubber tire tubes or little floats, like those which the lifeguard gave to two of the group.

Barney and I often left our snorkels behind when skin-diving, considering them a nuisance sometimes and tiring to the mouth. If the waters are rough, we feel safer without them too, as waves can splash into the tube and one can swallow a good deal of water.

But when going over a trail or a long reef, they are a decided advantage as one does not have to lift one's head continually to breathe. The snorkel is held in the teeth, the rubber flange that fits between the lips and gums sealing the water out. There are as many kinds of snorkels as masks, of metal, plastic and rubber and often having complex valves on bottom and top to keep water from entering. We used the simplest kind, with a crook at the bottom, and the rest straight and open at the top. When Barney was photographing on the bottom, he kept his snorkel on, and when he surfaced, blew out the water with a snort like our capybara, Helen of Troy.

Mr. Zani's people stood about, waist-deep, in bright swim suits, bikinis and some with jerseys like our against the sun; there was a child, a portly oldster, a blond long-haired woman, dipping their heads under and practicing conscious breathing through their snorkels and how to force or spit out water that got in. They floated and treaded water and coughed and tried again. And then they were moving out toward the Turtle Bay reef. We found it interesting, not spectacular like the Buck Island barrier reef. We followed the group, wanting to observe and not interfere with Naturalist Zani. He answered all questions briskly and described the common reef fish and identified the corals as the bathing caps and the tops of snorkels bobbed about him. Now and then, in the way of underwater guides, he stood on a brain coral he knew of while he explained. Barney kept descending to photograph the fish or rising to snap the swimmers. I liked the way my wrist was responding, no longer doubting that it would function well enough for me always while swimming. Barney also remained near and if I tired, obliged by letting me cling to his suit for a life raft.

When we came on shore, I decided to wait while he accompanied the next troop out. I listened to the high laughter and the calls back and forth from the tourists over the reef, slapping at the occasional sandflies that we had been told were sometimes a bother unless one remembered to bring along insect repellant. And then before long, Barney and Ranger Zani were back, and we were driving to the Underwater Trail at Trunk Bay. There were a dozen tourists on the beach and two or three in the waters as we entered. I took along a small life preserver that I had seen in the park jeep, so that Barney would be quite free over the trail, which was self-guiding. Mr. Zani said it was planned to elaborate it in time and to establish others and that the Buck Island Trail was the first to be marked in 1961; these markers were placed in 1962. The first one read: TRUNK BAY UNDERWATER TRAIL; Mr. Zani said the process involved taking two sheets of ten- by sixteen-inch glass and painting one marine blue. The text was inked upon this surface and the art work painted or glued on it. The other glass was cemented to it by a ribbon of epoxy. The complete glass label was applied with tile asphalt to a prepared recess in a concrete block.

We admired the trail which was short in comparison with Buck Island. In one of the deeper channels, as Barney went down and I was pushing my tube before me, gazing under, I felt a violent grip upon my shoulder and lifted my head. Beside me was a woman's face behind her full-face mask which was half-filled with water. Her vise-like hold was desperate and I shoved her hand roughly off me and pushed the tube toward her and called that she should pull off her mask. I felt if I stayed within reach she would drown us both.

She pushed her faceplate up and coughed and gasped, gripping the life preserver. "We're new to this," she said finally. "That's my husband over there."

"You've got the wrong kind of mask," I told her, "with that built-in snorkel and full face. You have no chance if water gets in."

"I don't know," she said, "the salesman said it was the best."

Her husband swam up. "Come on, Gladys. Don't be a sissy. Back to nature!" And he was off, floundering along.

"I wouldn't keep that mask." I urged her.

"I like to breathe through my nose," she explained.

I felt the danger to the couple, but that words would be of little use and assured the woman that she was welcome to keep the float. I would stay with Barney and the Ranger and would pick it

up in a little while. She accepted happily, unnerved but not comprehending fully what had happened, the way one often forgets a
near accident quickly. I knew that every year the number of
drownings of Americans at home and on vacation in other waters
was in the thousands, and that many were skin or scuba divers. The
underwater accident, in common with air accidents, has a finality
about it, unless a trained bystander is nearby with special equipment. Recent findings have shown a type of drowning, uncommon
before the advent of underwater interest, which is due to hyperventilation. I knew about the Oriental pearl divers who wore home-
made goggles and who had practiced their trade from childhood,
their bodies accustomed to high pressures. I knew that they forced
themselves to take deep breaths for three or four minutes in order
to saturate their bodies with oxygen before going down to remain
under for two and close to three minutes. The hyperventilation
results in blowing off a great deal of the carbon dioxide that is dis-
solved in the blood. Since the stimulus to breathe depends much
more on the presence of an excess of carbon dioxide than on a de-
ficiency of oxygen, people who have artificially lowered the level of
carbon dioxide in their blood are unaware of the fact that they are
running out of oxygen and are apt to lose consciousness. Persons
who have been rescued after this happening have said that there
was no premonition of trouble aside from a mild urge to breathe or
a sensation of giddiness or sleepiness.

The dangers of diving are many but usually are due to care-
lessness and the ignoring of basic precepts. Rules for amateur
snorkelers are to always have enough breath left in the lungs to
expel the water from the snorkel when surfacing, never to go out
alone if unable to float, never to swim beyond ones depth, never to
snorkel where you would not swim without one, and to know how
to handle oneself in rough water. If there is a cross current on a
reef and the waves become rough, one often does better to dip the
face mask in than to fight the water.

It is reported that deaths among scuba divers generally occur
among young men or women in the prime of adulthood; a survey

has shown that almost always overestimation of ability, solo diving or diving at a distance from the partner, contributed to the tragedy. Other causes were lack of equipment, defective equipment, failure to provide proper safety devices, diving under adverse weather conditions, or diving when not in the best of health.

I had heard of the painful and sometimes fatal bends caused by an excess of nitrogen in the blood. This occurs when a diver surfaces too soon after a long dive and the nitrogen is released in the form of small bubbles of gas. In mild cases pain is felt in the back, legs and joints, accompanied by dizziness; in severe cases the capillaries are clogged and death may result. The bends may be avoided by proper decompression, either in a special chamber designed for this or by ascending gradually and waiting at the proper depths for the recommended length of time, permitting the blood to be cleared of the excess nitrogen in a normal fashion.

A hazard for the deep skindiver, not the scuba diver, has to do with his lungs. The air in the lungs is compressed as the free diver descends, and if the lungs become small enough as the depth is swiftly increased, the ribs may crack and collapse. If a scuba diver conversely comes too quickly to the surface so that the pressure is reduced suddenly and the expanding air in the lungs cannot find outlet through the nose or mouth, the lungs may rupture and occasionally the accident is fatal.

In the underwater world, it seems it is as often the top men who are drowned as the novices; every year champions in the field and experienced men are reported fished up unconscious or dead. Nitrogen narcosis, also called Rapture of the Depths, is considered a greater threat than a shark for a diver who descends below a hundred feet. The condition is thought to be due to a buildup of nitrogen in the body and its action upon the nervous system. There is no pain connected with narcosis, either when it comes upon the diver or later; it is simply that the senses are drugged as when breathing the commonly used anesthetic gas, nitrous oxide. Jacques Cousteau, pioneer-philosopher in the sport, once lost one of the great divers on his team, who was brought up from near four hundred feet, his mouthpiece hanging loose about his neck; it is thought he had believed that it was no longer needed. When Cousteau referred to the Rapture of the Depths, he said, "I love it and fear it like doom."

It was past noon when we swam back over the trail. The woman who had been in danger was on the beach and we retrieved the life preserver from her. We were hungry and Caneel Bay was less than two miles away. Ranger Zani told us that tours were conducted once a week on the plantation, going through the sugar mill ruins or walking about the grounds, discussing the history of the island as well as the natural aspects. There were facilities for guests—over a hundred double rooms in the beachfront units and cottages to accommodate two hundred persons or more. The dining terrace was in the open with small clothed tables and a buffet fit for a gourmet: hollowed pineapple shells filled with fruits and cornucopias overflowing with exotic produce, every sort of cold and hot meats and accompanying sauces, vegetables and starches. We filled our plates and returned for more.

Laurance S. Rockefeller in 1952 sailed into a harbor of St. John and was struck by the isolation and the beauty he found. Before long he had bought the Caneel Bay Plantation of over a hundred acres—including ten beaches—and was beginning to dream a dream. Jackson Hole Preserve is a nonprofit conservation and education organization established by the Rockefeller family with Laurance Rockefeller its president and having its headquarters in Wyoming. Jackson Hole itself is situated in Grand Teton National Park, where John D. Rockefeller, Jr., purchased thousands of acres which he presented to the American people. Through funds donated by the Rockefellers, Jackson Hole Preserve began to acquire land on St. John. When five thousand acres had been purchased, the minimum required for the establishment of a National Park, they were offered to the people of the United States who accepted and on the first of December 1956, the Virgin Islands National Park was established and dedicated. More land has gradually been acquired and the park property on St. John, St. Thomas and nearby rocks and cays, now totals 9485 acres. Caneel Bay Plantation is operated by Jackson Hole Preserve, and the National Park Service of the United States Department of the Interior administers the entire park. We gazed out at the white sand, the yachts, the palms, the green-blue water before us, grateful for one man's dream.

We started out then to see St. John under the aegis of Mr. Zani. The roads were bumpy and dusty; the vistas offered views of turquoise bays under brilliant skies full of motionless clouds, in the foreground hibiscus and bougainvillea. We noted that there was a Centerline Road for St. John as there was for St. Croix, which crossed the ridge of the sunken mountain overlooking the scenery below. St. John like St. Thomas is of volcanic origin so that the mountains are abrupt, the valleys deep. We saw a grey King Bird; Ranger Zani said that the Brown Booby and the Green Heron were common as was the Little Blue Heron, the Blue-winged Teal, the American Widgeon, the Red-tailed Hawk, the Gallinule, the Spotted Sandpiper, the Laughing Gull, the Royal Tern, the Mockingbird, the Bananaquit that we had seen on Buck Island, and the Antillean Crested Hummingbird.

We asked about land mammals, and Ranger Zani said that although the mongoose and the rat and others had been introduced, the only native mammals were bats and that six species had been identified including the rare Red Fig-eating Bat. We knew that bats were the only flying mammals and that they were considered beneficial, being insect hunters, and that some ate fruit and the nectar of flowers and one species caught fish lying just below the surface, using its sonar ability to do so. We knew that the bat was as extraordinary as the porpoise in its adaptation to its environment and its equipment for echolocation. The creature sends out a beam of ultrasonic orientation sounds of high intensity by which it measures the position of obstacles and prey by the echo reflected back between one and six yards away from it. The species vary in their production of the sound, most using a specialized larynx and making the noise by a movement of the tongue; some use the nose which has a special fold it can control. It is not known exactly what the mechanism is, but the bat can distinguish its own echo, even when it is a thousand times weaker than an interference sound. The large flexible ears, combined with the mammal's dexterous and rapid movements, enable it to accomplish its aim with impressive accuracy. When fine wires between one-tenth to one-hundredth of an inch were stretched before a group of bats, they swerved to avoid them at distances of less than three yards. We knew that certain moths had developed protective devices against this prime predator; one was their furry covering, not characteristic of the day-moving butterflies, which absorbs the sound the bat produces; another was their sensitivity to the flying animal's sonic cries, so that if struck by one, they will fold their wings and drop to the ground instantly. We had had a pet bat in our country home, finding her gentle and retiring, rather like the nocturnal sleek-furred flying squirrels commonly kept as pets, which also have the layer of loose skin along each side of the body from front to hind legs, unique to these two families of mammals, and which the squirrel uses when outstretched—not to fly but rather to glide from tree to tree.

The bats of St. John throve in the jungle-like hillsides which were a typical rain forest. The Bordeaux Mountains to the east were spectacular, the highest point 1277 feet. There were few large trees, as the original stands were removed mainly during the days of the sugar plantations. We saw the Kapok Tree resembling the Banyan, and the Genip Tree with fruit like grapes in clusters that Ranger Zani said were edible. He told us that the Turpentine tree which we had seen before was also called the Naked Indian for its red bark. There were Acacias and Mangos. Some roads seemed to follow old trails and some were new, hacked out in the fifties after the island's protector, Mr. Rockefeller, had come. We went over a steep road where a native was working, spreading gravel.

Mr. Zani called, "The first rain will wash that all down the hill!"

The worker shouted back, "Then we'll put it back again." He said it smiling, "Weeee-ll poot eeet bock," speaking in the vernacular Calypso English.

We went through Mangrove swamps and our guide said, "Those are red mangroves on the left and white ones on the right." We saw the Machineel tree, familiar now with its contour and with the small green fruit that Columbus had called Death Apples. When we stopped the car, we noted the same lizards that lived on our balcony at Yacht Haven. We photographed the termite lumps and saw coral vines growing about. Everywhere the Zenaida doves flew up before us. We had noted a skunk odor and asked Ranger Zani if the animal lived there. He explained that it was the Eugenia, of the myrtle family, *Myrtaceae,* an evergreen tree and shrub of the tropics which has over fifteen hundred species, many of which yield a fragrant oil. The genera *Eugenia* and *Pimenta* of this family are the source of popular spices—allspice and pimento and cloves which are the dried flower buds of *Eugenia aromatica*; the guava belongs to the family too. The fruit of *Eugenia* is edible and is used for jellies and confections by the West Indians. We saw a spiny sharp-leaved plant resembling a yucca, and he said it was called a wild date and that the island story was that in old days they used to plant them closely about houses to keep the slaves from slipping away. There were Calabash trees forty feet high with spreading branches and melon-like fruit, a foot or more across, the hard woody shells employed for water vessels. We noted the Hoop Vine, used by the natives to make their fish traps.

Turning back toward Cruz Bay, we took what we were told was an old Danish carriage road, and we observed the remains of the slave-laid cobblestones. We stopped to look over the Annaberg ruins at the north of St. John on a tall hill above Leinster Bay with its backdrop of white clouds and spattering of boats, most rocking in the calm with sails drawn, in the distance the blue British islands of Tortola and Jost van Dyke. We were intrigued to find a Self-guiding Historic Trail here, the leaflets explaining it stacked in a box at the beginning of a series of numbered stakes. There was a horse mill, a windmill, a cistern and a factory, slave quarters, store rooms, a still and handcuffs fastened to a post. We gazed at the tall mound of a stone mill and its yawning archway. There were no other tourists about and it was not difficult to conjure up the old-time noisy scene while the same breeze was blowing in from the sea.

St. John had been uninhabited by man at the time it was claimed by the Danes spilling over from St. Thomas about fifty years after they had landed there in the ship *Faerø*. The plantation colony of St. Thomas had appeared a success and it was in 1718 that twenty planters, a third of them Dutch, arrived to colonize St. John. They brought five soldiers and sixteen slaves with them to establish the second territory of *Dansk Vest-Indien*. Before long a fort was rising above Coral Bay and by 1733 a lieutenant, one corporal and six soldiers manned it. There were stone windmills and treadmills everywhere, over a hundred planters settled in and all of St. John's tillable land was put into sugar and cotton. Because the island's well-being depended upon sugar cane and the factories converting it into raw sugar and molasses and rum, slaves were the basis of the culture, shortly far outnumbering the whites, over a thousand to the white population of two hundred.

The time was ripe for a violent insurrection of the captives, many half-starved; there had been a long drought and two hurricanes and an insect plague to compound the difficulties of the ambitious planters. And so on a hot morning in November of 1733, over a dozen of them gained entrance to the fort and murdered all but one within. A wave of destruction began. Armed with pistols, cane knives and flintlocks, the slave army grew to eighty. Planters were cut down and the mills and great houses burned. Everyone that was able fled to Caneel Bay Plantation, then the property of Peter Durlieu. With the aid of cannon, the uprising was held off; the women and children were put into boats and sent to St. Thomas. The men followed; for six months the slaves remained in possession of St. John. The planters asked for help from the English on nearby Tortola who cooperated by going along with parties to St. John to hunt down, capture or kill the fugitives. But the rebels, using guerrilla techniques, seemed to be holding their own. Then the Danes appealed to the French colony on Martinque, over two hundred miles down in the archipelago, and a ship arrived in Charlotte Amalie harbor carrying two hundred men. In a month's time, with the aid of the Frenchmen and their Creole soldiers, ruthless and persistent, the insurrection was quelled. It was said that the Negro leaders stood in a circle near the Annaberg Sugar Mill and each man shot the man beside him.

The assistance sent by the Martinique French was due to their private knowledge that a treaty between their king and the Danish West India and Guinea Company, not yet public, had been signed on the fifteenth of June, nearly five months before the November revolt, in which the merchant group paid 750,000 *livres* for St. Croix to the south. The King of France had been assured that the United Crown of Denmark and Norway would stand neutral and not interfere in his approaching war with Poland.

St. Croix's settlement was at once begun by the enthusiastic Danes and that agricultural island prospered, twenty years later coming under the crown officially as the third of the islands to compose the Danish West Indies. St. John never fully recovered after the slave insurrection, although many of the planters returned and rebuilt their estates. Neither St. John nor St. Thomas, of different geologic formation, had the fine soil of St. Croix. St. Thomas grew rich because of its superior harbor and its location as a center of shipping; St. John, of rugged terrain and much smaller, had none of their assets. When Governor General Peter von Scholten, in love with Anna Heegaard, stood on the balcony of Fort Frederik and declared the emancipation of all unfree slaves in July 1848, it was the death knell of the era. The year of 1867 ran its course of disease and natural disaster by smashing storm and earthquake, and then the jungle slowly took over St. John. On the seventeenth of January 1917, along with her sister islands, St. John was bought by the United States for twenty-five million dollars.

Thirty-five years later, Laurance S. Rockefeller sailed into one of
her bays and the present era began.

On our return to Cruz Bay, as we jolted over the roads, we saw a
notice that one could follow the foot trail to Petroglyph Falls and
see the Indian Rock Carvings. We were returned to a time long
before the restless white men had gazed at the Sea That Led To
The Wealth Of The Indies and sailed forth. The Arawak Indians,
agricultural and peaceful by nature, had once lived on St. John and
others of the Virgin Islands, and it is thought that these carvings
mark what had been a sacred shrine of theirs. On the arrival of
Columbus, the Caribs had been busy for a century subduing and
enslaving and wiping out their fellow Red Men, the Arawaks, of
another stock and with different mores. The Caribs were from the
south, excellent sailors of canoes and pirogues, and had been over-
running the Lesser Antilles in the way that Columbus' followers
would do in time. They imprinted their young on the rites of
scarification and fasting and the practice of cannibalism; the White
Man managed to practically exterminate them in turn, in about
the same span of a century.

It was close to five o'clock when we returned to the Park Entrance at Cruz Bay. We were grateful to Ranger Richard Zani, who
gave us brochures and let us take home a twelve-page paper he had
compiled that was a partial checklist of the marine fishes found in
and around St. John, which included common as well as scientific
names, and which we wished to have Xeroxed. The white sails were
up on vessels in the bay that were planning to return to St. Thomas
and our Captain Williams and his relatives were waiting on the
dock. As the skipper had predicted, the ride home needed all his
skills as he piloted us against the long running tidal waves across
Pillsbury Sound, the boat spanking into the sea for ten miles and
the water calming only just before reaching Charlotte Amalie
harbor.

At Yacht Haven, we found a message from Dr. Floyd Mowry,
that if we were not busy, he would like to show us another supper
place. While Barney called to arrange the time and to say that it

was our party, I rinsed off our diving gear and the camera, which we had been instructed to let dry before opening. I discovered a disaster: when I had removed the plug with the "o" ring sealer on the bottom of the camera, in order to put on the adapter and the flash attachment and photograph our friend, the Cruzan bartender, at the Club Comanche, I had neglected to replace them. The inside of the underwater camera was wet with salt water. I threw away the film and reported the event to Barney. He rinsed the camera out and recommended taking it to a shop on our return to Cleveland for repair.

Again we found ourselves on a mountainous road and were walking up steep steps to a breezy restaurant. We were seated in the open-air terrace under dim lights, with the panorama of Charlotte Amalie spread below. We ordered steamed and broiled fresh-caught wahoo and Spanish mackerel. Afterwards we returned to the Yacht Haven bar, reluctant to leave these islands. Dr. Mowry finally went home around one-thirty, but we stayed on, discovering that one of the entertainers was an admirer of my folksong-collector father, and he insisted upon handing over his guitar part of the time and calling for a family song. Equally firm, I rendered the Imprintation Song also, feeling that it too had an ethnic quality.

In the morning we collected our possessions and took a direct four-hour flight to New York's Kennedy Airport where we would transfer to Cleveland. I slept all the way for I had a monumental hangover, being more experimental with the local rum than Barney. Our light coats were crumpled in the bottom of one of the duffle bags. I was wearing a sleeveless dress and a sweater; an icy wind whipped about the corner of the terminal as we came out to hail a taxi to our next point of departure. The driver got into a temper when we told him, after he had started the cab, we were going to another part of the airport. We gazed at him in astonishment.

"Now I'll have to get at the end of the line again," he cried in a rage. "I've been waiting all morning for a fare. There ought to be a law!"

Unused to strong voices, chilled, we agreed. "We'll pay more," we offered, mild, but he was too stirred for reply.

As the next plane took us to our home, we talked of returning to the national parks of the islands. I felt that I would advise a visitor as innocent as myself to beware of camera attachments, unless one were a vigilant person, and of the local Cruzan rum and the fruit.

CHAPTER THIRTEEN

The Fog-Bound Coast

There is a pleasure in the pathless woods,
There is a rapture on the lonely shore,
There is society, where none intrudes,
By the deep Sea, and Music in its roar.

— Lord Byron: "Childe Harold's Pilgrimage"

IT was almost November, chill and sunny and clear when we boarded a plane for Oregon. Barney had medical dates in Klamath Falls and San Francisco and San Diego and Los Angeles, and I was invited along. We left Paula in charge of the various animals in our town house and The Unicorn's Lair garden. She drove us to the airport, Gustav, the huge black crossbred dog, in the back seat. Our trip would take twelve days and it was our opportunity to see the marine life refuges off the California coast. We would rent a car at Klamath Falls and go down through the redwood country and along the coastal route. After Barney's talk in San Francisco we would fly to San Diego and then drive up the coast to the Channel Islands National Monument and then to Los Angeles and home.

I had never been to the West Coast before and looked forward to it. Barney had been stationed in San Diego for two years at the end of World War II; he was familiar with the Pacific, and in the kelp beds there and along the shore had taken some of the first under-

water movies made, his camera encased in a rubber rebreather bag
from an anesthetic machine and the light meter in a Mason jar.
That was long before the advent of Cousteau and the present pro-
ponents of the diving sport. Barney ran off some of his early reels
for Paula and myself in the Red Room and we were startled at the
deep blue of the water, the greenness of the eel grass, the somber
wavering kelp where the Garibaldi swam by like distorted golden-
red flames. Barney said the kelp beds were to that coast what the
coral reefs were to tropical waters, providing a haven for marine
life. The theme was on a grand scale; whereas there were brilliant
often minute reef fish in coral-protected lagoons, in kelp, which
sometimes grew as tall as the redwoods, were large neutral-shaded
ones and not far off sometimes, monstrous California Gray
Whales. As the film flickered on, we saw more than a thousand
Western Gulls flutter up into a startlingly sunny sky and as many
seals humped upon the long rocky shore of one of the Coronados
Islands.

I packed our masks in the duffle bag with our binoculars and
books; we felt that the weather would be so cold we would likely
not go under. If we did, I would need my special faceplate and we
could always rent flippers. The camera we took along was fit for
shots above water only. When I had taken the underwater camera
to our shop and reported the disaster which occurred at St. John,
the man opened it and gazed in and shook his head, saying it
would cost as much to repair as to purchase a new one, so I gave
it to him to keep. When the photographs that were taken during
the time the salt water entered were developed, they had grotesque
streams flowing down the middles of them, but I placed them in
the album along with previous ones anyway, feeling that they gave
the account a dramatic touch.

We had written Secretary Stewart Udall of our coming trip and
had been advised that the National Park Service administered another marine area beside the Channel Islands National Monument, which would be of special interest to us—the Point Reyes
National Seashore just above San Francisco, which also contained

some underwater areas. The Channel Islands National Monument, we were informed, included two of the eight islands—Anacapa and Santa Barbara. The Superintendent of the Cabrillo National Monument in San Diego was in immediate charge of the Channel Islands National Monument, and we would see him about Rangers to guide us there. Transportation was to be arranged privately and boats were available for charter at the harbor near Oxnard. Few visitors came to the undeveloped islands; no accommodations or services were available; camping was permitted on Anacapa, but one must bring a supply of water and fuel and food as well as tents, since the island was famous for strong winds and varying weather. There were no telephones or public radios, but from the last week in June through Labor Day a Ranger was in residence and could communicate with the mainland in case of emergency by radio-phone.

Klamath Falls is just to the east of the great Cascade Mountain Range that is bordered by lakes and ponds and is one of the important flyways of the country. We were up every morning before dawn and our hosts and Barney shot tiny Blue-winged Teal and fat Canvas-backs, which flocked on the lakes and nearby marshes by the ten thousand along with Redheads, Scaup, Ruddy Duck, Gadwalls, Baldpates, Pintails, Mergansers, Mallards. The men took their catch to the terrace and plucked the teal and filetted the tough-feathered canvas-backs, the mountains standing blue in the distance. One dawn the season was open on pheasants too. We served the birds for every meal including breakfast, first pouring over melted butter and seasoning them and broiling them rare. I had no experience with a gun and my mending wrist gave me a valid excuse for not ever shooting again. But I always went out with Barney into the cold sunrise of the wet reedy swamp, valuing any purpose that took us there. I felt too, as we feasted on what they brought down from the sky, that their controlled act was like harvesting corn and not dangerous or offensive.

When the meeting was over in three days and we were breakfasting for the last time, one of the family spotted a small creature meandering along on the terrace, resembling a large rat, dark brown with a long hairless tail. Barney went out to catch the baby muskrat that had left its home too early and would be an easy prey for the hunting dogs of our host. We decided to take the mammal along with us and imprint it and bring it home for a companion for the capybaras. We called it Stewart Udall and it settled down in my hunting cap, content. We found Stewart amiable as we traveled and gave him crusts and fruit and salad when we stopped to eat. We obtained a box for him when we found that he liked to burrow under the car seat, a characteristic we had already observed with our house woodchucks, Sergo and Katrin.

I found the giant *Sequoia sempervirens* on U.S. Route 101 down the coast astounding. I knew that a century ago there had been two million acres of redwood forests from Oregon to San Francisco, and today less than a sixth remained. When we were having lunch at a roadside café, we heard a phrase that we were to hear more than once on our journey, "When you've seen one redwood, you've seen them all!" Up and down the highways we would overtake or find roaring toward us upon a massive semi-truck two or three sections of a single felled tree. We knew that the government in Washington was proposing a Redwood National Park which would encompass a particular watershed so that these Kings of Trees in that area could be maintained in a balanced ecology. We wished the conservationists luck, thinking of the situation of the Everglades. The government wanted also to preserve a little park, now owned by the Arcata Redwood Company, the Tall Trees Unit, where the world's giants were, over three hundred and fifty feet tall.

We drove through the misty cathedral-like forests, the sun streaming through lending to the unearthly feeling, where there were a few quiet tourists now and then and the trails were well-marked. Sometimes we saw deer in small groups on the bordering hillsides. Whenever there was a sign saying THE WORLD'S LARGEST TREE, we turned off the route. An elderly man would come out of an ancient cabin and direct us down a one-way pitted road where we would find a hand-painted sign nailed at a monster's base. We would photograph ourselves minuscule before the wonder. All through the afternoon, we seemed to pass through a tunnel of red-woods, many groves bearing the name of a private donor; these trees were a veneer, behind them usually the original timber-stripped land, sometimes being rehabilitated by a modern lumber company.

We stopped at an inn overnight, requesting a tub not a shower as our Stewart enjoyed it so much, swimming about me with enthusiasm, his brown fur appearing black when wet. We came down to the bar before our dinner bringing Stewart, dried and sleek in his cap, and found it full of energetic loggers, many of them young men, and wished that Paula were along. The man beside us, stocky, crew-cut, in a fresh white shirt and khakis, nodded, and Barney asked about his attitude toward the government's proposed park and he was all for it. He said that most of the lumbermen were, and that all they objected to was being censured by conservationists who viewed their living as immoral and unpatriotic.

He struck the bar with his fist. "My daddy was a logger and I was raised in a camp and it's all I know. My company's got all sorts of laboratories. We send men out to take cuttings and sprouts from the giants and use them in our selective breeding program to grow the fastest trees."

"How is it getting along?" Barney asked.

"Great. Take a look at the replanted areas while you folks are driving through." He peered around Barney at Stewart Udall dozing in my cap. "What's she doing with that rat?"

"It's a mascot," Barney said, "a baby muskrat. This is my wife."

"How do you do? Wait till I tell my wife. But don't let him out around here or he'll get into trouble and the tree-lovers will blame it on us!"

"How fast do the young redwoods grow?" I asked him.

"The point is," he said, "that there's an optimum time for harvesting timber and you've got to know when it is. After a certain point the tree's growth slows down. Our company's experimenting on finding it, and what's the best rotation system too and how thick to put the seedlings in. I'll say that dollar for dollar lumber's spending more on preservation of trees for the future than conservationists who want to keep all those old-timers around forever." He was fierce and hit the bar again.

"I've never seen so many big trees in my life," I said, placating.

"When you've seen one redwood, you've seen them all," Barney grinned.

In the morning, as we continued on our way, the fog was becoming thick and the sun disappearing into it. We turned into a primeval forest where our feet made no sound on the carpet of needles and our voices were muted by the vast foliage so high above. There was a wide stream which flowed in rapids and pools, and we took Stewart Udall from the car. After he drank, he wandered along the bank, pleased, and then waded in. We watched him dive and disappear and waved goodbye, fond, regretful of losing the creature's company, but feeling that the decision was his.

The fog still engulfed us as we took State Highway 1 which was uneven and bordered the shore and went down through Mendocino and then Sonoma County. Breakers rolled steadily and we could hear them when the Pacific was shrouded in the mist. We knew that certain shores lent themselves to spectacular pounding, that northward at Tillamook Rock, Oregon, a formidable stone weighing over a hundred pounds had been hurled by the waves into the air and through the roof of the lighthouse-keeper's home and that smaller ones had been tossed higher yet and even through the windows of the lighthouse itself, breaking them, and that a steel grating had had to be placed about the beacon. Further down the coast between Los Angeles and Santa Barbara, whole popular beaches had been moved away sometimes over a few years leaving rocky areas and clogging harbors. It is the movement of sand and stone by the action of the waves that causes the continual reformation of coastlines. Even on an inland water like Lake Michigan that I knew well, in the summers the gentle lapping carried the sand from the underwater slope upon the shore which made the beach build up, extending toward the lake; in autumn the storms would begin that continued through the winter, the surf pulling the sand back to the original slope of the bottom. Breakers are termed either "plungers" or "spillers." If the wave occurs on a gentle slope, the roll will continue for a long distance before breaking and these "spillers" are the delight of surfboard riders. The plunging breaker is born on a slope that is abrupt, and it is the kind that hurled the great stone through the Tillamook Rock Light.

About thirty miles before we reached San Francisco, we turned in at Point Reyes Station on the Sir Francis Drake Highway to view Point Reyes National Seashore as the Parks Department had recommended. We knew that it was here that the English Admiral, the first of his nation to sail around the world, had put in to repair the *Golden Hinde* before setting out across the vast western-stretching ocean in 1579. And we knew that a few years later Spaniards had come north from Mexico and had anchored in the same harbor calling it *Puerto de los Reyes,* Port of Kings. We followed the road to the promontory where the lighthouse was, wanting to look at Drake's Bay, but the fog concealed all and a chill wind blew. At the end of the point a large herd of sea lions were said to have their base, but we neither heard nor saw any. There were over fifty thousand acres in the site and we were impressed with the theme of undisturbed preservation rather than that of a vacation-land. Feelings of awe and the sense of history in the tourist were appealed to rather than sensuous emotions of self-gratification.

As we drove slowly on to San Francisco, the fog cleared but little. There we rode a cable car, climbed the steep streets, and went up the Mark Hopkins Hotel elevator to "The Top Of The Mark" that Barney had known in the days of the war's beginning and wanted me to see, gazing out, knowing that I for one would never view the Golden Gate Bridge which spanned the fog-bound Bay below. When Barney's lectures were over that night and late into the next morning, we had two days to spend before catching the plane to San Diego, and we took the road toward the Monterey peninsula where Point Lobos Reserve State Park was situated on the south shore of Carmel Bay. The fog had lifted somewhat and with it my hopes that we might photograph the rocky coastline the next day, as well as the colonies of Northern and California Sea Lions for which the park was named.

We lunched at mid-afternoon in Monterey on the breakwater, splitting plates of abalone steaks that we could cut with a fork and that tasted very like scallops, and black-shelled mussels sautéed in butter, their flesh orange-tinted, with cold ale on the side. There was a flock of sea lions out on the pier fifty yards from us, so tame that men were walking close by them. The waiter said they were there all year round and that the fishermen went about their business and occasionally threw fish and food out to the beasts, liking them and considering their presence good luck for the community. We listened to their barking and watched their sinuous movements. Barney was telling me about the abalones he had used to gather about the Coronados Islands during World War II.

Civilians had not been allowed to visit the Coronados because they were in Mexican waters, but Barney, who went there with a Navy recreation expedition sometimes, found hundreds of abalones growing just below the low tide level. Many would be coated with hydroids and plants but others would be swept clean by the surf and the iridescence of their mother-of-pearl lining would gleam like a jewel through the shell. I had seen them in the old movie reels he projected. Barney said that the abalone probably had more solid steak in proportion to body weight than any other creature of the sea. Its defense was to clamp onto a rock behind its shell using a muscled foot which was a chunk of hard white meat, six inches or more in diameter and several inches thick. Our steaks were tender and Barney claimed the method he used was to slice the muscle thin, pound it to break up and soften the fibers, keep it in a refrigerator for a day, then dip it in egg yolk and cracker crumbs and fry for a few seconds in very hot fat.

After a while we walked around Monterey, and I sang the song for Barney that my father had taught me back in the twenties when my sisters and I were small and had never heard of an abalone outside of the verses. My father had said that in Monterey there were pyramids of abalone shells stacked high, and that it was a world capital of abalone; at the lunch counters it was a favorite dish and the shells made shirt buttons by the carload. He told us the Lazzaroni were the homeless beggars of Naples.

> *In Carmel Bay the people say,*
> *We feed the Lazzaroni*
> *On caramels and cockle-shells*
> *And hunks of abalone.*
>
> *Oh, some folks boast of quail on toast*
> *Because they think it's tony,*
> *But my tom-cat gets nice and fat*
> *On hunks of abalone!*

We drove the few miles to the village of Carmel to look for a room for the night. I was beginning to sneeze and had a slight chill and felt that a long sleep might cure it. We found a place before too long, old-fashioned, overlooking the ocean, and with a warm bed. I had no aspirin and Barney said he would find some and get a newspaper and look at the town. I settled in to record the day in our journal and to doze. When Barney returned bearing a bunch of flowers, he was enthusiastic. He had been talking to towns-people and visitors and expected that we would see some otters the next day.

I was wakeful in the night, hearing Barney's light breathing and out in the dark the fog horns blowing. I thought of Drake and the early Spanish explorers sighting Carmel Bay from their ships, certain parties entering and camping by the *Río del Carmelo* and naming the *Punta de los Lobos Marinos,* Point of the Sea Wolves, three miles up the coast for the barking sea lions that I almost felt I heard along with the fog horns. There had been vast numbers of Sea Otters out there then, four feet in length including their foot-long tail, weighing up to eighty pounds, a glossy brownish-black, their feet webbed and resembling flippers. The sea otter was discovered by shipwrecked Russians in 1741 and almost at once their slaughter became organized and supported the fur trade. When the United States bought Alaska from the Russians in 1867 the rate of hunting increased, so that by the turn of the century the animal had become rare; ships that had brought back thousands of pelts were finding a dozen and the creature was believed practically extinct. In 1911 a treaty was signed by our country, England, Russia and Japan, outlawing the capture or killing of the sea otter. Twenty years later, rumors were bruited that the creatures had been seen in the kelp off the coast of California, and by 1938 a colony of close to a hundred was discovered just off the shore of Monterey where we had seen the tame sea lions on the fishermen's wharf.

Out there now were the sleek mammals, some of which we hoped to view riding the swells with their young on their stomachs, crooning to them as they are said to do. The creature spends much of its time in the kelp beds, coming onto shore only to ride out severe storms. They feed on sea urchins and shellfish—clams and the red abalone on which we had feasted, *Haliotis rufescens;* able to dive over two hundred feet down, they bring the food to the surface, sometimes with a stone with which to smash it. They have been seen rocking in the kelp, stuffing the morsels into their mouths.

In the morning I wore a sweater, though Barney went in his shirtsleeves, for it was cold and misty, the fog having thinned with the November sunrise. On the way to the park we saw a buck deer with spreading antlers on the grassy center strip of highway at one point trotting back and forth while cars went by; we felt the danger if the nervous creature were there in fog or dark, and admired his beauty. At the Park Headquarters' entrance, we spoke with the Reserve Supervisor, Mr. Don Rich, after we bought a ticket for fifty cents each. He said he had just been up to the coast and had seen fifty to sixty of the otters and that sometimes he could hear the babies crying in the kelp while the parents were fishing for them. The fog had lifted enough to view the sea lions also, and he recommended using our binoculars. Then he warned us of the fire hazard and against smoking except in the car and pointed the way.

The first turn-off led to Whaler's Cove that faced the mainland and Cannery Point looking out to Carmel Bay. Picnic tables were behind the rocks that outlined the parking lot. Back in 1861, the cove was full of small fishing boats and its banks with buildings for Portuguese whalers who had used it for their base. Not far inland was Whalers Knoll from which the once-abundant California Gray Whale, *Eschrichtius glaucus,* had been spotted as they migrated between the Bering Sea and their breeding and calving lagoons along the coast of Baja California and the water of southern California. When the quarry was harpooned and killed, forty tons and forty feet long, it would be towed into this cove and hauled up with the tackle and derricks, using rings set in the rocks. Iron caldrons were heated in stone pits, the oil was boiled off, smoke filled the air, flames hissed; we felt the old-time scene.

By 1884 the whaling industry was abandoned and Chinese fishermen huts began to appear along Whalers Cove. Before long an abalone cannery had been established. Imported Japanese fishermen, wearing wooden goggles and with nets roped about their waists, fished in ten-foot-deep water. The heaps of shells which remained could still be viewed. It was said that a man could sit on an underwater rock then and not change his position and fill a large basket with the red abalones, up to a foot long, selling for fifty cents a dozen. Now we knew that a lucky diver harvested a basketful in an hour, and that seven inches was the minimum that might be collected by law. We knew too that the Fish and Game Department had prohibited the shells being taken from the state and that nevertheless the species was being depleted.

A carful of tourists drove up and parked. Two couples got out, familiar with the place, the women with a bag of popcorn each. They went to the edge of the lot where Beechey Ground Squirrels came from their burrows to meet them. We asked and the men said that they came often to feed the delicate mammals, who numbered near two thousand in the entire park area; they accepted the blown kernels turning them over and over in their forepaws, nibbling. In a moment a pair of Western gulls, white with grey wings, yellow-beaked, and their immature dark-plumaged baby, lit nearby and began to beg from the women also, rushing after the popcorn. The baby, larger than its parents, kept bowing and squawking and trailing after them. The years of protection of the Point Lobos area had taught these creatures that they might associate freely with man.

The tourists spoke of the Monterey cypress for which the area was famous, containing the last primitive stand of that tree. The need for the preservation of the cypress, like the redwood, had been a strong factor in the fight the conservationists made to retain this park which now included 1250 acres. It had been established in 1933. The cannery had already been taken down, woods grew up where busy dwelling-places had stood and gradually the park trails were established. We drove down the one that led to Cypress Grove and Sea Lion Point, attractive weather-worn signs advising COL-LECTING PROHIBITED and that this included driftwood or shells, rocks or fossils. Visitors were to stay on the trails, to leash their pets, and, as at Point Reyes National Seashore, one understood the purpose of this park was to preserve the essentially primitive character of the place for the future.

As we shut the motor off in the car, we understood the name the Spaniards had given the creatures over the headland, for we heard them baying out of the fog beyond, sounding like a pack of wolves in pursuit of prey or the cries of a high-flying flock of Canada Geese. Carrying binoculars and camera, we went up the steep path, the mist from the sea blowing in steadily, the ground squirrels watching from their rocks as we passed, a brush rabbit loping before. I shivered as we came over the headland to the surf-charged coast. I knew that swimming was restricted to China Cove to the south, but that skin divers might come with a permit for observation or research and that the reserve contained 750 acres of submerged land. The breakers crashed below us; Sea Palms, *Postelsia,* of the phylum *Phaeophyta,* shining-plant, which is the brown algae group, clung to the rocks, their flexible stems flattened by the surge and rising again to their tiny palm shape when the breakers receded. This is the family which includes the Sargasso weed that breeds in the Caribbean but is broken off in storm and carried to the Sargasso Sea by the Gulf Stream. The kelp is the most spectacular of the brown algae—the West Coast beds famous for their thick growth which provides a haven for great numbers of fish as well as the sea otter. In the movies Barney had run off, I had noted the young Criles swimming in the long tendrils of bladder kelp, *Nereocystis,* and the kelp called Sea Pumpkin, *Pelagophycus,* and the vine kelp, *Macrocyctis,* with the typical buoyant air-floats along the stems. I had seen Barney trying to tear the tough tendrils. He said that if one got knotted about a diver, he must learn to keep his head, hold his breath and undo it before he can surface. The trick of swimming through kelp, sometimes seemingly tons of it, when a surge brings it over, is not to flail about, which knots it around one, but to hold the palms together over the head and go up through it, propelling oneself by the flippers, so that the kelp slithers off.

About the headland on which we stood and along the cliffs and shoreline were the Monterey Cypresses, a relic of the Pleistocene Age and found nowhere else in the world. It is a tree of vigor and tenacity; flat-topped, gnarled and weathered, it clung to the rocky cliffs overhanging the sea, resisting storm and salt-spray, dark green against the chaparral. The alien-seeming cypresses, the precipitous cliffs honeycombed with caves, the sea far below surging into the canyons and breaking upon the offshore rocks, seemed to lend to this moment a sense of timelessness as if the spot had not changed through the eons since it emerged out of the sea.

The yapping was continual beyond, out in the mists of *Punta de los Lobos Marinos.* We looked down into Devils Cauldron, avoided by seagoing humans, and next to it Sea Lion Cove. Barney was using the binoculars, examining the peaks which reared unevenly from the rushing sea. He handed them to me.

"There," he said.

And I saw them clearly with the glasses, brown against the black rock, one with nose to the sky, swaying his trunk and neck back and forth, lower down a gigantic male, motionless with reared head silhouetted vaguely against the sea. There were two species and they seemed lumped together almost as if lying on top of each other. Seals compose the order *Pinnipedia,* fin-feet, and there are three families: the walrus, *Odobenidae,* distinguished by its size and large white tusks and almost hairless hide, native to the Arctic; the seals with external ears, *Otariidae;* and the seals without them, *Phocidae.* To the latter family belong the common Harbor Seal and the great Elephant Seal. They are short-necked and must wriggle along on land as they cannot turn their rear flippers forward; there is not much disparity of size in the sexes. The sea lions that we were viewing all had small external ears, could stand erect on their large front flippers and also rotate their rear flippers forward so they could be said to walk on land.

The California Sea Lion is brown, black when wet, has a high forehead and is inclined to continually bark. They are six to eight feet long, the bulls sometimes weighing six hundred pounds and distinguished from the cows by their thick necks and sometimes being four times their size. The Northern or Stellar's Sea Lion males may reach over thirteen feet and weigh a ton. Besides their greater size, they differ from their fellow species in being yellowish-brown with low foreheads, their calls deep-toned, infrequent, and resembling lowing of cattle rather than barking of wolves.

We photographed the cragged rocks, the cypresses, the swirling crashing waves that sometimes wet the sea lions on the topmost part of the rock. Then we returned to our car to follow the park road to China Cove where we wanted to see Bird Island, the northernmost breeding grounds of the Brown Pelican. We saw what seemed a thousand of them, for it was the migrating season and many had come up from lower California and Mexico. No boats are permitted near the tiny rocky island for fear of disturbing the birds, which whiten it with guano. There is a small population of Pelagic and a great many Brandt Cormorants, most numerous of all ocean birds on Point Lobos Reserve. Barney had been told in Carmel last night that the noise made by low-flying jets often frightened the Brown Pelicans from their nests, which are completed in April, and by May the one to three eggs are being incubated. When the intimidated parent birds left, the gulls would come in and devour the eggs. It seemed that it took very little to disturb the precarious balance of nature.

An elderly couple wearing tweeds and walking boots, with binoculars in hand, were observing Bird Island. They told us that they came here every year to study the Point Lobos flora and fauna and were avid nature students. They advised us that they had just been watching some sea otters for the past hour in the kelp beds between Bird Island and Sea Lion Point. They said they had seen one of them crack an abalone on its stomach with a stone, tuck the latter under its arm and dive below for another shellfish, saving the tool. The otter did this repeatedly, the enthusiastic couple said, showing that it was no accident, and they felt it demonstrated the intelligence of the sub-anthropoid mammal, and we agreed. They said too that in the years they had been spotting sea otters, the creature's aversion to land was clear and if one were washed up by a wave, it would hurry at once back into the sea.

We went where they pointed, hurrying. After gazing with and without binoculars at the rolling surf and the swelling sea, at length we saw our first sea otters, a female on her back in the kelp in typical pose, a pup on her belly. We watched them awhile and then drove back along the road, stopping at China Cove too to search for more of the sea creatures. A group was diving and playing a short distance from shore and reminded us of our capybaras as a pair rose simultaneously, facing each other and embracing a moment before submerging. There was another sea otter mother too, with a youngster clinging to her. We counted sixteen in all in the kelp. We stopped to speak with Mr. Rich, as we left the park entrance, to tell him how we admired the conservation practices that had made the trip memorable. We mentioned the otters we had watched and the sea lions. He said that on quiet summer

nights he could hear the latter here at his house beside the Headquarters, particularly the bass voice of the Northern Sea Lion.

We headed back to the village for another night at our old-
fashioned hotel, planning to be on the road early. Barney was due
at the meeting in San Diego at two the next afternoon and we had
a plane to catch. My cold was better, but I was glad to return to the
comfortable room. We left Carmel at seven, the fog thick upon the
road. Barney drove as fast as he felt was safe and I read aloud from
a novel we had brought along to distract myself. By the time we
had dropped off our rented car at the airport, we had to run for the
plane. In San Diego there was some misunderstanding about our
reservation at the Rent-a-Car booth, holding us up, and afterwards
we had trouble finding the parking entrance at the huge modern
hotel. I held the car at the curb until Barney found someone to
park it for us, and then we hurried to the desk.

The clerk gazed at us mildly while Barney spoke impatiently,
"My wife will check us in. Just tell me where the meeting is!"

He shook his head and ruffled through his cards again. "I'm
afraid the meeting isn't until tomorrow, doctor. You're a day early
and your room's occupied. We're full. Would you like me to call
another hotel?"

"Really?" we said. "Look again."

But it was true and Barney was pleased. "Have you ever been to
the Baja California part of Mexico? We'll drive down to Ensenada
and stay overnight and come back in the morning. Do you want
to?"

"The fog's confused us," I told the clerk.

He found the man to bring back our car and waved us off.
"Happy days, folks!"

We felt we were escaping the bad weather, for as we moved
southward the sun made its way through the mists and we gazed at
the blue sky again. At the border we sped down the cluttered
streets and past the flesh pots of Tijuana; the customs men waved
us through and the sun glistened on the highway ahead. We could
see the jagged outline of the Coronados' rocky peaks out at sea,

that Barney said were of the same original mountain chain which made up the Channel Islands. The road skirted the high cliffs that dropped off occasionally onto caves into which the swells of the Pacific rolled and broke green and foaming on the glistening sand beach. There were long stretches as we continued on the coastal road, where the cliffs fell directly into the caldron of foam below among the black sharp rocks. During the war Barney had tried to dive for lobster and abalone here, giving it up because he had been bruised and scratched unduly on the rocks by "plunger" waves.

We sang as we drove along, feeling the introspection that often accompanies rain or fog leaving us. At five we stopped at the Rosarita Hotel, almost closed down as it was out of season, our footsteps echoing in the tiled and marbled and decorated rooms, the one for dining filled with tiny tables, and out to the bar that looked to the seascape. We ordered Margueritas, the specialty of Baja, made with tequila distilled from the juice of the Mexican century plant of the Amaryllis family, tasting as if flavored with motor oil, I felt. The Mexicans who relished the apéritif endeavored to conceal its origins, I thought, by frosting the rim of the glass with salt before filling it. Stubborn, I would drink one in the evening too, feeling it was the wine of the country and must not be ignored.

Suddenly I pointed up the coast. "Look!"

There it was, rolling down from the north after us, in ten minutes engulfing the sun and continuing south—the fog. On the road again, we made Ensenada by twilight. We strolled about as night came on and lights blinked in the warm mist. We purchased a small guitar to take when we traveled and a Mexican dress that I would wear in the country in the summers. We liked the town where the tourists were few and the people smiled easily. For breakfast we ate *huevos rancheros,* which the waiter said was the only item worth eating—fried eggs with a red pepper sauce, refried Mexican beans, and thin browned ham, all served on flat Mexican tortillas, made with unleavened cornmeal. The morning was hot with no breeze; we drove back to San Diego over the desert land, pleased with the gift of the extra day. The same clerk was at the desk.

"And did you go to Ensenada, doctor?"

I showed him the guitar. "See?"

Barney's meeting was over late in the next afternoon and I had the car packed and waiting. We had three more days of vacation and Barney's talk in Los Angeles was on the last. We were going to La Jolla ten miles up the coast, to stay at the Beach and Tennis Club. Then we would drive to the Cabrillo Monument in the morning on San Diego Bay, where the Superintendent was in charge of the Channel Islands National Monument. We would arrange with him for Rangers to guide us and the chartering of a boat.

We checked into our rooms at La Jolla—a kitchen, living room and two bedrooms, spare and old with sink and stove and utensils designed to accommodate a family, the windows looking into the fog-cloaked sea, a hundred yards away. Barney, nostalgic, declared that there was no beach on the Pacific coast so sheltered, calm and strikingly beautiful beneath the overhanging cliffs where the cormorants and gulls roosted, and with its rocky sea-swept stretches and its tidewater areas that he had found so rich in octopus and lobster and marine life! He said that at La Jolla cove there was an underwater cave where tourists could visit and we would go there. And he would call a friend of his in the morning, Dr. Hankins, who had a boat and might be persuaded to take us out to look at the Coronados Islands so like the Channel Islands to the north in their ecology.

As night fell, we walked in the fog up the beach to the restaurant built almost upon the water's edge. The lights shining out illuminated the wavering shoreline where the water flowed in and retreated and in the space between small flocks of Sanderlings ran, a kind of sandpiper, whitish, plump, with a wingstripe, on stilted legs, feeding. The waitress told us that in the morning we might see the tame California sea lion that frequented the area, swim-

ming with the children often and coming up on shore sometimes.

Later we returned along the sand again, carrying our shoes, the
silical grains cold, listening to the washing water and the occasional
distant foghorns. Barney said, "I might write a poem when we get
in." And he did.

We walked tonight along Pacific sand
In the breaking surf of the fogbound shore,
Where the spring tide was drawing out the waves,
Leaving the land strewn with the spawn of the sea.

Flights of Sanderlings in a patch of light
Dodged the waves or caught the gifts they gave;
The air had sent the birds to limit the hatch;
There was a balance there in all we saw.

Hand in hand we witnessed the display
Of serenity in life and sea and sky;
We thought on needless troubles in our town
And felt perhaps we knew the reasons why.

CHAPTER FOURTEEN

The Tidewater

When you were a tadpole, and I was a fish,
In the Palaeozoic time,
And side by side in the ebbing tide
We sprawled through the ooze and slime.
—Langdon Smith: *The Scrap-Book*

AN offshore wind was blowing in the morning; the fog was gone, the sky a brittle blue, Barney had called his doctor friend and we looked forward to having lunch with Hank and his wife and then going out to visit the Coronados Islands. As we walked through the corridor to the Beach Club's breakfast hall, we passed two young men with their girls, all wearing full-length wet suits, carrying their flippers and masks, heading for the beach. We asked and they said they were biology students from nearby Scripps Institution of Oceanography and had permits for certain specimens and were collecting for a project. They were vigorous and the girls had long hair; we watched them running to the water's edge, where they put on their gear and the girls covered their hair and like black monstrous frogs walking upright, the four entered the bright waters. A family at a nearby table, proprietary about it for they had been there a week, told us that the sea lion which frequented the beach had been out there since dawn; we saw it in a while, bobbing after the skindivers who were heading south where the rocky cliffs were, and then cruising back up the shore where it remained playing up and down before the Beach Club.

Barney talked about studies that had been made over the past hundred years, lately with increased interest, with diving animals, such as Elephant and Harbor Seals and sea lions, water birds, and with dogs and men, to understand the slowing of the heart beat, which takes place when a creature is immersed either forcibly or when trained to go under. Human subjects respond similarly whether they are skilled divers or amateurs who duck their faces in water. In seals or geese, the beat may slow to a tenth or more of the normal rate; in man to half. Also the flow of blood to the muscles and outer limbs is constricted and the circulation which remains is directed to the vital brain and heart muscle. This is a normal response to being under water and causes no discomfort and is not even noticed by a diver.

We knew that Antarctic seals, of the same order as the tame sea lion out there, were being studied for clues to man's survival in unnatural elements, including perhaps the moon, that it was found they could endure tremendous cold, dive to a depth of 1970 feet, stay under water as long as three-quarters of an hour, sleep under water without apparent breathing and that they used echolocation to find their way in the dark under the thick ice to their occasional breathing holes. In an expedition to the frozen wastes, the seals were heard hooting and yelling under the ice and these sounds, like the porpoise's squeaks and clicks, are assumed to be their sonar and communication system. It was reported too that they paid no heed to the landing helicopters, having no hereditary knowledge of them as a danger, and we thought of the history of so many of these naïve creatures in the days of their discovery by man. The new trend toward the study rather than exploitation of the wild, seemed obvious as we looked out at the four tiny black frog-like creatures visible at the rocky bend and at the brown one closer by us.

After a while we headed for the Cabrillo National Monument, taking the Pacific Highway to the Marine Corps Base where we turned to follow the signs onto Point Loma, at the tip of which was the monument. We stopped in at Superintendent Thomas Tucker's office and were told that he was directing some Rangers outside and would be back shortly. We walked about while we waited, gazing at the enormous statue of Cabrillo, done by a Portuguese sculptor and given by that country to the state of California and overlooking a stunning view of San Diego Bay. Juan Rodríguez Cabrillo, fifty years after Columbus discovered the New World, arrived here, a Portuguese mariner serving the Spanish Crown with enthusiasm. He was with Cortés in the taking of Mexico City and had helped Alvarado overcome Guatemala; with two ships under him, the *San Salvador* and the *Victoria,* Cabrillo sailed from Navidad on the west coast of Mexico, crossing the Gulf of California and skirting the coastline, after three months spotting the Chumashan Indian camp fires along the peninsula of Point Loma on the twenty-eighth of September 1542. When they landed, the Indians shot arrows at them, wounding three, wary already of the White Man's way, for the ambitious Spaniards to the east had a reputation for bringing disaster and the Red Men's villages were peaceful and prosperous and numerous due to their unique sea culture. During Cabrillo's stay he noted their skill at navigation and the friendliness of the chiefs when approached with courtesy. Then the two ships had continued north, stopping now and then. In the second week of December, Cabrillo broke his arm and infection set in. The expedition passed the Channel Islands and Point Reyes where we had visited and when a storm forced the vesssels to turn back, they retraced past Drake's Bay until they came to San Miguel, the farthest north of the Channel Islands, then called *Isla de la Posesión,* where they landed and took refuge. Cabrillo was fatally ill by now from the infection; before his death he admonished his successor "not to fail to discover as much as possible all along the coast." His crew buried him wearing his helmet and with his jewel-studded long sword, a fact which Barney, a confirmed treasure hunter, found of interest. The men renamed the island *Isla de Juan Rodríguez* before setting forth to follow their leader's injunction.

We returned to the office and then Superintendent Tucker arrived with two of his Rangers, Vernon Betts and Vern Appling.

Mr. Tucker apologized for the delay, saying that there had been a dedication at the monument the day before and that Secretary Udall had been there. A boy had slipped on the pavement outside and was slightly injured and they were wondering if the area could be made safer in some way. We said firmly that we thought their time should be spent upon the monument and that the public should take care of itself, and he smiled, indulgent. We asked about a guide to Anacapa and arrangements to get there and he said that Rangers Betts and Appling could accompany us the morning after next if it suited our plans. We accepted and asked for help in chartering a boat. Mr. Tucker replied that he would take care of it and while we withdrew to the next room with the Rangers, he put a call through to the Cisco Sports Fishing Association at Channel Island's Harbor, asking that a boat be held for charter the day after next.

The town of Oxnard, sixty miles up the coast from Los Angeles, was close to the harbor, and the Rangers said they would make reservations for us at a motel tomorrow night and would meet us in the lobby at seven-thirty on the following morning. We asked if they could bring flippers for us both as we had packed only face-plates and they agreed. I said I was not handy at sea, and they would arrange for a ladder for me to get in and out of the boat and also a dinghy so that we could explore the caves where sea lions and sea elephants were to be seen. We mentioned the other island belonging to the monument—Santa Barbara, and they said it was thirty-eight miles off the coast, opposite San Pedro, the port of Los Angeles, and assured us that a visit to Anacapa, ten or so miles from Channel Island's Harbor, would give us a sufficient idea of the terrain and fauna and flora of both places.

We could hear Mr. Tucker in the next room, "We will send two Rangers along . . . four in the party . . . want to go ashore." When he joined us he said that there was no Ranger in permanent residence on Anacapa. "It's a rugged and lonely island. Santa Barbara is even more so; it is almost impossible to land there. The cliffs are unscalable and the kelp is thick and the surf is high."

Plans were under way to make the island more attractive to tourists, he said, improving the camping accommodations and the access and arranging for tours, guided or self-guided. Mr. Tucker spoke too of the government's long-range plans for the development of the northern group of five islands. Already 538 of Anacapa's 700 acres were set aside, the Coast Guard administering the rest. And 582 of Santa Barbara's 650 acres, as well as thirteen-acre Sutil Island. He said it was hoped that eventually the three other islands would come under Park Service control—Santa Cruz, Santa Rosa and San Miguel. Santa Cruz was the largest of all the Channel Islands, containing over sixty thousand acres and being twenty-one miles long and five wide, with many sea caves, the largest called Painted Cave, its entrance close to seventy feet high; it was held by the Stanton and Gherini Ranches that grazed livestock there. Santa Rosa, the second largest, with fifty-five thousand acres and owned mostly by the Vail and Vickers Ranch, was rocky, with dangerous shoals and surrounding beds of the bladder kelp, *Nereocystis,* found in waters up to a hundred feet deep and thriving in turbulence. San Miguel of fourteen thousand acres, with ten-acre Prince Island offshore, a seabird rookery, was a long run from the harbor, the farthest away of the Channels and controlled by the Navy. On that island was one of the largest colonies of sea elephants known, as well as extensive herds of two species of sea lions, and fur seals too. We knew that it was there that Cabrillo's unmarked grave was said to be and that a stone cross had been erected: JOAO RODRIGUEZ CABRILLHO / ISLE OF BURIAL 1543 and that before the Navy took the island over many treasure seekers had been there with the jeweled sword in mind that Barney had noted.

Mr. Tucker said it was thought by some archaeologists that these islands were occupied by primitive man as far back as 29,650 years, and that the fossil bones of prehistoric elephants or dwarf mammoths predated to an earlier time. Over two hundred village sites and many burial grounds and numerous artifacts have been unearthed. The region may be one of the oldest inhabited of North America. He said that for various reasons the remaining three

Channel Islands were not now proposed for inclusion in the national park—Santa Catalina was already well developed as a resort, San Clemente was being utilized as a bombing range, San Nicolas was too remote to make proper administration possible, being at the southern end of the Outer Santa Barbara Channel.

The policy of the National Park Service, Mr. Tucker told us, was to not assume responsibility for wilderness areas under the supervision of a State Park Service. They were interested in areas difficult or impossible for individual states to preserve. Thus in California here, where the state had already set aside sections of the coast for littoral preservation, the federal government controlled none of the sea shore and was interested only in the Channel Island group, ten to fifty miles off the coast. The three men felt that if the wildlife there was to be preserved, it was essential that all of this come to pass soon, otherwise these once inaccessible islands were bound to be plundered by the ever-increasing fleets of sport boats that dotted the harbors all up and down the California coast.

As we left we were impressed again with the dedication of the Parks people, which seemed as strong as Cabrillo's had been to his cause. The two Rangers accompanied us outside, urging us to look around. We said we didn't have time, as we were meeting the Hankins for lunch and would go on to the Coronados Islands in the afternoon. We mentioned the sea otters we had seen at Point Lobos and they told us of an interesting ecological development since the creatures' depletion. The sea otter is fond of feeding on the white sea urchin, which lives in kelp. On the death of the urchin, its skeleton is discarded, leaving the sea bottom so cluttered now that the kelp cannot anchor properly, and the beds are being gradually killed off. The rangers said that sea otters had been reported recently on San Miguel, but that they had not as yet been able to authenticate the reports.

We told them we looked forward to seeing them soon. Barney asked what the temperature of the water was now, and they estimated about sixty-three degrees, the temperature varying from about sixty in the coldest of winter to seventy in the summer. "Invigorating, but not paralyzing," Barney said as we shook hands and got into our car.

Mrs. Hankins had lunch ready to put on the table when we arrived at their house on the outskirts of San Diego, little local lobsters caught yesterday, one apiece and pots of melted butter. Then we drove to the marina where a new large cabin cruiser was moored at the pier, encased in white canvas. Barney and Hank stripped the protective covering from the windows and hardwood panelling and we were off, the sun still blazing and only a slight mist over the open sea where we headed. Hank had an auxiliary wheel up in the top deck, to guide the boat from there, and I sat with him enjoying the brisk wind, the waves, the blue water, the last view of the white buildings upon the shore. We were alone on the sea and no boat in sight, our course set upon the Coronados.

"Look," Mrs. Hankins called.

"Where?"

Off our side were three or four sea lions, peering at us, whiskered. I thought of Richard Eberhart's poem about the seals he knew in the channels and coves about Maine's coast and declaimed some lines down to the two on the decks below:

> Resting on the oar and lolling on the sea,
> I saw their curious images,
> Hypnotic, sympathetic eyes
>
> As the deep elapses of the soul.
> O ancient blood, O blurred kind forms
> That rise and peer from elemental water:
>
> I loll upon the oar, I think upon the day,
> Drawn by strong, by the animal soft bonds
> Back to a dim pre-history.

We were outside the harbor perhaps ten miles from shore, and had been on the water less than an hour when we saw a murky haze ahead. Within five minutes we were in an engulfing fog.

Visibility fell to ten feet and I sensed the terror of it; we could scarcely see the bow ahead.

"You can always expect one of these but you never know when," Hank said.

Barney laughed from below in a way I had become familiar with which he reserved for crises. "This isn't a bad spot for a sea serpent, Helga."

Hank cut the motors down and we chugged along, barely moving. He stayed in the top deck and Barney climbed out on the bow for a lookout. Hank told me, "Sometimes you go through one of these. It might be clear just a hundred yards ahead."

"And it might not," I sighed.

After a long while at slow progress, Hank shouted down, "What do you say, Barney? Do you want to turn back? We can go to the Coronados anytime. It's up to you two."

"I wanted her to see them," Barney called. "Try cutting the motor and maybe we'll hear the sea lions barking on the island. We ought to be close by now."

Hank did so and we rocked on the swells for a few minutes. There was no other sound. "We'll run up on the island before we see them in this," Hank said.

And then we saw it approaching out of the mist, a fify-foot looming yacht on a course diagonal to ours so that she was crossing in front of us. Her fog horn blasted and she swerved and skirted us with ten feet to spare before disappearing into the white blanket. Hank started the engine again and wheeled slowly for our return. I could hear Mrs. Hankins speaking below.

"We never know whether it's better to get out of here fast and take a chance on hitting another boat or to go slow and get run down by one."

As we moved slowly through the fog, no one speaking of the edge of worry, I thought of old-time sailors who believed that tides were caused by the breathing of the earth, and that the Atlantic was a river running around the rim of land, and that monsters lived in the water, particularly far off, who came to the world of

men now and then, possessed of a wish to destroy them. Scandinavian seamen spoke of the Kraken, a creature a mile and a half
around, of a circular flat shape with seaweed growing upon it so it
resembled an island, and how it had a way of embracing a ship and
sinking it. It was said there were fish out there ten times the size of
a bull; there was a whiskered serpent that had been born at the
same time as the world and was as long as a river; there were lobsters so huge they would reach up their claws and pull down innocent sailors standing at the rail; there were sea snakes that coiled
about a vessel and crushed it, devouring the little two-legged creatures who fell into the water. And on islands here and there,
beautiful songs were heard that entranced frail men, luring them
to where sea-maidens sat on rocks with their tails curled about
them and combs in their pretty hands to get the seaweed from
their long wet hair.

We ploughed on steadily and then as abruptly as we had entered
it, we were out of the fog and the sun was shining on the shores of
the harbor. Everyone began to talk, the burden lifted. Barney said
we should buy lobsters to have for supper in our Beach Club
kitchen, his appetite whetted by the little chicken lobsters Mrs.
Hankins had given us for lunch, and so Hank skirted the fishermen's piers along the shore in one area where little flags were
strung and the creatures were kept together in tanks of grating just
below the surface. We stopped at a sign announcing LIVE BAIT, and
a fat woman in jeans came out of the shed. We stepped onto the
planking to make our decision. One lobster was a giant, larger than
the rest and weighing perhaps seven pounds and Barney said that
one would do. The woman put him in a pasteboard box with fresh
wet kelp, and we returned to the shore. I was sorry not to see the
Coronados, I told the Hankins, but glad to set foot on my natural
element again. As we drove back to town with our lobster, I suggested to Barney that now that I was beginning to realize the reality of our excursion to cold Anacapa the day after next, I would
not mind owning a wet suit. We stopped at a shop for diving equipment in La Jolla and bought one; when we got home, Barney said

I must put it on and he would photograph me holding the dark red monster, so that I could show it some day to my grandchildren.

The mist was beginning to come inshore at our beach when we reached it around four o'clock. I put on the suit, the lobster clacked and objected and the picture was taken. We decided then to explore our own shoreline since we had the end of the afternoon free and I was properly clothed against the cool breeze and Barney was becoming nostalgic again. By now the mist was thickening, the air becoming still and the sun was a white disc which floated over the horizon. It was the time of the minus tide, the lowest for the day and people could be seen moving toward the tidewater area under the sharp cliffs as if magnetized by the stranded creatures of the sea. When they reached the rocky place, none of them walked erect or had any air of briskness; all were bent over in an absorbed attitude. They started when one spoke to them and we were surprised at the diversity of the nationalities. A Korean with his wife and three children, exhibited a gunnysack-ful of octopuses, when we expressed interest. He said he was snagging more and we watched him work, feeling into the little crevices of the kelpy rocks of the tide pool with a bamboo wand he carried, locating the soft creatures by their feel and the way they clung to his wand. Then he would motion to his wife who carried a plastic half-gallon jug of Chlorox; he squirted the fluid into the hole which drove the creature out, and as it swam by the family, jet-propelled by the water it ejected from its siphon, one of them would grasp it and drop it into the sack. A teen-age couple holding hands were watching a schoolboy of perhaps eleven, who was turning over stones and had a pail by him in which he was collecting shrimp crabs and tiny fish for his aquarium; he had a wee octopus, its body half an inch in diameter with tentacles outspread that made a drop of purple ink when the boy disturbed it. There was a Japanese, his child-like wife at his side, collecting top shells and seaweed; he had a few small black abalones and a large crab which his wife showed us in their sack which she held. A stalwart Portuguese man was there too, half-submerged toward the seaward side of the area, searching the deeper holes for octopuses with a small gaff-hook and a container of what he called lye. I wondered what the noxious fluid did to the neighboring fauna and the flora anchored to their positions, and Barney said that years ago before the use of toxic chemicals was outlawed, fishermen would use copper sulfate which killed all the plant and animal life for a good distance. The short-acting acids or alkalis like Chlorox or vinegar did less damage to the tidepool life.

As we waded through the eelgrass or made our way from rock to rock, Barney said that once there had been great quantities of mussels and abalones at these tide lines and numerous lobsters too. In the shallower pools had been limpets of the same family as the abalones, but smaller and remarkable for their homing instinct; they may leave the particular place on a rock where they live during a tide but invariably return as soon as low tide occurs; I was sorry not to see any. It seemed to me that all of this huntng was perhaps harmless, for there was an abundance of sea creatures here, but I wondered how long that state would remain, and thought how pleasant it would have been to wade through the area and observe the life in its elemental profusion before the coming of man.

Barney was silent and withdrawn by now and I felt his melancholy and an empathy with him too, I had never known salt water as a child, but I understood its excitement as I viewed the engrossed various people about us, who apparently understood the habits of the creatures of the tides as well as the tides themselves. As the moon, because of its nearness causing twice the effect on the tide as the sun, swings daily about the globe, all of the oceans are set into motion, and on the side facing the moon the waters are pulled out. The sun negates or enforces the moon's gravitational pull depending on its position, and the various high or spring tides and low or neap tides result and all of those between. The coincidence of tides with wind, storm or underwater eruptions are the cause of disaster.

The tides seem to control the breeding habits of certain sea creatures, although it is held by some marine biologists that the phenomenon is due to the higher temperatures at the time of the spring tides, caused by exposure to the sun, as well as the variabilities of water pressure and augmented food supplies. The chitons or sea cradles which we saw, marbled or bristled, and which will roll up like armadillos when threatened, invariably spawn in May or June when the low tide occurs in the early morning. A tiny species of clam lays its eggs only at full moon during one of the summer months; certain jellyfish congregate during a single flood tide; a variety of marine worm, *Odontosyllis phosphorea,* a fraction of an inch long, may be seen swimming about at dusk as a sparkling of phosphorescence in tidal pools. When biologists moved these latter worms into an artificial tank, they continued to spawn at their original time although there was no simulated tide; it has been speculated that the moon's gravitational power may be responsible for their spawning activity. It is also possible that as in the migration of birds, the phenomenon is related to a pattern established back in the early part of the Paleozoic Era when simple marine life first appeared.

Barney had told me of the running of the tide-conscious grunion, with which he was familiar and had participated in when he lived on the West Coast. This species, *Leuresthes tenuis,* six to eight inches long and found from San Francisco to Baja California, comes to the sandy shore to breed during the months of March to August under an exact built-in device timed to the tides. A quarter of an hour after high tide, a few nights after the highest tide of the full moon, they ride in on a breaking wave. With her tail the stranded female digs into the sand, three or four inches, and while the male hovers above her head, drops about two thousand eggs which he fertilizes with milt. The process takes a minute or until the next surf swirls in, riding the pair out to sea again. The spawning process of the different couples continues for an hour; the eggs will remain in their burrow protected by the sand over them until the next high tide two weeks later at which time they hatch and the young are carried out to sea.

When Barney lived here the Running of the Grunion was advertised as a tourist attraction, and he was startled at the response of the local people when the call was given, "The grunions are running!" The residents grasped the shining slippery creatures with bare hands and even feet, for the law of the state prohibited their being taken any other way; then the hunters built fires on the moonlit beach and grilled or fried the little smelts, eating them whole—guts, heads and all.

Here in this boundary zone between earth and sea where the eelgrass, *Zostera,* flourishes we saw the sea hare, *Aplysia Californica,* said by our mentor Aristotle, when viewing it off Lesbos in the Aegean, to be "named the 'aplysia' or the 'unwashable,' from the circumstance that it cannot be cleaned." He assumed the sea hare to be a sponge and noted, "They are distinguished in the sea from ordinary sponges from the circumstance that the ordinary sponges are white while the slime is in them, but that these sponges are under any circumstances black. And so much with regard to sponges." The common name sea hare derives from its earlike tentacles and it belongs to the order *Opisthobranchia,* gills-behind, which includes the sea slugs—marine snails which have no shells. We knew that this West Coast one we viewed sometimes would grow to fifteen inches; it had two large fluted flaps along the back of its slimy spotted body and they waved in the pool's movement. When Barney picked the creature up, it discharged a purplish fluid like the tiny octopus we had seen.

We knew that sea hares often camouflaged themselves in accordance with the vegetation on which they grazed through a mechanism which extracted the color from the food; if it were grazing on brown weeds and then moved into green ones, its basic color, not the typical dark rings or spots that remain permanently, changed with the vegetation. In this way it differed from the octopus, the grouper, the chameleon and the host of species that have chromatophore cells in their bodies and may camouflage swiftly. We knew too that the creature was hermaphroditic and could act as male or female and that as many as a dozen of them have been observed coupling, very occasionally in a complete circle. The thread of spawn that the creature extrudes may be fifty feet long and contain half a million eggs, which along with surviving larvae are consumed by starfish, flatworms, crabs, sea anemones, hydroids and other predators.

Nineteen hundred years ago in Rome, Pliny the Elder cautioned of the dangers of the small beast: "Wonderful things are related of the sea hare. To some it is poison if given in drink or food. . . . Struck by it a human being smells of fish; this is the first symptom by which such poisoning is detected. Furthermore, the victims die in the same number of days as the hare has lived." We knew that wizards and witches used to employ the sea hare in their concoctions and trusted that it would continue to prosper here since man found it unpalatable, in the same way that certain weeds and buttercups and marigolds and May apples along the banks of our ponds and streams are ignored by the grazing goats and deer and capybaras and wild fowl and flourish therefore.

It was chilly and I watched Barney moodily strolling in the distance among the humps of exposed algae-covered rocks, bending now and then to examine something that took his interest. The octopus hunters and their families were making their way down the beach, back to their homes or vending places; the lovers and children and tourists were going too. And then Barney was returning and we were finding our way to our home. There were no pots large enough for our *pièce de résistance* among the utensils in the kitchen and Barney went down to talk to the chef about his problem. He came back after a while with a huge iron pot and a bottle of California Riesling. When the water boiled, he took the scuttling monster from its seaweed and dropped it in, the claws hanging over the edges.

The lobster apparently feels no pain when it is immersed in boiling water which may be due to it being a creature of the sea where water never gets hot and there is no reason for the sensation of heat to be experienced or avoided. It is only after a delay that the lobster seems to sense the change of environment and is presumed to react to the lack of oxygen in the hot water by struggling briefly before dying. After twenty minutes, Barney lifted the creature out and split it; he removed the shell-like stomach and the dark line of gut which leads through the white tail, preserving the soft grey succulent liver. He placed the halves of the giant red shell on plates and brought them to the table in the living room where the windows overlooked the dark sea.

Barney said that in relation to the tides out there and the moon's singular influence on certain of the creatures, one must not forget that the white satelite has held a unique position in the poetry and literature of man and in the relationship which man calls romance. Then we toasted with the local wine to the luck of our trip to the Channel Islands and hoped that the fog might hold back for once.

CHAPTER FIFTEEN

The Sunken Peaks

The ocean is a wilderness reaching round the globe, wilder than a Bengal jungle, and fuller of monsters, washing the very wharves of our cities and the gardens of our seaside residences. Serpents, bears, hyenas, tigers, rapidly vanish as civilization advances, but the most populous and civilized city cannot scare a shark far from its wharves.

—Henry David Thoreau: *Cape Cod*

ON our way out of San Diego at noon the next day, we stopped in at Sea World, an oceanarium on Mission Bay, to take a look at a live performing monster, a killer whale or Grampus called Shamu who had been trained like the porpoises we saw on the East Coast and was closely related to them. Sea World occupies fifty-five acres and was established in 1964; they obtained Shamu a year later. As we stood at the side of the enormous tank bordered by a hundred visitors, we felt that the account we had read had been inadequate. The beast seemed as exotic or strange as some fabled one might be, fourteen feet long, her body velvety, the texture due, it is said, to the oil which she exuded to destroy all friction in the water she cut through with such speed. Above the wide blunt jaw line where the forty-four pointed cone-shaped teeth showed, she was jet black, below her white coat continued up on the sides near the tail; there was an elongated white spot behind each tiny bright eye too, set back so she could see to each side as well as forward.

In the tank with Shamu was a companion, a Pacific porpoise called George, who had been with her since her arrival and who swam about her as she performed. She took her cues from her trainer, who blew a whistle or gave hand signals from his platform. She rolled on her back to be patted, squirted water from her mouth, slapped her tail, had her teeth brushed, let the man put his head down into her mouth like a lion act, licked his cheek in an enormous kiss, and finally leaped clear of the water, returning with a splash which sent water over the screaming spectators who would not retreat although warned.

We knew that the education of the monster was due to an understanding of her sonar mechanism. Like the porpoise and others of the family, the killer whale is equipped with a special vibrating organ within the air chambers which leads to the blowhole and with which it produces a pulselike click, slowly when hunting and with increasing rapidity for accuracy when closing in on prey. Besides the clicks, it produces high-pitched whistles and squeals made by a mechanism in the larynx and related not so much to the location of food or obstacles or predators, as with the intra-species communication having to do with mating and alarm signals. It is believed that the sound-receiving system of the *Cetacea* is picked up in long narrow oil-filled channels in their lower jawbones and that their large brains are involved in their sound-beaming ability.

Like the rest of the order of *Cetacea*—the Latin *cetus* meaning a large sea animal—the whale is a re-entrant. Its body has become enormous and streamlined; its fins contain vestigial forelegs complete with finger-bones; its hind leg bones have disappeared altogether; its nostrils have moved to the top of the head to become one blowhole, which has a muscular flap that closes on submersion and which enables the monster to breathe an inch or two above the surface without exposing itself. There are two suborders of whales; the Toothed Whales, *Odontoceti,* and the Baleen Whales, *Mysticeti.*

Among the Toothed Whales are the White Whales, the Sperm Whale, *Physeter Catodon,* that Herman Melville made so famous;

and those of the family *Delphinidae,* including the unicorn-horned Narwhal, the Beluga, the Pilot and Beaked Whale, porpoises and the Killer Whale, all of them traveling in packs, having teeth in both jaws, and being carnivorous. The smaller species feed on fish, squid and cuttlefish; and the largest, the Killer Whale, the males twice the size of the females and running to thirty feet, called the Sea Wolf, *Orcinus Orca,* and considered the most cunning and deadly of the creatures of the waters, feed upon porpoises, seals, sea lions, penguins, walruses, fish, and other whales.

The Sperm Whale is fond of the giant squid, which ranges fifteen to fifty feet, measuring from mantle top to the end of its tentacles, and which the whale finds by echolocation. It is thought by some that ambergris is the result of the Sperm Whale swallowing squids whole and being unable to digest the parrot-like hard beaks, vomiting them up in the form of ambergris; it is said by others that only old or unhealthy whales have the ability to manufacture the sticky grey, black, yellow or variegated formation, spewed up and floating or again washed upon the shores, the treasure of the sea which Barney as a child sought on the Atlantic beach. A fifty-pound mass of ambergris has been found in a single whale, and we had heard reports of an even larger piece being discovered on a Bermuda beach by some ship's crew who deserted and fled with their booty. Soluble in alcohol, the value of ambergris is due to its ability to fix the scent of perfume; it has never been perfectly replaced by a synthetic substitute.

Baleen Whales have no teeth but a series of plates of whalebone, or baleen, hanging from the roof of the mouth with which they strain plankton, pressing their tongue against it and swallowing the mass that remains. The baleen is thick and tough and has a multitude of hair-like fringes at its extremity; the weight of the baleen from one whale may come to a ton. These whales pasture in the upper sunlit layer of the ocean, mainly in the Antarctic, in the top thirty feet, sifting out plant and animal plankton and retaining a larger plankton animal, called krill by whaling men, which is almost exclusively their food—*Euphausia superba,* up to two and a half inches in length, bright red, shrimplike, sometimes so packed into the water that there is a red hue and so abundant that it extends for hundreds of square miles. It is estimated that a growing whale will consume six to eight hundred pounds of krill a day, and it is thought that they locate denser areas of krill by use of their sonar ability. The echolocation system used by Baleen Whales differs from that employed by Toothed Whales. The former have not been observed to produce the recognizable clicks, but rather to make a sustained groaning, moaning or mooing rather like a herd of cows and familiar to whalemen.

The Baleen Whales include the Gray, Right and Finback Whales, and the most famous of the Finbacks is the Blue Whale, the largest animal that has ever existed within man's knowledge, weighing up to a hundred and fifty tons and occasionally reaching a hundred feet long. Its calf may measure twenty-five feet at birth and the cow, like the female porpoise, has two teats and pumps its milk mechanically and swiftly to the air-breathing mammalian baby who could not suck under water; it is estimated that a ton of milk a day is supplied to a Blue Whale calf. The whale cow has a reputation for its affection for its mate and young, holding firmly to the former and fiercely protecting the latter, which it will not forsake in case of danger, a characteristic employed to the benefit of old-time whalers who used the captured baby to lure the cow whale into reach of their harpoons. Whalers have reported too that if a pod of female whales are traveling together and one is struck and wounded, her companions will not flee, but remain in porpoise-fashion swimming about the stricken one, a trait used also for the benefit of the hunters, who can send out many boats and capture the entire group.

The extermination of the Blue Whale, if accomplished as seems likely, will mark the first time this has happened to a known species of whale. After the invention of explosive harpoons and the subsequent factory ships with gun platforms, radio, sonar, radar and helicopters, the population of the Blue Whale rapidly fell; in 1929–1930, twenty thousand were harvested; in 1963–1964, a little over a hundred. The sounding whales are pursued until exhausted; if the four-foot barb is improperly placed, a whale may tow the heavy boat for hours before giving up. Like porpoises, the great creatures are reported to squeak plaintively when harpooned and to have a gentle and rather timorous and inoffensive attitude toward divers who have swum with them.

On leaving Shamu's tank, we joined an enthusiastic crowd who were watching a troop of Brown Pelicans march about a stage, awkward, short-legged and heavy-winged, the only bird with all four toes connected by webs, the hind toe being turned forward and linked to the inner front one. Then there was a strange cry off in the wings, very like the trumpeting of an elephant. Flopping into sight came a creature that seemed as large as one, close to 4000 pounds, dwarfing his trainer—an elephant seal. In common with all true seals, his flippers were fused to the tail and he was unable to rotate his rear limbs forward, so his progress toward the pedestal upon which he finally placed his flippers was clumsy. The man patted him familiarly and put him through his paces, occasionally tossing him a fish. The creature lifted his great head, his proboscis, a foot long, hanging before him; again came the uncanny bellow as from some primordial age.

At last we turned away; we took the coastal route. It was under two hundred miles to Oxnard and we proceeded in a leisurely way. It was twilight when we reached the little town and checked into the motel. Our reservations were in order, and we went across the road to a tavern for supper and turned in early. We were up at seven and breakfasted hastily in the coffee-room of the motel. There was a slight drizzle and it was cold and the sky was dark; we watched restlessly for a sign of Rangers Betts and Appling who were due to meet us at seven-thirty. When an hour had nearly gone by, we concluded that we had misunderstood and that they had gone ahead. Barney put a call in to the Channel Islands Sport Fishing Center to be sure that the boat was being held for us, and we left a note in case the Rangers called to say that we would meet them at the dock.

There was a café at Channel Islands Harbor, many sailboat and yacht conveniences and a privately owned marina with close to three hundred boat slips, most of the craft rocking at their moorings in the grey mist. As we were arranging for the chartering of the boat, the park men joined us; they had stayed in the same motel as ours and had assumed they would see us at breakfast in the coffee room, where we had eaten so quickly. At eight-thirty, they decided to ring our rooms and found our message. I was wearing a heavy sweater and rain parka, Barney had on his jacket and our Ranger friends were clad in short-sleeved cotton shirts in which they seemed comfortable. The captain of the boat arrived, tall and quick, his brown face seamed, and we shook hands.

"If I'd of thought you folks wouldn't mind, I'd of asked my wife to come along," he told us.

"Call her up," Barney said. "We'll wait."

"It wouldn't do," he said. "But I take her along whenever it's not too crowded, if the passengers don't give a care."

He had some grocery sacks full of supplies, and bringing our two duffle bags, we made our way along the pier to the *Sea-Jay*, blue and white and with a red dinghy aboard and the little ladder we had requested and a supply of flippers and masks. We settled ourselves, the captain started the engines and we were off. Our destination was ten or eleven miles from the shore.

The water was calm and Western Gulls circled overhead, white with dark wing tips and yellow beaks and occasionally a dappled immature one; their feet were tucked under their bellies like retracted landing gears. They were screaming as we made our way out of the harbor; the skipper gave me part of a loaf of bread from one of the bags, which I broke and tossed to the crying birds, who caught them in mid-air. A flight of Ruddy Turnstones passed by, their harlequinesque black-and-white pattern striking, their backs brown in fall plumage, a shore bird, a little larger than a sandpiper. We saw a few Brown Pelicans flying low, and the Rangers said old-timers of the area talked of thousands of them here once and that they had been reported nesting on Anacapa since 1898 and would be seen carrying seaweed in their bills for their nests. Nowadays there was still a good-sized colony and gulls reared their young on Anacapa too. In the season when the young of the latter had just hatched, it was hoped that people could be discouraged from going near their sites because the alarmed babies would walk right off the cliffs. The gulls that I fed followed for a mile or more before most of them turned back; two remained to accompany us. But for them, we were alone it seemed, in the cold mist on the silent and empty sea. I thought of the contrast to the sunny Virgin Islands and it seemed proper somehow to visit a tropical country in hot weather and a forbidding seascape like this in the present season, intensifying the experience.

For half an hour we ran seaward without seeing a living creature except the pair of birds gliding above our wake. Then again ahead of us were gulls, an immense flock feeding in their usual way, following a school of splashing bait fish being pursued from beneath by predators. A sea lion reared up beside us, its eyes soft and dark; and in a moment two more, coming up together to embrace and then disappear. Mr. Betts, who is a naturalist, said that there was trouble with fishermen who shot them, claiming that they tore up their nets on purpose; he said that the damage done was negligible and that the shooting was to be deplored. Sportsfishermen in fast boats made a problem too, because in the fashion of a special breed of hunters found every place and renowned for firing at cows and jays and even whooping cranes, they desired simply to test their marksmanship. The poachers would be observed, but by the time the Ranger reached them, there would be no case against them, for either they had slipped the killed creature back into the ocean and assumed an innocent posture or they would gun their engines and speed away. Due to this poaching problem and the island's accessibility, the sea lion colony on Anacapa was barely sustaining itself.

Ranger Appling was motioning. "There it is."

In a moment, I discerned an uneven low line along the horizon through the persistent mist. I thought of the name—*Ana* or re-

peated, and *capa* or cape. As we came closer the Rangers pointed
to the natural bridge formation off the east end with the sea running under it—Arch Rock. The sunken peaks of Anacapa are a
five-mile chain of three islets called East, Middle and West Islands,
all about a half-mile wide, rugged, their south sides composed of
high cliffs and steep slopes where prickly pear cactus, *Opuntia
oricola,* flourishes. West Island, the largest and tallest and where
we were heading, rises to about nine hundred feet; the Chumashan
Indians that Cabrillo had admired lived there at the time he discovered California; it has subsequently been inhabited by sheep
herders, sporadic fishermen and a lone character after which the
place we were just heading for was named—Frenchy's Cove. Here
the Rangers said there was a boat landing and after circling the
island, we would drop anchor by the Coast Guard's buoy which was
fifty yards offshore near a rearing rock. There were tide pools here,
especially just across the spit of land bordering the cove, where all
the tidewater creatures were plentiful—the sea anemones and
striped shore crabs and sea hares; there were black mussels, poisonous sometimes in summer, and red abalones at low tide. In this
area no spearfishing was permitted and the skindiving was excellent.

I gazed into the formidable water and listened to the enthusiastic Rangers in their shirtsleeves. In the eelgrass and seaweed were
purple sea urchins, opaleye and smelt, and black abalones in the
deeper waters. The cove had been noted for years by angler fishermen who came to camp on the land for a week or so, occasionally
employing Raymond LeDreau, Frenchy, for a guide. The latter
had arrived in 1928 and moved into a shack he found there; staying about thirty years until one day he was gone; the shack was torn
down; and only his name remained. As we began to skirt Anacapa,
the Rangers said that the fog horn we kept hearing was automatic
and based at the lighthouse perched on the easternmost end of East
Island near Arch Rock, manned by a small crew of Coast Guard
men. We were preparing to pass by West Island first, noting the
pock-marked character of the cliffs ahead, whose caves resembled

eye-sockets in skulls. We asked about the terrestrial mammals of the island. The white-footed mouse is common, as is the Black Rat *Rattus rattus* that lives everywhere a ship has neared; there were domestic cats run wild since Frenchy had kept many; and there were rabbits on East Island introduced first for emergency food supply for the Coast Guard Light Station during World War II, some escaping and at one time overly abundant. We understood that Anacapa Island did not deal with virgin fauna, for sheep had been there in numbers too once and it had to be considered in some respects a disturbed environment rather than isolated and original.

The slopes we saw were nearly treeless, except for scattered wild cherries and eucalyptus, and we were told that there were live oak, *Quercus tomentella,* in the arroyos. The vegetation seemed mainly a scrubby growth of prickly pear cactus and cholla ice-plant, the leaves of the latter covered with particles which sparkled like ice. And there were wild sunflowers, now grey and shriveled and dormant, the Giant Coreopsis, *Coreopsis maritima,* that will rear up to eight feet, tree-like, the yellow blossoms that would come in April and May being five inches or more in diameter. The Rangers said that when in bloom the golden spectacle was visible to ships ten miles off, and that Santa Barbara to the southeast, the other Channel Island belonging to the monument at present, had the largest single stand of the Giant Coreopsis in the world.

The cliffs at the summit of the bend were white from the guano of pelicans and cormorants and gulls that roosted there. We saw Black Oyster Catchers on the rocky beach below, fat and black-backed, feeding on barnacles and clams, having a red bill that looked like plastic; Ranger Appling told us that when the sun shone the bills seemed to glow like neon lights. No eagles have been seen in this area for a long time, although in the early part of the century many nests were noted. The Western Meadowlark is common on all three islets, and migrating birds use the land as a resting place.

There was a strong current like a rip tide as we rounded the bend. The Captain said it was going six knots which would sweep a swimmer away from a moored vessel and it would be impossible for him to return; moreover, the water shelved off deeply right from the shore and even when it was extremely clear, the bottom wasn't visible. We saw buoyed lobster pots and Barney was surprised, since it was a national park. There were trawling and fishing boats speckling the sea here and there and we saw many as we circled the island. Mr. Betts said that there had been no attempt by the government to stop commercial fishing and as a naturalist, he wondered whether it would be a good policy to do so. It seemed that the ecology of the island had adapted over the years to the depletion and perhaps it would be thrown out of balance if the practice were abruptly halted.

As we neared Middle Island, we were told of a sandy-bottomed cave there and how bat-rays bred in it commonly. Also we heard of caves where Black Sea Bass lived of the family *Serranidae*, relatives of the groupers that we had seen in tropical waters, curious, fearless, and easily tamed so they would follow divers like dogs. They traveled singly and stayed in their chosen lairs. Spearfishing is allowed in the area and recently they said that a fisherman had killed eight of the creatures, the largest weighing 325 pounds. I was silent and appalled, thinking of Captain Ahab and the jewfish Moby Dick in the waters off Fort Jefferson. There was another cave called Cathedral Cave, the light in it being greenish and which extended a hundred feet back and where sea lions were occasionally noted. We had seen none of the creatures yet and then as we reached the end of Middle Island we had our first glimpse—a big bull and a cow on a rock and another on the pebble beach nearby. Ranger Betts said that individuals of the Guadalupe Fur Seal, closely related to the sea lion, had been sighted over recent years, a species long thought to have been extinct—dark brown with a silver grizzle about the head and neck, its muzzle pointed.

Ranger Appling motioned to the misty shoreline where a few brown pelicans floated. "That's a seal rookery."

"I don't see any," I sighed.

"Look there," said the Captain, "an elephant seal."

I saw it plunging then from its rock perch, monstrous, like our friend at the oceanarium, and disappearing under. They told us about capacious Sea Lion's Cave, and how the sea poured in among the rocks and the creatures would lie on the ledges back in there. The Rangers said that it could be dangerous for swimmers who persisted in going back in the island's caves. Even on calm days there could be an occasional "sneaker" wave, the huge one which unexpectedly sweeps in from the vast expanse of ocean and may hurl a skindiver against the jagged rocks. Our skipper said that once he was caught by a "sneaker" when in the dinghy and he got banged against the roof of Sea Lion's Cave, escaping with a few scratches. And Ranger Betts said that he had seen a huge bull sea lion in the cave on the rock above him one day; the animal had been as startled as he and leaped toward the craft barely clearing it, almost swamping it before plunging in on the other side.

The south edge of Anacapa was dappled by prickly pear as we passed, nearing Arch Rock. On East Island we saw the white lighthouse with its red top where the fog horn continually moaned and sea birds soared above. There were a series of hoists which were used to bring material up to the lighthouse, barnacles covering their bases. At the bend were thick kelp beds where Calico Bass lived and the friendly Garibaldi, *Hypsypops rubicundus*, the largest of the flashy Demoiselles, which we had seen so commonly in the coral reefs, the adults golden-red, the young green with jewel-like blue spots. Here the kelp's gigantic stalks grew up to a hundred feet from the bottom, the brownish fronds on the surface buoyed by their natural floats. It is off this side of the island that the Broad-billed Swordfish run, open to the ocean with freighters passing continually on the horizon, employing the Outer Santa Barbara Channel. Our captain said he often took fishermen out and recently had sighted seven of them in an afternoon, his guests catching three, averaging four hundred pounds each. Out there too were the marlin, occasionally reaching a length of fourteen feet and a thousand pounds, numerous down on the Mexican coast.

The Channel Islands were famous for big fish—halibut running over sixty pounds with thirty pounders common, yellowtail over forty pounds, and the black sea bass, four hundred and fifty now and then. Even in inclement weather he said that quiet waters for smaller fish could be found on the lee sides of the Channels.

The men began talking about the beasts of the sea. Barney spoke of a Giant Devilfish or Manta Ray that he had seen snagged when he was a child on holiday in the Florida Keys. A dark flat surface had loomed before the boat, their captain had hurled the spear hooking the right wing, the three hundred feet of heavy rope had rushed and amid confusion the boat had taken off, a fleck of foam in the distance guiding it. For two miles they followed, the line taut; then the beast surfaced and the rope slacked and everyone hauled it in, until with a rush the line burned through their hands as the ray sounded. The family had played it, until suddenly the rope gave way, the brilliantly polished creature floated to the surface, flapped lazily and disappeared; their skipper had pronounced it twenty-two feet across and weighing a ton and a half. The Devilfish has its name for the fins like horns on either side of its head, used to gather plankton into its mouth, which it filters the way certain whales and sharks do; it does not bottom-feed as a sting ray will. It is often seen basking in the sun with the wing tips protruding above the water; it has a habit of leaping high, fifteen or twenty feet, before splashing noisily back in; the name Manta is after the Spanish word for blanket. There is a Little Devilfish which may reach five and seven feet, but the *Manta Birostris,* the Giant Devilfish, ranges to twenty-five feet across and may weigh 3500 pounds. Tales are told of boats that have been pulled across the ocean by the monster, often to their destruction.

There were more great beasts of the sea out there, nearly as impressive as the fabled ones reported by returning seamen who had perhaps glimpsed a true monster. The Kraken that the Scandinavian sailors had seen, is thought to have had its foundation in the Giant Squid. Squids are of the same class as the octopuses, *Cephalopoda,* head-foot, since the foot is developed into a circle of tentacles around the mouth, which has a parrot-like beak. Like the great whales, the Giant Squid's appearance is menacing, but they too live in the remote deeps of all the seas and are not known to attack man. They may be observed cruising slowly, using the fins alongside their mantles to propel themselves; when feeding or escaping predators, they move more swiftly than any other inhabitant of the sea except perhaps the game fishes. They are able to move backward or forward with ease, their power like that of the retiring-natured octopus, being in their instant reverse thrust; they draw water into their mantle cavity and by changing the position of their water-ejecting siphons control the direction, sometimes simultaneously discharging a dark camouflaging fluid.

We had once eaten squid on the *Sea Diver*, bought by the pailful from a shrimp boat, dragged up from the bottom in their nets, each creature identical to the next, four inches long, pale with dark tentacles. The Greek cook Johnny cut off the head ends, dusted on flour and dropped them in hot fat for a minute or two on each side; he served them with lemons to squeeze over for appetizers. The meal itself was the bodies cut in slices, making small rings since the mantle cavity is hollow, and stewed in a red spicy sauce Johnny had learned to make in Athens; it was glutinous and tasted a little like macaroni.

The squid's eyes are extraordinarily sharp and resemble the human eye closely, having an eyelid, a cornea, a pupil which contracts and expands and a complex lens; they are able to tilt their eyes and to use each independently; one species, the sail squid, has eyes of differing sizes, each adapted to a different use. Being predatory animals, the squids depend for their existence on speed and quick reflexes. Their ability to change color rapidly due to the redistribution of the pigment in their chromatophores is well-known. They are voracious and feed on plankton, every sort of fish and other squids. The battles between sperm whales and the giant squids commonly fifteen feet from the tip of the tentacles to the top of the mantle and having been measured at close to fifty feet, the world's largest invertebrate, are legendary. As are the stories of tentacles of the giant creatures pulling small boats down. The beak of the squid is like the parrot's except that the lower closes over the upper; it is able to cut a heavy wire; the suckers at the ends of the tentacles are equipped with teeth too, to help them hold their vacuum grip.

The tentacles of the cephalopods are used for reproduction as well as food-catching or locomotion. Aristotle noted it: "That is to say, they unite at the mouth, by an interlacing of their tentacles." During copulation, the tentacles of the male quid grasp the female and one of them, especially developed and with smaller suckers, is inserted behind the female's head to transfer the sperm. In a certain species of octopus, the paper argonaut, which produces a translucent papery shell as an egg case, the tentacle is actually broken off from the male and left in the female and was long thought to be a separate worm-like creature. Octopuses have eight arms of equal length, inhabit the bottom of the sea and crevices and are solitary and nocturnal in habit; squids have ten tentacles, two being longer than the others, and often travel in schools, Certain of the deep-living squids have organs which make a blue-green light resembling that made by chemical reaction in the common firefly and being either embedded in the body or simply a sparkle upon the skin; this organ may be located at the tip or within the entire tentacle or else above the eyes. The Bobtailed Squid in the dark depths, when pursued uses another kind of lighting; certain luminescent bacteria live in a small gland near its ink sac and are ejected at the same time as the camouflaging fluid, causing it to glow. Squid ink varies from light brown to black; a relative of the squid, a cuttlefish called Sepia, has been employed for over two thousand years as a source of a brown pigment that artists use and which is the base of India ink.

Out upon the oceans, among the creatures man feared, was the great white shark, weighing up to four tons, famous for its attacks on bathers on our Atlantic coast when the temperature of the water is over seventy degrees. And then there were the killer whales, their food seals and porpoises, warm-blooded and of the

same size as the five of us on the *Sea-Jay,* and which when drawn
into the company of man, like Shamu at Sea World, and communicating with him, could be persuaded to kiss the cheeks of movie
stars and beauty queens who visited them.

As we passed sea-swept Arch Rock, a cold rain started blowing
up; out on the misty water we could see two freighters heading for
the channel; we felt the rugged grandeur and the barren nature of
the area. We were returning to Frenchy's Cove and the Rangers
suggested that we all go down. I stated that I for one, would not.
The Rangers, bare-armed in the rain that began to pour, appeared
disappointed. The Captain said he wouldn't mind returning to
land since his boat was chartered for the day and it made no dif-
ference. We turned to Barney, who sneeezd and said he was glad
for any excuse to stay on deck. In his visits to the Coronados during his service with the Navy, he had become familiar with the
underwater and tidewater ecology of islands like Anacapa. I had
viewed his movies and understood the differing character of cool
kelp beds and warm coral reefs. We agreed too that we were there
to write about the place and should behave the way a casual visitor
might.

And so the *Sea-Jay* was heading again into the ocean, the salt
spray driven back into our faces and mingling with the downpour.
I had hoped to see quantities of sea lions, I told the Rangers, which
I had viewed covering the Coronados' beaches in Barney's twenty-
year-old film. I said I had also been intrigued by a baying handsome group at a Monterey breakwater where we had lunched a
few days before. Ranger Betts explained that often many were seen
here, but that it was true that most had retreated to Santa Barbara,
which was less accessible and where they were not disturbed consistently and there was an established rookery on the southeastern
coast. There the sea elephants congregated too in their cove on the
northwest. The Rangers said again that if they were not shot at
here, likely the sea lions would return and adapt again to Anacapa
and mankind.

The noise of the moaning lighthouse was not audible anymore;

we were on the open swells again, our wake churning whitely behind. No gulls accompanied us; the far-off freighters had disappeared in the curtain of rain. We stood in the cold continuous
flood feeling almost as if we were under the sea. We knew that we
would come back sometime to these sunken peaks when the gigantic sunflowers bloomed turning them golden and when the tide
pools were warm and when man no longer molested the sea lions,
who would be sprawling in contented hierarchical flocks on the
rocks and pebbled beaches.

CHAPTER SIXTEEN

The Treasure

We travel not for trafficking alone:
By hotter winds our fiery hearts are fanned:
For lust of knowing what should not be known
We make the Golden Journey to Samarkand.

—James Elroy Flecker:
"The Golden Journey to Samarkand"

WE drove to Los Angeles in the late afternoon, seventy-odd miles from Channel Harbor, in the sporadic rain. Barney had a medical talk to give that evening and we would stay overnight with his host, an old friend, Dr. Rex Ross, before returning to Cleveland in the morning. Rex met us at the gate of his walled garden just off Sunset Boulevard. In the twilight, oranges hung like burning lanterns on the trees of the lawn that sloped up from his patio, isolating his half-acre. The rain had stopped and after bathing and dressing for the evening, we sat outside before going on to the meeting. Avocados hung ripely nearby, grapefruit studded some of the trees and hibiscus bloomed in pots about us.

Barney and Rex talked of the complex problems of smog and pollution vexing our country and how concern even now is beginning to center upon man's massive chemical intrusion into the waters of the world. It is well known that life-threatening concentrations of DDT and other insecticides have been detected in birds and fish on and near land, and it is recognized that due to these concentrations the butterfly has been added to the list of endangered creatures in the United States, its population down to twenty-five percent of what it once was. It is common knowledge too that traces of pesticides have been noted even in Antarctic Penguins and deep-sea Tuna. Now it has been determined that trade winds as well as water bear these poisons all about the world from the Coral Sea to the Arctic, from the fields of Europe and Africa and Asia to the cities of Australia. The noxious traces are various; in our country 100,000 tons of car exhaust lead are air-borne yearly and when carried seaward and precipitated, the natural lead content of the oceans is overloaded. Unless the ways of the earth—the currents of air, the oceans which appear so infinite, the rivers and lakes upon the land masses—are examined and understood and acted upon, posterity may indict us as we do those who devastated our own country and creatures.

I knew that the lake of my childhood, Lake Michigan, and the lake beside which I now lived, Lake Erie, were both dying, their fatal illness known as eutrophication, an affliction of ageing lakes, once balanced but now not so. Barney said that the term eutrophism, well-nourished, ought to be hypertrophism, over-nourished, and that the disease in lakes was as serious as its human counterpart, obesity. The process is characterized by a change in biota, which is the plant and animal life of the water. The public beaches along the edges become stained with blue-green algae which grows in ridge-like formations in areas of the once-clear lakes, and the screens of the water-filtration plants of the cities become clogged, drinking water is discolored and deep sludge banks are noted along the lake perimeters. When the algal bloom dies and decays along with other plant life and sinks to the bottom to decompose, it absorbs oxygen from the water. Without oxygen the marine life proceeds to die, adding to the decomposing mass of organic sediment. The eutrophic lake begins to be filled with this and perishes inevitably. Man is hastening this process by his use of lakes as dumpage spots. It has been suggested that if interceptor sewers were built about the waters, the nutrients might be diverted

to some of the freshwater rivers. Barney said that because the
oceans to which the rivers run are now beginning to show signs of
pollution, it might be wiser to spread the wastes on the land, employing them as fertilizers or for other specific purposes. Complex
research is going on to determine solutions to the accelerated eutrophication due to this pollution as well as to the problems of
changes in fish population and the fishing industry itself.

Barney and I were eager to be home and had an early plane to
catch and so after the meeting we went at once to bed. In the morning Rex's Mexican housekeeper Josephina brought plates of
huevos rancheros out to the patio where we sat in the warm air, a
pot of marmalade made from the fruit of the trees about us glowing in the sunlight on the table. And then Rex was speeding us to
the airport and in a few hours our plane was landing in the cold
winds of Ohio, a thin glaze of early snow everywhere. We wanted
to go to the country for supper and would drive the twenty miles
out there as soon as I had unpacked and Barney had gone through
our piles of mail.

Paula met us with various news. Ed and Marion Link had called
yesterday. Marion was sad; Little Sea Diver was chewing all the
salty ropes of the *Sea Diver* and was in continual mischief and she
felt the young capybara might be extraneous to a busy boat filled
always with expeditions of scientists and divers. They had just returned from the Tongue of the Ocean where they had completed a
seven-hundred-foot lockout dive from the little yellow submarine
Deep Diver off Great Stirrup Cay and were now planning a thousand-foot dive. Ed said they would be meeting other boats,
equipped with scientists, divers, photographers and complex equipment, in the coming spring in the waters off British Honduras, on
a project called SHARK, to study those creatures and try to ascer-
tain among other things which stimuli repelled or attracted them.

"Mrs. Link said she would put her child on the plane today, air
express," Paula told us, "and he'll be here in two hours. I was hoping he'd arrive at the same time as you both."

"Wonderful," I said.

"You've been wishing Little Sea Diver would come ever since we brought him to the Links, haven't you?" Barney said.

"A husband for Helen of Troy," I told him.

"How are things in the country?" Barney asked Paula.

"Lenore is gone," Paula sighed.

Barney and I were not surprised. We would miss the gentle affectionate two-year-old Turkey Vulture, called the Andros Eagle in the Bahamas. We had let her wings grow out, hoping that she would remain around, but we knew too that we were taking a chance. When a winged creature is grounded during its imprintable early life it becomes accustomed to the contours of its home from that view; if released and seeing the land from above, it is possible that it may not return. We had decided to let Lenore go anyway, for the migration season was nearing its end and we felt she should be true to her impulses. We would watch hopefully for her return in spring and perhaps look around for another baby vulture too.

"What else?" I asked Paula.

"A four-pound book came from John and Lauri DeWeese on American sea shells. There's a letter from them, too. And half a dozen letters from all over the country from the National Park Service."

At home, while I leafed through the DeWeeses' heavy book with its multitude of color and black-and-white plates, Barney read John's account of the underwater trail that had been installed at Fort Jefferson. It had been John's summer assignment; there were twenty-two markers placed at intervals along the sea side of the north and northwest moat wall where we had spent so much time. A different labeling method had been used than at Buck Island and the markers were smaller also. The illustration or photograph and the text describing the fish or marine growth was sent out for plastic lamination; when returned it was secured to aluminum backing with a silicone sealout. The markers had to be cleaned weekly and abrasives could not be used on plastics because of scratching and John was experimenting with a glass face using the same silicone sealout; he also planned to increase the size of the markers for better visibility as soon as practicable. John said that at Fort Jefferson the development of underwater trails was still in an experimental stage and he thought it would be some time before they would come up with a permanent solution to the problems involved, but that with or without labels or markers the beauty was there for all to see that so desired, and Lauri sent her love.

Paula headed back to the airport to pick up Little Sea Diver; Barney brought the mail upstairs and opened it while I unpacked. He put aside the letters from the Department of the Interior; we would look them over in the country later, responses to ones we had sent out to certain national parks which were adjacent to marine waters like the Point Reyes National Seashore that we had visited on our way to Anacapa and, we had been informed by park people, might in some ways be classified as underwater parks. We were interested in the amount of scuba or skindiving done in them and wanted to know their restrictions on the taking of wildlife in any form.

We had lost track of time and Paula was back with Little Sea Diver before we knew it. Barney's gold Swiss watch that he had obtained in the duty-free port of Christiansted on St. Croix for twenty-five dollars had been behaving erratically lately and now had halted. It was late in the day before we got onto the throughway and then the mile of bumpy gravel road which led to The Unicorn's Lair. Paula and Barney and myself were in the front seat and in the back was Gustav with Little Sea Diver leaning into his warmth. Gusts of wind out of the northwest assailed the car and spits of snow crystals came with them now and then.

As we braked and got out, a flock of thirty Canada geese, calling hoarsely, were arriving for a landing on the lake beyond the small house. It was the restless season for the creatures who dipped their heads in the dark water and flapped their wings and then moved in unison toward the feeding station of shelled corn fastened to the bank. We had a brooder lamp installed in the flight pen attached to the house where Helen of Troy lived along with a goat, a few long-haired guinea pigs and various wild and tame birds. Helen came out nickering to greet the newcomer; he accepted her swaggering air and soon lay beside her in the straw of the warm corner.

During that evening we talked with Paula of the future of the seas of the world. We knew about the wealth they contained, of the quantities of food. The Japanese already were profitably farming not only oysters and mussels, but shrimp too, and soon crabs and lobsters might be added, and choice fish. Around our Great Lakes, where the loss of the once-abundant pike and trout and other prize fish has long been lamented, there is good news of late. A few years ago the coho salmon, a game fish from the Pacific coastal waters and streams, was introduced into Lakes Michigan and Superior and just lately into our Lake Erie. The coho seems to thrive on a trash fish, the alewife, six inches long, which has glutted these polluted waters for years. Coho roe and fingerlings were planted in the creeks; by their third season, two feet long and fifteen pounds or more, the coho salmon headed back for the water of their youth to spawn and die. They were met by thousands of boats and lines of hundreds of angling fishermen, the latter waist-deep, elbow-to-elbow and fifty yards from shore. Over 30,000 cohos were caught in the first season and the number is expected to multiply vastly every year. Now the streams about Lake Michigan are being stocked with king or Chinook salmon which will weigh over fifty pounds each at maturity. We thought perhaps the very pollution we've been trying to avoid may, by its largely organic nature, supply a food chain which will end in an incredible supply of desirable fish. Barney and I considered writing a song about our Lake Erie: "Pollution Is the Solution."

We spoke of the vastness of the seas, which contain 300,000,000 cubic miles of water. The massive icebergs of its frozen areas, towed to warmer ones, might be storehouses of fresh water for thirsty cities. Below the ocean bottom are unprobed oil and gas and mineral reserves representing immeasurable wealth. Originally the seas had been considered to belong to no nation. The major fishing countries claimed what waters were within range of a cannon

shot—three miles—of their shores. This was extended to about
twelve miles and of late that limit has been questioned and chal-
lenged. Who owns the world's waters? we asked. Forty-two nations
signed a covenant in Geneva in 1958, which assigned the ownership of the Continental Shelf, and the agreement stopped there.
We thought of the dangers as technology developed and the competition grew greater for sovereign rights to underwater lands.

Archaeologists are continually dredging up sea treasures, objects
of beauty as well as historic value. We knew of the new research
into the ocean as a source for drugs and medicines, of the unoccupied areas which might be presented to colonies of restless confined mankind, and finally that portions of the seas were becoming
popular for the pursuance of the sport of viewing the underwater
scenes.

Barney said that it was not until the 1950s that the interest in
skindiving and snorkeling became widespread. For its enjoyment
there needed to be clear water, preferably warm, and something to
see. Coral reefs were ideal but were easily despoiled and something
needed to be done to protect them for future generations to enjoy.
The existing national underwater parks were too few and too inaccessible. There were two possibilities; one was for the states to
claim and protect a littoral strip of their land holdings. There
should be free access for the public to the offshore areas just as
today, but owners would be responsible for the protection of the
underwater property and could prosecute anyone who took living
creatures from it.

We opened the letters from the parks. We learned that at Padre
Island, stretching for 113 miles off the east coast of Texas from
Corpus Christi to Mexico, spearfishing was regulated by the Texas
Parks and Wildlife Service, mollusc collecting was permitted, and
that tropical fish such as Damsels and Butterfly Fish might be captured for home aquariums. The waters were semi-tropical, but
since they were murky and often rough, diving activity was usually
limited. Padre is a barrier island as is Fire Island National Seashore, extending thirty-two miles along the Atlantic Ocean off

Patchogue, New York. A barrier island or beach is formed when sand is blown by the wind into dunes which may, as at Fire Island, rise to a hundred feet. Barrier islands may vary in width from a a few yards to a mile; they may be dozens of miles long and are separated from the mainland by shallow bays, marshes or tidal lagoons. We were told that at Fire Island the waters were not the best for diving because of poor visibility. And there, too, state conservation laws restricted fishing and shellfishing.

Cape Hatteras National Seashore contains forty-five square miles of barrier islands off the coast of Manteo, North Carolina. With the exception of certain species of waterfowl in the controlled hunting season, all flora and fauna is protected. Here the snow geese winter as well as Canadas and varieties of ducks and large numbers of whistling swans. The currents are strong, the sands are continually shifting and, due to the roiling of the surf and the absence of coral reefs, little skindiving is done. Shipwrecks of interest are a long way offshore and can be reached only by seagoing craft.

We had a letter also from the Cape Cod National Seashore, a peninsula which juts seventy miles into the Atlantic from the mainland of Massachusetts. Hundreds of thousands of migrating birds following the Atlantic flyway nest or rest on Cape Cod. Divers, including local residents are there for a purpose; the surf is rough and the shoreline sandy and they are after lobsters. The license fee is ten dollars, spearing is prohibited and the creatures must be taken by hand. Spearing of striped bass, the popular sport fish of surf casters there, is outlawed, and fishing is permitted in accordance with federal, state and local laws. Here too, we were told, wreck diving was not a great attraction since the severe winter storms broke up the ships and the sands buried the remains. David Henry Thoreau named Cape Cod the Great Beach, saying, "A storm in the fall or winter is the best time to visit it. . . . A man may stand there and put all America behind him."

A letter had come from the Glacier Bay National Monument in southeastern Alaska, which comprises 4400 square miles and encloses sixteen active tidewater glaciers. Scuba divers in special gear have occasionally gone into the icy waters to check hull damage to vessels. The upper part of the bay is silt-ridden from the many glaciers terminating at salt water and the visibility is poor. No life other than fish and shellfish may be removed. We had heard of spectacular slides there due to glacial activity and how ten years ago, 90 million tons of rock had broken loose from a cliff and a slide was created, which on its way down tore a thousand feet of ice from the base of a glacier. When the slide crashed into the water, the wave surged to a height of 1720 feet; maintaining a great size, the wave moved toward the sea, eight miles away, completely destroying the forest along the shores on its way. In the waters of the monument are killer whales, sea lions, porpoises; on the land are mountain goats, sitka deer, brown and black bears and some- times a glacier or blue bear; there are all varieties of waterfowl, bald eagles, ravens, and in spring flocks of sandhill cranes migrate through.

Our last letter was from Isle Royale National Park, just below the international boundary of United States and Canada, the largest island in Lake Superior, forty-five miles long and nine ac- ross at its widest point. Midsummer temperatures in Lake Superior range as a rule from 44 to 49 degrees, cold for even an enthusiastic diver. Barney and I were familiar with the dangers of swimming in cold water, especially if there was a strong current. Once in mid- winter, when the temperature of the water was near fifty, we had gone off an anchored boat to swim in an old wreck nearby. We just made it and were badly barnacle-scratched as we hung onto it in the rough tide, trying to get our breath.

The cold water reflex somehow inhibits breathing and the enormous increase in metabolism which results from trying to keep up the temperature of the body, increases the need for oxy- gen. In water just above the freezing point, as in the North Sea in World War II, there was little need for sailors or aviators to have life preservers, for they would die of exposure to cold within ten minutes, regardless of whether they were supported or swimming.

Tests made in 40-degree water have shown that swimmers become exhausted in about half the time they do when the temperature is in the seventies. It was also demonstrated that a layer of fat such as the re-entrant mammals have evolved, and women have as a secondary sex characteristic, is good insulation against the cold; fat swimmers last longer in cold water before breathlessness sets in than thin ones. It is mandatory, therefore, to wear full wet suits when diving in water as cold as that around Isle Royale.

The Superintendent of the park wrote also that for highly experienced diving groups there was much opportunity for adventure. Every year about sixty members of diving clubs, each preconditioned to cold water diving, dove off one or more of the twelve shipwrecks in Isle Royale waters. Anyone diving there was required to obtain a special permit from a Ranger Station, where equipment was checked and local diving conditions reviewed. And he added a statement which we thought noteworthy, "Federal Regulations prohibit the collection of any wildlife, mineral specimens, or historic artifact (shipwrecks or any portion thereof) by scuba divers at Isle Royale."

Outside now as night fell, the spatter of snow was becoming a steady fall. We put on the floodlights under the eaves to watch it blanket the garden. We talked of a naturalist neighbor of ours who communicates with wild creatures not by using human speech, but their sounds which he took the trouble to learn, carefully mimicking each so that his work with them is most successful. He has raised a variety of naturally different species of birds and animals together. The wood duck, the most beautiful of American wildfowl, is notoriously difficult to rear because its food consists of flying insects, and the duckling does not comprehend that ground grains are food. When our friend raised newly hatched wood ducks and mallards together, the former followed the eating pattern of the latter as well as their roosting habits, so that now adult, they come together nightly to roost in his hen house, safe from the abundant Great Horned Owls in the bordering woods.

A small conservationist may live like our naturalist neighbor on a piece of country land or be a city resident with a back lot in which he raises a little flock of protected wildfowl; he may be a hotel-keeper or a corporation with an ocean front that is a haven for seals and coral life and jewfish; he may be the private owner of a lake lot who objects to spearfishermen walking out into his waters. And then he may be ourselves at The Unicorn's Lair, which is a sanctuary for wildlife from Canada geese to Lepidoptera, from fox and flying squirrels to red-spotted newts in the caves nearby, from bobwhites to a variety of alien animals and birds that we enjoy.

We went to the door and stepped outside to feel the way the wind had fallen and to listen to the scarcely audible movements of the geese that had landed on the lake beyond. On a small pond close in, a pair of Mute Swans, a dozen wood ducks, three or four mallards and several Canadas circled, some imprinted birds and others wild; they would keep the ice open during the long Ohio winter ahead. Under the hemlocks by the pond's edge were the two white fallow deer, Bliss and Sheba, their undercoats prepared to keep them warm in any weather, and Hase, the long-legged hare, equally ready. Within the burrow she had built into the bank by the side door, the woodchuck Katrin was curled where she would remain until some late March or early April day when she would emerge, sleepy and yet fat. From the flight pen there was no noise from the dozing long-haired guinea pigs in the straw by the capybaras and the goat, or the roosting ringneck doves and pigeons, the peacocks and Chinese silky hens.

As we turned to come in, I thought of the wilderness of the sea and the places we had seen and how, in the great and small wild creatures of the waters, generations to come could find the same pleasure we had found in mingling with the wild life of the land and could discover for themselves what we believe to be the true treasure of the sea.

Index